WITHDRAWN

THE REVOLUTION
OF 1854 IN
SPANISH HISTORY

Oxford University Press, Ely House, London W.1

GLASGOW NEW YORK TORONTO MELBOURNE WELLINGTON
CAPE TOWN SALISBURY IBADAN NAIROBI LUSAKA ADDIS ABABA
BOMBAY CALCUTTA MADRAS KARACHI LAHORE DACCA
KUALA LUMPUR HONG KONG

THE REVOLUTION
OF 1854 IN
SPANISH HISTORY

BY

V. G. KIERNAN

OXFORD

AT THE CLARENDON PRESS

1966

TO

MY FATHER

WHO FIRST GAVE ME

AN INTEREST IN

SPAIN

CONTENTS

INTRODUCTION

The Revolution of 1854 in Nineteenth-Century History

In its broad outlines the history of nineteenth-century Spain has
been known for a long time about as well as it is known today, or
is likely to be for a long time to come. Years ago Altamira complained of the obscurity covering much of what happened in that
age,[1] and more recently another Spanish historian has talked of the
efforts required to fill in 'not gaps in our knowledge but whole
seas of ignorance'.[2] From the present generation of Spaniards it
is in some ways more remote, and separated by greater barriers,
than it is from observers in other countries. A contribution by a
foreigner may therefore have some utility; and for the purpose of
an exploration in some detail of one limited section of the period,
the 'Bienio', the two years opened by revolution in 1854 and ended
by counter-revolution in 1856, may be a not unsuitable choice. It
occupies a mid-century eminence commanding a prospect backward towards the beginnings of the Liberal movement and onward to its decline. It brought into action veterans from the first
decades of the century and newcomers, some of whom were to be
active in the last decades. Brief as it was a great deal of history was
concentrated in it; nearly all the persistent problems of modern
Spain—political, economic, cultural—asserted themselves forcibly; nearly all the parties of the next epoch had their roots in it.

The hundred years may be fairly readily divided into three
phases. There was first the stage of struggle against the *ancien
régime*, down to 1840; then the attempt to consolidate and expand
the reforms achieved, down to 1875; finally, with a restored
Bourbon monarchy, stagnation. The first impetus came from outside. When Napoleon sought in 1808 to put his brother on the
Spanish throne, he dragged a forgotten part of Europe back into
history. Much as he was hated, his armies kept open for a few
years a chink through which light from the outer world could

[1] R. Altamira y Crevea, *Temas de historia de España* (in *Obras completas: Serie
histórica*, Madrid, 1929), vol. i, p. 15.
[2] *Bibliografía histórica de España e Hispanoamérica* (vol. i, 1953–4, with *Índice
histórico español*, Barcelona, no. 7), p. xx.

percolate. Spanish Liberalism came into existence, and in 1812 a first Constitution. This lasted only two years, for most patriots were fighting for anything but progress and reform, and applauded when Ferdinand VII came back from France in 1814 and swept it away. But the nation closed its eyes again in vain; Napoleon had murdered sleep, and Spain was to sleep no more. In 1820 the Liberals regained power and kept it for three years before being overwhelmed by a monarchist and clerical reaction, which this time required the aid of a French royalist army. Too much was changing in Europe, and loss of empire in America quickened many currents of change at home. Towards the end Ferdinand's own rule was shifting from blind medievalism towards semi-enlightened despotism of the eighteenth-century school.

Dying in 1833, he left his crown to an infant daughter, Isabel II, under the regency of her mother María Cristina, his Neapolitan niece and fourth and last wife. His brother Don Carlos demanded it from her in the name of the Salic law. Under dynastic schism lay the two opposing creeds of absolutism: Don Carlos was the choice of the ultra-conservatives in Church and State for whom it was heresy to admit the thought of any change at all. Cristina was shrewd and adaptable enough to strengthen her position by coming to terms with the Liberals, or the less exacting among them, and during the seven bitter years of civil war they were able to establish themselves in power and to carry out irreversible measures. It was now that Mendizábal, their most effective organizer in the struggle, suppressed the monasteries and sold off their vast estates, in order to raise money, weaken Carlism, and create vested interests committed to the Liberal side. Carlism was hemmed in slowly inside its two main strongholds, Catalonia and the Basque area, where provincial separatism favoured it. In 1839 its chief had to retire from the field, and a few years later he 'abdicated' in favour of his eldest son, who called himself Carlos VI or Conde de Montemolín and settled at Naples, where a superfluous princess was found for him by the local Bourbons. Carlism was not dead, but Montemolín made an uninspiring figurehead: he was five feet five inches high, knock-kneed, with protruding discoloured teeth, an oblique nose and a squinting eye, and his other qualities were not much more prepossessing.

Characteristic of this era of the crumbling of the *ancien régime* was the slowness of the reforming movement to draw in behind it any large volume of support. Most Spaniards were peasants; and when the Spanish transformation is compared with the one that started in France in 1789, a factor of critical importance may be seen in the absence of any widespread revolt of the peasantry alongside of that of the urban middle classes. Agrarian revolt in Spain was delayed by the influence of a Catholic Church that survived the eighteenth-century Enlightenment less enfeebled than in almost any other country, and then by the diversion of rustic energy into the heroic but in many ways reactionary fight against Napoleon. His removal of the Bourbons in 1808, and the dynastic split of 1833, gave Liberalism the chance to work its way into power without a direct confrontation of classes like that of 1789–94, and without any serious mobilization of the peasantry. As a result it was tempted to merge with, instead of destroying, the old semi-feudal landowning class. With the selling of Church lands, which had started even before 1814, too many Liberals turned landlord, and former landlords turned Liberal in order to get more land. Had the peasantry been aroused as effectively as the *sans-culottes* of the towns, the civil war could have been far more easily and rapidly won, and Carlism more thoroughly eliminated. As it was the new régime entered on the task of reconstruction with reform prospects already gravely compromised.

There had always been under different names a left-wing and a right-wing faction within the Liberal ranks, and during the civil war these hardened into two rival parties, Progresista and Moderado, each seeking support from the improvised armies and their hastily promoted chiefs. An army mutiny paved the way for a constituent assembly and the fairly radical Constitution of 1837; and when the fighting came to an end General Espartero, the Progresista paladin, was able to get the better of Cristina and her Moderado friends. In 1840 she was pushed out of the country; it was Espartero who took her place as regent. But his party rested on too narrow a basis to be either stable or united. Rivalries of individuals and cliques, jealousy between politicians and soldiers, speedily reduced it to disarray, and in 1843 Espartero found himself helpless in face of Moderado risings, chiefly military. He fled to England; insurrections with a republican tendency in Catalonia, Aragon, and Galicia were crushed; Cristina returned, and the Moderados in partnership with her embarked on a long spell of eleven years in office. Their sword-arm was Narváez, another successful commander from the Carlist war and now Duke of Valencia, who believed in ruling the country very much as he ruled his army.

The Moderados soon tore up the Constitution of 1837 and replaced it with the more authoritarian one of 1845.[1] In this the balance between Crown and executive on the one hand, and Cortes and public on the other, was heavily weighted in favour of the former. Yet monarchy no longer had any valid *raison d'être*. Its mild reformism of the eighteenth century lay too far in the past to be remembered, and the Spanish Bourbons could scarcely be regarded as, like the Hohenzollerns, bound up with national strength or prestige. They had played no part in the war of independence, their achievement since then had been to lose most of the empire, and Spain had no position in Europe to depend on them. Monarchy was surviving, with powers far more than nominal, because Liberalism was divided and Moderados wanted to make use of it against Progresistas; also, more fundamentally, because they wanted to use it to control the mass of the people, still royalist in sentiment because too little tangible benefit had come to them from the Liberal dispensation to wean them away from old habits of mind.

In this opportunism of the conservatives lay the risk that they themselves would be unable to keep control of the Crown; and the young Queen was no sooner of age to meddle in politics than there were signs of this beginning to happen. The Court was tampering with the Constitution, and finding pliant ministers to aid it. When San Luis was appointed premier near the end of 1853 the danger seemed acute; for San Luis, a master of corridor politics and tactics, was one of a swarm of venal careerists who would be a menace to parliamentary government as long as there were reactionary interests ready to hire their services. Resistance took at first the form of an army plot, initiated by a Moderado general, O'Donnell. His *pronunciamiento* in June 1854 met with little response: the army, which had been Liberalism's substitute for a mobilization of mass forces against the old order, had never won the confidence of the people. But the rising gave the signal for

---

[1] The texts of the Constitutions of 1837 and 1845 can be found in H. Abad de Aparicio and R. Coronel y Ortiz, *Estudios sobre derechos políticos* (Madrid, 1863–6), vol. ii; J. Muro Martínez, *Constituciones de España . . .* (Madrid, 1881), vol. i; A. Padilla Serra, *Constituciones y leyes fundamentales de España (1808–1947)*, (Granada, 1954).

more popular outbreaks in the big cities, which quickly brought the Court faction to its knees. Espartero was recalled from retirement to head a government mainly of Progresistas, though it included O'Donnell, and a fresh constituent assembly was elected. This met in November with a clear duty not only to deal faithfully with the Palace but to place Liberalism on a firmer footing by extending its benefits to far more Spaniards than could hope for any direct gain from any merely constitutional reform.

Opportunity seemed great. At this moment the country had broken further away from the old moorings than at almost any other point in the century. One indication of this was the astonishing feebleness of a renewed Carlist effort at rebellion in 1855. The constituent assembly was to be described by its historian, not unwarrantably, as the most outstanding in the entire constitutional epoch.[1] In 422 sittings packed into twenty months it toiled at the task of renovating Spain and left behind it nearly two hundred laws. On the side of material development it gave the economy a decided impetus. It provided the indispensable minimum of modernization—a railway programme, for instance—to keep Spain going and postpone to the end of the century the collapse whose outward sign was defeat in war with the United States. But the sins of omission of this Cortes, only in part explained by the short time allowed it, were at least as striking as what it accomplished. It did no more than talk desultorily about the running sore of slavery in Cuba. It quarrelled with the Church, but did not try to dig up the roots of intolerance and superstition. It erected no firm bulwark against monarchical reaction. This could probably only have been done by a change of dynasty, and in 1853–4 some very moderate men had been contemplating such a change, yet the restored Progresistas could not muster the moral courage to send Isabel and her family packing when it would have been easy to do so. Worse still, they did too little towards the emancipation of the common people from their burdens, conscription and excessive taxation, and the ignorance fostered by bad or no education. Worst of all they made scarcely any effort to rescue the peasantry from insecure tenure, rack-renting, usury, unemployment. On the contrary they embittered the situation by completing the transfer of the Church estates to a landlord class

[1] J. del Nido y Segalerva, *Antología de las Cortes desde 1854 á 1858* (Madrid, 1911), p. 668.

for the most part inefficient and parasitic, which found in bigger
fields and higher rents an easy substitute for better farming, and
by beginning a vast new transfer, the sale into private ownership
of the village commons.

Every revolution has something of the apocalyptic quality
that Hazlitt saw in the great French Revolution: it brings suddenly to light things that have long been taking shape. For the
first time the engrossing of all the profits of Liberal reform into
a few hands was forcibly challenged from below. Among the
peasants, especially in some southern provinces where their lot
was most miserable, the Bienio was the starting-point of a hundred years of agitation. Industrial workers, a newer class, were
quicker to begin thinking about conditions and trying to alter
them, and they had been a cause of alarm to the respectable for
some time; but it was in 1855 that a general strike in Catalonia
marked the beginning of active struggle. This rejection in both
village and town of law and order and orderly starvation came
as a shock to the propertied classes. Liberals might have argued
from it that private property, as well as Church and monarchy,
must submit to restrictions. Instead, while the vested interests
drew away from them they refused to strengthen themselves
by welcoming the dispossessed classes into their camp. They
drifted consequently into isolation. In July 1856 Espartero
was manœuvred out of office, and O'Donnell in league with the
Queen took his place. Armed resistance by the people, in which
Espartero and most of the Progresistas took no part, was crushed
by the army.

In 1854 O'Donnell's liberal-conservatism had been left behind
by the swing towards revolution; in 1856 it was left behind by the
swing towards reaction. In October he was dismissed and replaced by Narváez, and next year Narváez was removed to make
room for ministers more under the thumb of the Palace. But like
its opponents the Palace faction was too narrowly based to be
capable of ruling alone, especially after the stimulus given by the
Bienio to national opinion and the national economy. Isabel was
compelled to turn back to O'Donnell, whose 'Liberal Union'
represented now Spain's political centre of gravity. What it
amounted to was a banding together of all types of property-
holder old and new against those who wanted either to put the
clock back or to put it forward. One of O'Donnell's moves was to

reach in 1859 a full settlement of the differences with Rome which had led to relations being broken off during the Bienio. The stability thus achieved was paid for by a slackening of the country's economic as well as political momentum. Mass poverty restricted the home market, and a true *bourgeoisie* was still scarcely in being except in odd corners of the country. The salient figure in industry and finance was Salamanca, a businessman of creative vision who made and lost several fortunes by the kind of methods without which enterprise on a grand scale was impossible; half politician, more than half adventurer or swindler, in 1854 he had narrowly escaped lynching. Stability was marred, moreover, by irresponsibility at the top, as well as by discontent below. The monarchy required a sharper lesson than that of 1854 to teach it, and Isabel personally was incapable of ever learning, that it could function only as one partner in a conservative ring. All the same O'Donnell was laying the foundation of a system that was to prevail for long after his own lifetime. 'The whole policy of Restoration Spain was here roughly sketched out. This was its first dress-rehearsal.'[1]

Meanwhile mass discontents swelled, but the readiness of progressive politicians to take account of them did not keep pace. The task of organizing true political parties of any complexion was one that Spain found difficult; it is a touchstone of the moral heritage or psychology of any modern country, whether in Europe or beyond. Official interference always complicated it, and one of the most damaging failures of the Bienio, never made up for later, was that parties were even then not fully recognized and ratified and allowed to build themselves into compact national bodies. After 1856 some Progresistas lapsed into Liberal Unionism, others into inactivity. It was chiefly their radical wing, which had separated off during the Bienio to form a Democrat party, that tried to keep up the struggle. Too much of its energy went into conspiratorial tactics on the Carbonaro model, a proliferation of lodges and secret rituals; a reversion to the tactics of Liberalism in its nonage, when it worked under cover of Freemasonry. Democrats masked and cloaked like this were more effectively disguised from the public than from the police.

Out-of-date methods went with an out-of-date programme. At bottom the Democrat programme was still no more than the old

[1] A. Ramos Oliveira, *Politics, Economics and Men of Modern Spain* (London, 1946), p. 85.

Liberal creed, carried to the logical conclusion of universal suffrage. The old simple cry of Liberty had served well enough with the small urban classes—artisans, shopkeepers, clerks— among whom Liberalism recruited its fighting-force, the national militia which got its best and last chance in the Bienio. But this social stratum, heterogeneous and individualistic, can exert a strong pressure on events only when the State is weak and in confusion, as it was during the Carlist war, or in France in 1789– 92. In Spain it still included a considerable part of the population, because the pace of industrialization was slow, but it could not be an autonomous force in politics now that a new and stronger State machinery had been set up. To the peasantry and factory proletariat the old watchwords made far less appeal, and they were moving away from Liberalism faster than it could make up its mind to move in their direction. When their support was forth- coming it embarrassed militant radicals more than it heartened them. In 1857, for example, there were disturbances in Seville province. What the Democrat leader Sixto Cámara was aiming at there was a republican rising against Isabel and Narváez; what came about was an agrarian rising of landless men who saw Narváez much more as a landlord and friend of landlords than as an enemy of Liberty.

Democrats argued a good deal among themselves during the sixties about the mild notions of social welfare that had first cropped up during the Bienio and been denounced by orthodox Liberals as socialism; but the majority remained faithful to *laissez-faire* individualism, and no agreement was reached on even a modest instalment of social reform. Shortly before the revolution of 1868 García Ruiz, who was helping to prepare it, wrote that the hunger devouring Spain was regrettable because hunger bred blind mutiny instead of sage political aspiration.[1] This refusal to see that without hunger there would be no real mass movement, and without this no real political advance, was fatal. A good deal of the old religious dualism of soul and body lingered on in it; every outlook inherits much more from the past than it is aware of. Some of the more ardent found an alternative in Federal- ism, an ideal of provincial autonomy which grew out of the de- centralization policies practised or projected during the Bienio and then promptly scrapped. It could claim practical merits in

---

[1] E. García Ruiz, *La revolución española* (Paris, 1867), p. 54.

a country so unevenly developed, but by itself it could solve no essential problems, and in the long run it divided Democrats or republicans without uniting them with the masses. Among its advocates were the men most anxious to improve the lot of the poor, notably Pi y Margall whose anarchist philosophy, first outlined in 1854, shaded into that of Bakunin; but their practical proposals hardly got beyond Proudhon.

Because of these blockages in their thinking, when 1868 came the radicals were still unable to sustain themselves except in alliance with those army chiefs who were willing for a time to co-operate with them. There was little to hold the two groups together beyond agreement on the necessity of getting rid of Isabel, and Prim and the other generals, some of whom had been with O'Donnell in 1854, were joining the revolution even more obviously than then in order to keep it from going too far. All the unanswered questions of the Bienio now asserted themselves again, and more explosively because in the intervening years they had grown less capable of solution within the limits of Liberalism. When in 1870 a new sovereign was found and the experiment of a new dynasty launched, it was too late. A foreigner owing his crown to the ballot-box could not satisfy traditionalist sentiment, and no king of any sort could conciliate the republicanism now far more widespread than in 1854. Amadeo gave up in 1873 and went home to Italy. The Republic that followed was torn by feuds among the Democrats themselves, reflecting the erratic tendencies of the petty *bourgeoisie* they depended on. The less extreme men like Castelar joined forces with the generals to quell Federalist revolts in the south and to maintain conscription, and thus made it easy for the army to close the Cortes—as in 1856—and take things into its own hands. Meanwhile another Carlist war broke out in the north. Carlism seemed to have reached a dead end in 1860, when Montemolín made a foolish landing on the coast, was captured at once, and released after a humiliating renunciation of his claims; he had died the next year, childless. Yet here was a nephew, a new Pretender, in the field as Carlos VII. As if there were not enough troubles at home, a desperate servile war raged in Cuba.

By the end of 1874 the generals were ready to bring back the Bourbon monarchy: not Isabel, but her son Alfonso XII, who might be expected to prove more docile. The Restoration was stage-managed by a conservative, Cánovas del Castillo, who

entered politics in 1854 as a young O'Donnellite conspirator. In
Alfonso's first Cabinet could be seen the Marqués de Molíns,
who had been in that of San Luis, and Salaverría who had been in
O'Donnell's first ministry in 1856. A system of limited monarchy
was established under which most Spaniards found their rights
strictly limited indeed. A make-believe of parliamentary rule was
kept up by a Conservative party led by Cánovas and a Liberal
party led by Sagasta, another youthful rebel of 1854 and mellow
cynic now, taking turn and turn about in office. Cánovas lasted
until his assassination in 1897, Sagasta till 1903. Behind the
façade *caciquismo*, rule by jobbery and bribery through local
bosses, resumed and extended its sway; and behind this in turn
stood the vested interests, especially landlordism, and the great
corporations, army and bureaucracy, Church and Court, with
nothing to fear so long as they took care not to fall out again
among themselves. As for the peasants, they consoled themselves
with religion or turned to Anarchism, equal if opposite modes of
abandoning any thought of a rational social order. If Federalism
tried to dissolve the nation into cantons, the Restoration, or 1856
and 1875 together, succeeded in dissolving it into classes and ways
of thinking with scarcely anything except force to bind them
together. Every revolution divides, but the more fruitful ones
reunite nations in a new pattern, restoring that degree of homo-
geneity, that sense—however imperfect—of a communion of
interests and beliefs, without which there can be no continuing
development. Spain's fate has been to experience civil wars rather
than revolutions.

Throughout the century Spain was acted on by influences
from abroad; also by political pressures, being neither strong
enough to make her own history nor insignificant enough to be
left alone. Here too the Bienio was a landmark. It saw full recognition of the fact that Spain was part of Europe, after awareness
of this had been gathering for a long time, and its programme of
reforms was consciously intended to europeanize the country
more thoroughly. But to be europeanized, or modernized, meant
also infection with novel social maladies. Uneasiness stirred up by
the strife of capital and labour was played upon by those who were
planning the coup of July 1856; and they had French backing,
potent because Napoleon III was at the zenith of his fortunes and
because during the Bienio foreign, mainly French, capital was for

the first time flowing into Spain on a big scale. The Paris Commune of 1871 had the same unnerving effect on the propertied classes as the Paris fighting of 1848. In the last years of the century Liberalism was on the ebb in Spain partly because it was ebbing elsewhere, in Germany for instance. In Germany, however, industrialization was opening another door to the future. Spanish Liberalism had pushed this door ajar during the Bienio, but no more; and the conservatism that supplanted it was too archaic and irrational, and by contrast with Germany or Japan too little under the spur of any need to equip the country for modern warfare, to promote modern manufactures by State aid from above. Thus Spain ended with only a pinchbeck industry, surrounded by a derelict agriculture, as well as with only a shadowy parliamentary life; it was as if the country had been assimilated into South America rather than into western Europe. The consequences of this retardation were to be grave for Europe as well as for Spain.

Few personalities of the Bienio were much known abroad, fewer still are remembered today either abroad or at home. It may not be out of place to add some further introduction at this point of some of the most conspicuous, or most representative, among them, beginning with Isabel. Her tutors' failure to educate Isabel into a Spanish Queen Victoria was part and parcel of the Liberal failure to transform the old Spain at large. Her mother, while always putting her own interests before everything else, had been obliged to make her own way in the world, and was at any rate realistic and experienced. Isabel, unlike Cristina, was Spanish, a queen at the age of three, accustomed from infancy to romantic adulation as the symbol of the struggle against Don Carlos. She grew up imprisoned within a vast unwieldy palace piled up on the western rim of Madrid, and within a monarchical tradition still powerful though now obsolete, and resistant to any adaptation to modern conditions. It was part of the tradition that Isabel should address every Spaniard from duke to dairymaid with the familiar *tu*: every Spaniard was the monarch's vassal or servant. It was part of it also that she should grow up an obedient daughter of the Virgin of the Atocha church at Madrid, the protectress of her dynasty, and through her of the whole Catholic Church, mortal enemy of Liberalism in Spain and in Europe. Altogether she was bound to be a rallying-point for all forces opposed to progress which judged Carlism too intransigent, or doomed to defeat.

Isabel was not without native abilities, early displayed: she had a strong memory, a lively wit, a gift for manipulating individuals. But in so contradictory an historical situation, on a throne with no rational basis, her qualities all took a bad turn, only relieved by a profuse generosity, itself half vanity, in giving away endless heaps of money without troubling about who had to provide it. The private situation of this young woman indecently married off by her elders was equally anomalous, and her natural but indiscreet attitude to her marriage vows deprived her of the decorous respectability that nineteenth-century royalty everywhere had to acquire, or to affect. In these circumstances the constitutional monarchy dreamed of by Liberals as a fixed point of rest between the excesses of Carlism and republicanism was a dream and no more. July 1856 and the fall of Espartero put an end to any possible coexistence between her and real Liberalism, and even to the diluted Liberalism of O'Donnell and his friends her ineradicable habits of intrigue and double-dealing made her a continual nuisance. From her freakish angle of vision they for their part were refractory upper servants who had got into bad habits. 'The army is solidly Liberal', she wrote absurdly to the pope in 1865, apologizing for the hateful necessity of recognizing the new kingdom of Italy.[1] She was allowed to go on till 1868 only because the politicians dreaded another explosion like 1854. In exile she settled down with something of her mother's resilience to enjoy life's little comforts, after at last shaking off her unbearable husband, until in 1904 it was time for her to make the final journey to her old residence of the Escorial, in whose vaults she lies among her kin.

Baldomero Espartero was the great name of Liberalism in the twenty years before 1856, though he was the man least of all capable of explaining what it stood for. Born in 1792 in a poor family in south-central Spain, he served as a volunteer against the French, and then from 1815 as a regular officer against the South American rebels—less appropriate training for the champion of freedom. On his return he had the good luck to marry a small fortune at Logroño on the upper Ebro, where he made his home. In the Carlist war a mixture of luck and dash brought him

---

[1] C. Llorca, *Isabel II y su tiempo* (Alcoy, 1956), p. 165.

glory, and it fell to him to finish the contest off and win the title of Duke of Victory. Political ambition was by this time well alight in him, fanned by the Progresistas who needed his name and his sword. As regent he showed small skill, and was notoriously in the hands of a clique of intimates. Thereafter he was in exile in England, and in retirement at Logroño. Yet he remained a name to conjure with, because more than any other single man he embodied the forces and passions astir in the Spain of that chaotic epoch. He shared the romantic impulsiveness of his countrymen, their fits of magnanimity and of savagery, their ill-informed self-esteem, physical courage, and mental indolence; their incapacity for patient exertion, their oscillation between soaring hope and despair. With his needy childhood and his dukedom he personified the career open to talents; as vanquisher of Carlism he represented the fitful alliance between Spain's new army and progress; his stay in England, where he was lionized, gave him ties with the nation that all progressive Europeans looked up to. His peculiar virtue was that he, almost alone of public men, had admirers among both high and low, and that he could arouse a tumultuous enthusiasm such as none of the aloof men of the Liberal élite, or the more aristocratic army chiefs like Narváez, could call up.

But Spain was changing, while Espartero's mind stood still. Not long before the revolution of 1854 he was writing to let his old friend Lord Clarendon know that his principles were the same as ever: he desired for Spain 'una libertad bien entendida'.[1] What he meant by 'liberty properly understood' he signally failed to make clear after the revolution swept him back into power. His party's submissiveness towards him during the Bienio betrayed its lack of self-confidence, while it ruled out the kind of positive programme, including social legislation, which alone could make its position secure. The year 1856 was the end of the road for Espartero, as for much besides. For the rest of his long life he was content with his garden at Logroño, where he faded little by little into a legend, as his shortcomings were forgotten and public veneration gathered round him like moss round an old oak. In 1875 young Alfonso made a pilgrimage to listen to a lecture from the grand old man on the duties of a constitutional monarch. He died in 1879; his statue on horseback still looks down on the Madrid that once strewed flowers in his way.

[1] 14 Mar. 1853; Clarendon Papers, vol. c. ix.

Leopoldo O'Donnell was not a man to become a popular hero, but he was willing, as Narváez never was, to practise demagogy. Like Narváez he came from the small 'service' nobility, but his family roots were less in the land and more in the army. He too distinguished himself against the Carlists; he was a colonel at twenty-four, and came out of the war Conde de Lucena, blessed also with a wealthy young widow who made him a devoted and intelligent though retiring wife. A plotter against Espartero's regency, he was rewarded by the Moderados in 1844 with the captain-generalship of Cuba, the richest plum that any Spaniard could win. He suppressed a negro revolt with exemplary cruelty, though subsequently he seems to have tried to improve conditions, not from humanitarian but from economic motives, and came home with a sharpened craving for power. A novice as yet in politics, meagrely educated like most men of his class and time, he developed before long into an exceptionally shrewd, unemotional calculator.

His formula of 'Liberal Union', which meant the banding together of all the satisfied classes, was not his own invention, for the idea of a party intermediate between Moderado and Progresista, drawing on both of them for recruits, was floating in the air before 1854. O'Donnell was the leader destined to bring it to fruition. He began feeling his way towards his goal while working with Espartero during the Bienio, whose barrenness in the vital field of social reform was to a great extent due to him. His grand opportunity came in 1858, when Isabel found herself growing isolated and was obliged to invite him back to office. He remained premier until early 1863, an immensely long stretch as Spanish ministries went, and it was in these years that the foundation of a good understanding among all sound, solid, selfish men of property was laid. For other Spaniards he made some provision, in the form of patriotic excitement, by his war in 1860 against Morocco. This wretched affair, which made him Duke of Tetuan, distracted those other Spaniards only temporarily. O'Donnell was in power again when in June 1866 Madrid once more resounded with gunfire, and this time reprisals against the rebels were far more vindictive than ten years before. He died in 1867 and was buried in the ornate church of the Salesas in Madrid. In the carved relief on his tomb he may be seen riding not towards Vicálvaro, where he fought against Isabel in 1854, but towards Tetuan.

None of the civilian statesmen stood out so prominently as these military men; a revealing commentary by itself on Spanish politics. Among them were many individuals remarkable enough in their way, whose abilities would have brought them to the front in any parliamentary arena. Much of what was best in the more conservative circles of Liberalism was represented by Ríos Rosas. A lifelong preacher of official purity and probity, more surprisingly he practised in office what he preached in the wilderness. He was besides a firm constitutionalist, but one who was held back by a nostalgic monarchism and Catholicism, both linked with mistrust of common humanity, from any belief in democracy; between his dual convictions there was a contradiction of which his entire public life may be regarded as the working out. A southerner, born in 1812, son of a lawyer, he practised law, and wrote poetry as well as better things—it was the Romantic age of Spanish politics, and nearly everyone versified—and in 1837 entered the Cortes. He was soon a well-known Moderado orator, though too angular a character to win the good graces of the party chiefs. In 1854 he entered or at least lent his name to O'Donnell's plot, as a protest against San Luis and corruption, and he was an outstanding member of the constituent assembly. He treated parliamentary business with intense seriousness, not to say solemnity, and ought to have been happy in this Cortes, one of the few where freedom of speech and debate prevailed; but the pace of progress, far from dizzy though it was, alarmed him, and in 1856 he accepted office under O'Donnell. When the latter returned to power Ríos Rosas was the man chosen to go to Rome and negotiate the settlement of 1859. Disillusioned with the Moderado party, he had made himself the philosopher of Liberal Union; inevitably he was soon disgusted with it too. Yet the lesson that public decency and legality would never be safe until Spain was more democratic always eluded him. Bewildered by events after 1868, he put up with Amadeo as less bad than a republic, and died in 1873, honourably penniless.

Olózaga (1805–73) was another born parliamentarian who looked on politics too much as the affair of an educated minority, and supposed that the churning river of history could be turned into a placid parliamentary canal. He was a doctor's son from Logroño in the north, and was in jail and then in exile before the death of Ferdinand. On his return he became an eloquent

Progresista spokesman, and was a principal architect of the Constitution of 1837. In 1843 he was briefly in power, after combining with the Moderados to turn out Espartero and his officer friends, against whom he represented the civilian wing of the party. The Moderados then turned him out, and tutored the girl queen to give false testimony that nearly cost him his life and did cost him another banishment. Ever afterwards a vendetta against Isabel helped to stiffen his genuine radicalism. But there was another side to his character. Tall, well-built, vain, a cosmopolite more at home in the drawing-rooms of Paris or London than in most Spanish gatherings, he had a weakness for rank and ribbons; and there was too little in his environment, in the absence of a mature middle class, to counteract this, or to keep him at the hard perpetual grind of party work. The disparity between his ambition and his energy was never more in evidence, or more harmful to his party, than during the Bienio when he led, by fits and starts, the radical wing that wanted to be more independent of Espartero. His career closed in a futile repetition of what he had done long before. After the fall of his old enemy Isabel he shone in one more Cortes, superintended as in 1837 and 1855 the drafting of a new Constitution, and went off to Paris for one more term as ambassador which lasted him till his death in 1873. The Progresista party that had come to be identified with him was already defunct.

It is another sidelight on the progressive movement that the Democrats should have found their leader in a ninth marquis. Courage was not wanting among them, but this man possessed also, as his biographer said, a certain aristocratic audacity and instinctive knowledge of the enemy's weak points.[1] José María de Orense y Milá de Aragón was born in 1803, was an émigré of 1823, and entered the Cortes in 1844. His peerage of Albaida, which he succeeded to in 1847, did not hinder his sturdy radicalism from growing into republicanism, and after an active share in the insurrectionary attempts of 1848 he was in exile again until 1854. Orense was often miscalled madman because detractors failed to comprehend how a grandee of Spain could be a democrat unless he were mad. In fact he was a sensible, practical man, a careful manager of his estates and business interests, including iron-works he had built up: a better *bourgeois* in spite of his blue blood than

[1] R. M. de Labra, *Estudios biográfico-políticos*, part 1 (Madrid, 1887), pp. 35 ff.

most middle-class Spaniards ever were. Sanguine, energetic, good-humoured, he was neither a brilliant orator nor an original thinker, but an impressive speaker and pamphleteer in a plain unvarnished style too seldom heard in Spain. His error was to mistake Spain for England or the United States, and not to realize that freedom in Spain needed other buttresses than the free competitive capitalism of happier lands. Having helped to bring about the revolution in 1868 he refused to compromise with monarchy, and when Amadeo departed he was elected president of the constituent assembly; but he was equally unready to come to terms with the socialistic forces now stirring on the left. The republic he had striven for all his life brought him only disappointment, the Restoration one more of many exiles, and in 1880 he died, like so many of the best men of that ill-starred age, in the greyness of defeat.

I

THE CONDITION OF SPAIN AT MID-CENTURY

BY the time the fires of the Carlist war had burned themselves out in 1839 a good part of the old Spain had been consumed, and by the middle of the century the country looked a very different place from what it had so lately been. The Church above all, the grand support of the old régime, looked as if crippled beyond recovery.[1] Most of the clergy had been and many remained at heart Carlist. They had few able leaders, for with loss of wealth and power the profession ceased to attract able and ambitious men.[2] Tithes had vanished, and been replaced by a meagre and irregular subsidy from the State. A visitor to Madrid was struck by the scanty attendance at Sunday mass.[3] Like the Gallican Church before it, the Spanish Church thus debilitated was growing ultramontane, turning its face towards Rome more than it ever did in its days of pride and prosperity. But Rome itself was a weak prop to lean on now.

The *ancien régime* survived in a hundred corners of town and village and of men's minds. Foreigners were disappointed at the drab European clothes that were ousting picturesque national costumes; yet to many of them the land of 'the languid, lounging, smoking, idle, procrastinating Spaniard'[4] appeared antediluvian. A more discriminating Frenchman saw a dual society everywhere, the age of the Cid and the age of Napoleon side by side.[5] Progress, real but uneven and inadequate, could be seen most clearly in the country's economic life. To stimulate change there was for one thing a growth of population; there were about fifteen million

[1] See, for example, T. M. Hughes, *Revelations of Spain in 1845* (2nd ed., London, 1845), vol. ii, chaps. 9–11.
[2] 'No man of any respectable family now enlists himself under the banners of the clergy' ('An Old Resident', *Roman Catholicism in Spain* (Edinburgh, 1855), pp. 41–42).
[3] W. E. Baxter, *The Tagus and the Tiber* (London, 1852), vol. i, p. 214.
[4] W. Thornbury, *Life in Spain: Past and Present* (London, 1859), vol. i, p. 125.
[5] E. Quinet, 'L'Ultramontanisme', 1844: *Œuvres Complètes*, vol. ii (2nd ed., Paris, 1873), pp. 142–3.

Spaniards in 1850 instead of the ten or eleven of half a century before.[1] Customs revenue increased from 90 million reals (about £900,000 in English money of the same date) in 1843 to 126 million in 1849, 177 million in 1855.[2] Industrial output was aided by tariff protection, though there was immense smuggling, especially from Gibraltar, and in 1857 could be roughly reckoned to have doubled itself in fifty years.[3] Iron-working showed the biggest increase; by 1850 there were twenty-five foundries profitably operating. Cotton mills represented the largest single investment, and employed 120,000 hands.[4] Most manufactures were small-scale and old-fashioned; in 1860 a census showed about 660,000 artisans, compared with 150,000 factory workers and 23,000 miners. In larger undertakings foreign capital and management, chiefly British and French, played a prominent part.

In Catalonia especially, an industrial revolution was being hastened by the presence of numerous French mill-owners as well as workmen.[5] Barcelona was the great smithy. Its population of 150,000, second only to that of Madrid, included 50,000 out of the 90,000 mill-workers of Catalonia.[6] Steam, a fabulous genie still to most of the country, was a common drudge here, and construction of locomotives and steamships was being taken in hand. In his trade report for 1853 the British consul, while lamenting as everyone did 'the deficiency of all kinds of statistical information in Spain', put the number of 'establishments' making machinery and castings in the city and its environs at fifty-two, with 1,100 hands. In 1834 all Spain's cotton-mills had required 7 million pounds of raw cotton; in 1840, 18 million; in 1853, 36 million. Catalonia, in exchange for its manufactures, depended

[1] The first serious modern census was held in 1857, and gave a figure of 15,464,340: *Anuario Estadístico de España* (Madrid, 1859), p. 243. This was believed to be somewhat below the true figure.

[2] J. Becker (y González), *Relaciones comerciales entre España y Francia durante el siglo XIX* (Madrid, 1910), p. 48. The standard coin, the silver-copper *real de vellón*, was worth about 2½d., so that 100 reals made roughly £1.

[3] N. de Cabanillas, *Colección de los artículos publicados en el 'Diario Español'* (Madrid, 1855–7), vol. ii, p. 207.

[4] On iron, see S. T. Wallis, *Spain: her Institutions, Politics, and Public Men* (London, 1853), pp. 342–3; on cotton, J. Illas y Vidal, *Memoria sobre los perjuicios que ocasionaría . . . la adopción del sistema del libre cambio* (Barcelona, 1849), p. 52.

[5] On the growth of Catalan industry see, for example, J. Cortada, *Cataluña y los catalanes* (San Gervasio, 1860), pp. 39 ff.; F. G. Bruguera, *Histoire contemporaine d'Espagne 1789–1950* (Paris, 1953), pp. 183–4, 206–7.

[6] F. Garrido, *L'Espagne contemporaine* (Brussels and Leipzig, 1862), p. 232.

on other provinces for three-quarters of its wheat.[1] Modern industry, in fact, was too closely confined to two regions, the coastal strips of Catalonia and the Basque provinces, though odd towns elsewhere, like Malaga in the south,[2] were copying their example. Catalans and Basques, moreover, were by language and tradition at least half alien. In the civil war their hill-men had been the mainstay of the Carlist army; it was a similar though opposite recoil from the life of the rest of Spain that made their townspeople the readiest to adopt foreign economic modes. In Catalonia by mid century the fermenting mixture of social forces old and new was about to begin precipitating, in accordance with a primary equation of nineteenth-century history, a movement of national separatism.

Railways held out a prospect, the first in Spanish history, of the heterogeneous regions being joined together by a common circulation of goods and thoughts, instead of by a more or less artificial political framework. Barcelona of course led the way: in October 1848 its railway line to Mataró, sixteen miles long, was opened. Elsewhere development was slow. Few projects got beyond the stage of blueprints, nearly all were enveloped in job-bery and intrigue.[3] Many other enterprises failed likewise, and a feverish boom in the later forties collapsed in a commercial crisis.[4] Capitalism in Spain bore too many traces of its archaic origins. Money-lending was its most lucrative activity, at every level from village usury, a plague Asiatic in its virulence, to the operations of the ring of financiers who kept an always needy Treasury going with short-term loans at monstrous rates.

Most Spaniards were still villagers, and most men of means still preferred land to any other form of investment.[5] Loss of

---

[1] J. Baker to Earl of Clarendon, Foreign Secretary, no. 7, 21 Jan. 1854, in F.O. (Foreign Office Records) Class 72 (Spain), vol. 851; Public Record Office, London. In 1855 was founded 'La Maquinista Terrestre y Marítima', an engineering firm that has lived to celebrate its centenary: chap. 3 of its history by A. del Castillo (Barcelona, 1955) covers 1850–6.

[2] On progress at Malaga see S. T. Wallis, *Glimpses of Spain . . . in 1847* (New York, 1849), chaps. 7–9.

[3] On the early days of the railways see F. de A. Cambó y Batlle, *Elementos para el estudio del problema ferroviario en España* (Madrid, 1918–20).

[4] There is a good account of the boom in R. de Mesonero Romanos, *Nuevo manual . . . de Madrid* (5th ed., Madrid, 1854), pp. 555–6. Cf. Conde de Romanones, *Salamanca, conquistador de riqueza* (Madrid, 1931), p. 62.

[5] See A. Moreau de Jonnès, *Statistique de l'Espagne* (Paris, 1834), chap. 3; Cabanillas, pp. 191–7; M. Colmeiro, *Historia de la economía política en España* (Madrid, 1863), vol. ii, pp. 89 ff.

empire and imperial tribute forced on Spain the necessity of feeding herself; transfer to private ownership of the uneconomically managed monastic estates stimulated production on them. A food deficit was turned into a food surplus, and grain could now be exported—on condition of a great many Spaniards being kept on very short commons. But little of the money invested reached the fields as fertilizing capital in the form of better tools, seeds, methods, or water-supply. 'It seems strange', an English expert observed, 'that a people who are so unanimous about the necessity of irrigation should do so little towards supplying that great want.'[1] Sun, mule, and primitive Roman plough continued to bring forth their scanty harvests;[2] bad or non-existent roads hindered produce from finding its best markets.

At bottom the causes of stagnation lay more in social than in merely technical backwardness. The *bourgeois* revolution in the countryside had been made only from above, and as a result agrarian problems instead of being solved were in some ways worsened. Reforms since 1810 had erased such palpable evils as seigneurial courts or banalities; entails had been extinguished.[3] But the old feudal estate survived, not much changed in essence, and with it a labyrinth of old habits, obligations, and injustices. Dissolution of the monasteries stimulated rack-renting as well as production. Absenteeism of bad landlords left villagers at the mercy of worse stewards.[4] Minute fragmentation of holdings into scattered strips wasted infinite time and made for infinite litigation.[5] Lack of any systematic cadastral survey, or register of land titles, promoted usury, by impeding rural credit, and made a fair allocation of tax burdens impossible.

[1] J. P. Roberts, *Irrigation in Spain* (London, 1897), p. 3.
[2] M. M. de Reinoso (Reynoso), *Informe presentado á las Juntas Generales de Agricultura* (Madrid, 1849), pp. 10 ff., surveys the deficiencies of agriculture under nine heads. Cf. E. Abela y Sainz de Andino, *Memoria sobre el estado de la agricultura en la provincia de Madrid* (Madrid, 1876), e.g. pp. xxi, 85–88, 172.
[3] See F. de Cárdenas, *Ensayo sobre la historia de la propiedad territorial en España* (Madrid, 1873), vol. ii, chap. 4; A. Cabezas Díaz, *La reforma agraria* (Madrid, 1932); R. García Ormaechea, *Supervivencias feudales en España* (Madrid, 1932), shows how imperfectly agrarian feudalism had been brought to an end, e.g. pp. 50–51, 60, 98.
[4] G. Brenan, *The Spanish Labyrinth* (2nd ed., Cambridge, 1950), p. 115, points out that two thirds of the latifundia of modern Andalusia arose from nineteenth-century sales of monastic and common lands, but are indistinguishable from those of old feudal origin.
[5] On the evils of fragmentation see J. García Sanz, *Manual de agricultura* (Madrid, 1861), p. 428; Abela y Sainz de Andino, p. 85.

In the south-west the cultivator was a labourer working in a gang, if he could find work at all, at starvation wages on a big estate.[1] In over-populated Galicia[2] extreme sub-division of holdings was driving thousands to emigrate to America. In the Castiles the small tenant-farmer was harassed by rents that were too high and leases that were too short. Valencia was exceptional in being actively and intelligently cultivated, but exorbitant rents kept tenants poor in spite of incessant toil. Only in a few areas, chiefly in the north and notably among the Basques, did similar toil yield a modestly decent livelihood to peasant proprietors and tenants with long leases and security. Village commons were still extensive, and helped, even after the disappearance of monastic charity, to keep the hard-pressed countryfolk from destitution. But pressure by tax-collector, money-lender, and landlord was helping to swell a growing army of landless or almost landless labourers, of whom the census of 1860 showed more than two and a quarter million.[3] If the nineteenth century was the age of the emancipation of property in Spain, as an enthusiast declared,[4] it was also one of emancipation, for the majority, from property.

Altogether the meagre yield of the Liberal revolution had been very unevenly distributed. In 1851 a writer on the social problem calculated that only the ninety thousand citizens qualified to vote could be possessed of incomes of more than 3,333 reals (£33) a year. He believed that, taking Spain and Portugal together, the completely destitute class had grown from a twentieth of the population in older days to at least a twelfth, and that in Spain nearly half the breadwinners earned less than the minimum required for decent maintenance.[5] For this state of things Liberalism seemed to have no solution, or even concern. It had seen its

---

[1] The best contemporary survey of agrarian problems is Fermín Caballero, *Fomento de la población rural* (3rd ed., Madrid, 1864). See also D. E. Aller, *Las grandes propiedades rústicas en España* (Madrid, 1912); C. Viñas y Mey, *La reforma agraria en España en el siglo XIX* (Santiago, 1933); Brenan, chap. 6.

[2] See R. Pasarón y Lastra, *Informe sobre el estado en que halló á los colonos pobres de Galicia el hambre . . . de 1853* (Madrid, 1853).

[3] *Censo de la población de España* (Madrid, 1863), pp. 732 ff. Half a million others were classed as tenants, one and a half million as proprietors. The various categories overlapped, however.

[4] M. Danvila y Collado, *El contrato de arrendamiento y el juicio de desahucio* (Madrid, 1867), pp. 125 ff.

[5] N. Fernández Cuesta, *Del pauperismo, sus causas y su remedio* (Madrid, 1851), pp. 88–92.

mission as the sweeping away of glaring evils and anachronisms; for the building of new things in their place it trusted too much to the free play of private energies. In a country so long shackled and bled as Spain these energies were too feeble for the task, and Liberalism had no notion of how to reinforce them. To the generation it had first and most vitally appealed to individual freedom seemed, naturally enough, a be-all and end-all. Distrust of public direction or ownership of any kind was in a way the worst legacy of the old régime.

Liberalism was still imprisoned in the towns, surrounded by peasants suspicious of it even when, as sometimes happened, its programme was in harmony with their interests. They had eagerly hoped that the revolution would give them land, and they had been disappointed. Inside the towns themselves too little of a solid *bourgeoisie* solidly committed to modernism had developed. Property was scattered among landowners blue-blooded or up-start, bankers, traders, higher functionaries, successful soldiers. To detect where in such a chaos resided the real power and re-sponsibility of State, to identify in other words a ruling class, is not easy. The old landed aristocracy had long ago handed over the business of governing to monarchy and Church; by 1835, when these were crumbling, it could be dismissed as 'a body with-out a soul, a class destitute of all influence, moral, political, or social'.[1] By 1850 a new plutocracy was beginning to form.

It was a matter of frequent remark that the old moral fabric, the philosophy of life stereotyped by the Church, had disinte-grated, but that no new one had filled the gap. Doctrinaire belief in individual freedom easily ran into an egotistic freedom from any social morality. Liberalism, which in the years of struggle had not been without its heroisms and sacrifices, was the less able to resist such degeneration because it had never ceased to be an exotic growth transplanted to a thin soil. A new corps of pro-fessional politicians competed for prizes that were not all specified in the Constitution. Law and journalism were their two chief highroads, eloquence the indispensable qualification: many of these new men were recruited from the voluble south. All careers were open to talent, though not always the best talent: Spain was being run, if not ruled, by parvenus sprung from the provincial

[1] Anon., *Madrid in 1835* (London, 1836), vol. ii, p. 99; cf. Hughes, *Revelations*, vol. ii, p. 58.

petty *bourgeoisie*. The parties they joined had only painfully and imperfectly emerged from the secret societies or Masonic types of organization imposed by the struggle against absolutism. Each was a loose league of scrambling factions; fifteen Cabinets came and went in the eleven Moderado years after 1843. Of regular structure they had little, of bona-fide programme less.[1] Reduced opportunity in the Church and the colonies fostered *empleomanía*, hunger for government jobs, and the exchequer was burdened not only with the salaries of an inordinate number of functionaries, but with pensions to another swarm dismissed to make room for those whose friends were in the ascendant.

The Constitution of 1845 inaugurated a régime that was, as Castelar said of it later, an imitation of the July Monarchy in France.[2] It prided itself on knowing how to equip the country with an up-to-date machinery of administration, and how to run this efficiently; in performing its work it receded a long way from Liberalism towards enlightened despotism. While the sovereign was still a young girl the dominant politicians could treat her prerogatives as their own; and wide powers were vested in the executive, which could govern by decree or 'royal order' over an ill-defined area.[3] Both Senate and Lower House were packed with government employees. A narrow electorate, chiefly composed of taxpayers liable for 400 reals or more in direct taxation, was managed with equal dexterity. Police coercion, falsification of voting rolls, trickery at the polls, all aided *caciquismo*, the sway of the *cacique* or local boss and vote-maker.[4] Reactionary critics were free to assert that parliamentarism, so young in Spain, was already discredited.[5]

[1] On this defective state of the parties and the resulting incoherence of politics, see, for example, Fernández Cuesta, *El porvenir de los partidos*, p. 5; C. de Mazade, *L'Espagne moderne* (Paris, 1855), pp. 32–34; A. Borrego, *Estudios políticos. De la organización de los partidos en España* (Madrid, 1855), e.g. pp. 201–2.

[2] E. Castelar, *Recuerdos y esperanzas* (Madrid, s.a.), vol. i, p. 293.

[3] The structure and working of each department of State are described in P. Madoz, *Madrid* (Madrid, 1848), pp. 271 ff.; Baron J. von Minutoli, *Spanien und seine fortschreitende Entwickelung* (Berlin, 1852), pp. 87 ff.; A. Ramírez Arcas, *Manual descriptivo y estadístico de las Españas* (Madrid, 1859), pp. 166 ff.

[4] On this kind of trickery see G. de Azcárate, *El régimen parlamentario en la práctica* (new ed., Madrid, 1885); A. de Figueroa y Torres, *El régimen parlamentario* (Madrid, 1886), e.g. pp. 137, 141, 153; J. Costa Martínez, *Oligarquía y caciquismo* (Madrid, 1903).

[5] e.g. P. García Cabellos, *La revolución del siglo XIX* (Segovia, 1848), p. 232; J. Canga Argüelles (y Villalta), *España ante la Asamblea Constituyente* (Madrid, 1854), pp. 58, 60.

Moderados believed in centralization, whereas Progresistas had more sympathy with local self-government, and in 1849 powers formerly divided were concentrated in the hands of the provincial governor, an understudy of a French prefect.[1] Each of the forty-nine 'provinces' into which Spain had been arbitrarily cut up in 1833 was supplied besides with a military governor, and each of the fourteen groups of provinces had a captain-general with something of the character of a viceroy or satrap. Some part of their time-honoured autonomy was still clung to by Navarre and the three Basque provinces; Catalonia on the other hand was more often than not under special, more or less military, control from Madrid. The army now held the country together, indeed, much as the Church had formerly done. It was a consequence of society being so ill articulated, and the gulf between property and pauperism so wide, that a great deal of the work of governing devolved on the army. Well over a hundred thousand strong, it could be described as 'a distinct and independent power of the realm';[2] happily a spoils system of its own kept it too much divided to be able to dominate the country by itself. Civil war had swollen beyond measure a complement of officers already extravagant: in March 1850 there were 6,604 of them, including 650 generals[3] or one to every two hundred other ranks, and they were in a continual ferment of jealousy and intrigue. On balance the army's affiliations were Moderado more than Progresista, and Narváez took pains to strengthen them.

Essentially the army was a gendarmerie scattered over the country to maintain order and authority, in particular by over-awing the bigger towns; though its rank and file consisted of highly reluctant conscripts, chosen by lot for eight years' service. Provincial quotas of both conscripts and taxes were allocated to districts by the *diputación provincial* or county council, and individual tax dues by the *ayuntamiento* or municipal or district council. Hence these local bodies mattered much more than the Cortes to many Spaniards; whoever was top dog there could see to it that his friends did not pay more than they ought, and his enemies at all events not less than they ought. The Moderado fiscal system

[1] On local government see A. Posada, *Evolución legislativa del régimen local en España 1812–1909* (Madrid, 1910).

[2] *North British Review* (Edinburgh), vol. xxvi, no. 61 (Nov. 1856), p. 285.

[3] F. Pérez Mateos, *La villa y corte de Madrid en 1850* (Madrid, 1927), pp. 91–92.

was put in shape by Alejandro Mon in 1845,[1] and was designed to ensure that the costs if not the blessings of the new Spain should be very widely spread. An important item was a twin pair of taxes which could trace their ancestry back to the alcabala: the *puertas*, or octroi duties, and *consumos*, or excise.[2] Both were violently unpopular, partly because they raised the prices of necessaries like meat and oil, partly because they brought a rapacious flock of harpies to every town gate, where peasants and their market-carts were kept waiting for hours. Hardly less detested were the State monopolies or *estancos*, responsible for dear salt and for vile as well as dear tobacco.

Direct taxation, a new departure in Spain, included a roughly graduated levy (not an income-tax) on *industria y comercio*, embracing all trades and professions;[3] and a *contribución territorial*, or tax on real estate. This was payable by all cultivators, including the multitude of very small peasant proprietors and tenant-farmers; the great majority paid less than 100 reals a year. Trifling as the average payment was, it cut sharply into their infinitesimal incomes, and the inequitable distribution of the burden was notorious.[4] Arrears, harassment by tax-collectors, forcible distrainment, followed in its wake. Yet budgets were never balanced, salaries and pensions were paid spasmodically, and interest on much of the debt,[5] especially the foreign, was never paid at all.

Of this jejune polity Madrid was an appropriately artificial capital. By origin an outgrowth of the royal court, it had not been, like London or Paris before it, the heart of the Liberal revolution. But centralization, and such economic growth as Spain could boast, were engendering a more real need for a national centre, and provincial rivalries found their balancing-point only in this 'least Spanish of all Spanish towns'.[6] Finance made Madrid its

[1] Mon's system is described approvingly in J. M. Piernas y Hurtado and M. de Miranda y Eguía, *Manual de instituciones de hacienda pública española* (2nd ed., Madrid 1875). For a recent survey see J. M. Tallada Pauli, *Historia de las finanzas españolas en el siglo XIX* (Madrid, 1946), chap. 6.

[2] On these taxes and their evolution see A. Dutard, *L'octroi en Espagne* (Toulouse, 1909), chap. 1.

[3] See M. Alonso and A. Cereceda, *Manual de la contribución industrial y de comercio* (3rd ed., Madrid, 1862).

[4] For complaints about unfair tax-quotas, see, for example, Hughes, *Revelations*, vol. ii, p. 390; G. A. Hoskins, *Spain, as it is* (London, 1851), vol. i, p. 267.

[5] See L. M. Pastor, *Historia de la deuda pública española* (Madrid, 1863), pp. 180ff., &c.

[6] W. G. Clark, *Gazpacho : or, Summer Months in Spain* (London, 1850), p. 33.

metropolis, and on the Bourse financiers and politicians peeped into one another's pockets and souls. Year by year Madrid was growing into more than a mere administrative centre. Its Ateneo was Spain's intellectual forum; its university had five or six thousand students; there was a big book trade.

Above all there was buzzing activity in journalism.[1] Not much journalistic effort went into reporting news; the chief weight of each paper lay in its leading articles, which expounded the philosophy of the editor or his backers as forcibly as censorship permitted. A Madrid newspaper as a rule consisted of one double sheet, or four pages of five columns each, a serial story occupying half the front page and advertisements half the back. Often it was ephemeral: fourteen dailies perished between 1848 and 1852. The thirteen extant in 1850 had circulations ranging from a few hundred to ten thousand or so and totalling barely 35,000.[2] All the same, by this time every faction needed its organ, and among these dozen papers were the only three or four in the country that could claim a degree of national significance.

Economically Madrid was still very much a parasite on the rest of the country. Population was estimated in 1831 at 150,000, in 1854—by Mesonero Romanos, Madrid's great chronologer—at 270,000.[3] By 1854 there were some ten thousand civil or military posts,[4] with, allowing for a swarm of domestics, something like a fifth or a quarter of the total population dependent on them. Industry lagged, water being scarce and living costs high. There was a gasworks, some iron-working, some production of cloth, a good deal of printing and building labour, and a tobacco factory. A survey a few years earlier reckoned 11,049 *jornaleros* or day-labourers.[5] They lived in the *barrios bajos*, the 'low quarters', slums of the wretchedest sort. The working class of modern character was small, but it was growing, and the pauper-populace

---

[1] Chap. 4 of E. González-Blanco, *Historia del periodismo* (Madrid, 1919), covers 1808–50.

[2] Pérez Mateos, pp. 58–59, 169–70, with details of the papers and their political affiliations; see also F. Silvela, 'Orígenes, historia y caracteres de la prensa española', in *La España del siglo XIX* (Madrid, 1887), vol. iii, pp. 238–9.

[3] *Nuevo manual*, p. 172. The 1857 census figure was 281,170.

[4] Anon., *Las clases pasivas en España* (Madrid, 1856), p. 16. The writer adds that without their income of eleven million reals a month Madrid would dwindle to a mere township.

[5] Madoz, p. 471, with figures for each district. There were more than twice as many domestic servants as day-labourers.

of older days was being assimilated to it. In the revolution of 1854, which first fully vindicated Madrid's claim to political primacy in Spain, this working class was to play its part.

Narváez was after his own fashion a believer in constitutional government as now by law established. He set out, that is, to rule on behalf of and in harmony with the propertied middle classes.[1] The shortcomings of these amorphous and immature groups, as well as the temper of the 'fiery duke' himself, made him more dictator than premier, but his régime showed itself robust enough to survive armed challenges from both Left and Right. In 1846 he beat down a rebellion in Galicia, and in 1848, when their day of wrath overtook Europe's principalities and powers, two ill-planned attempts at insurrection in Madrid by a few Progresistas were snuffed out with ease,[2] and then made the pretext for an exercise in intimidation. Similar risings in Catalonia were also dealt with. So was a separate Carlist revolt, smouldering there since 1846, the war of the *Matiners* or dawn-raiders.[3] Much more markedly than the war of 1833-9 it failed to spread beyond a limited area, chiefly in the Catalan hills. Carlism still had a reservoir of rustic sentiment and clerical blessing to draw on, but for men with anything to lose the old allegiance had become, like Jacobitism after 1745, more a mood than a programme.

Friends of order were perturbed by a new and worse peril, social instead of merely political. Once their fears were aroused they slid quickly into a panic that was authentic enough even if fomented and exploited by alarmists for purposes of their own. Though little happened during 1848 in Spain, the spectacle of happenings abroad, especially in Paris, convinced many that they too were about to be gripped by the 'social problem', that disease of modern Europe. Its advent was most frighteningly apparent at Barcelona, whose mills were drawing in recruits from far as well as near and subjecting them to all the hardships of an unregulated industrialization as they earned their ten or twelve reals a day by a dozen or more hours' labour.[4] These workers inherited or

---

[1] 'Narváez era representante de la mesocracia . . .' (A. Révesz, *Un dictador liberal: Narváez* (Madrid, 1953), p. 191). Cf. J. and M. Prados López, *Navdez, el espadón de Loja* (Madrid, 1952), p. 132.

[2] See E. Rodríguez-Solís, *Historia del partido republicano español* (Madrid, 1892-93), vol. ii, pp. 395 ff.

[3] See R. Oyarzun, *Historia del Carlismo* (Bilbao, 1939), chap. 15; J. Carrera Pujal, *Historia política de Cataluña en el siglo XIX* (Barcelona, 1957-8), vol. iv, chap. 2.

[4] F. Garrido, *Historia de las asociaciones obreras en Europa* (Barcelona, 1864), vol. i,

acquired the temper that had made Catalonia's history one of rebellion; they were 'turbulent, disloyal, and democratic', as a foreign visitor noted reprovingly. French proximity intensified agitation as well as investments—'the French socialist is nightly haranguing in the cafés';[1] though on the other hand the half-foreign character of industrial Catalonia separated its workers as well as its *bourgeoisie* from the rest of Spain.

To many timid men of substance a revolt of the masses seemed imminent; a new Dark Age, as several writers expressed it, coming to engulf civilization, with the factory workman for barbarian invader.[2] Few now harboured the illusion, a legacy of the old somnolent days of priest rule, that Spain unlike other countries contained no serious class enmities. 'There was not a conservative paper in all Madrid', wrote an American resident, 'that did not daily and principally enlarge upon the horrors of the socialist doctrines.'[3] These doctrines were still very nebulous, but this in a way only added to their terrors. And elemental and scattered as the forces of social revolt were, they were nevertheless gathering; and at this intermediate, indeterminate point in history State and society were so much out of joint that a wholesale overturning of things was perhaps less impossible than either earlier or later.

The question now was whether Liberalism was capable, before Socialism arrived to supplant it, of broadening its foundation. Reformers pointed out that the masses were realizing how little it had done for them yet. Liberty must no longer be left to seem the emblem of poverty and suffering, one veteran publicist wrote in 1851.[4] A terrific upheaval under communist banners was preparing, declared the radical Sixto Cámara, who came of a poor family in Rioja, if those in power remained deaf.[5] Another urged that the masses should be afforded protection if they were not to mutiny like the Israelites wandering in the desert.[6] One newspaper

---

pp. 62–64. Cf. on working-class conditions his *L'Espagne contemporaine*, pp. 232 ff.; and on the background of Catalan labour disputes, L. Martín-Granizo, *Apuntes para la historia del trabajo en España* (Madrid, 1950), chap. 15.

[1] J. M. Mackie, *Cosas de España* (New York, 1855), pp. 238, 254–5.
[2] e.g. J. Canga Argüelles (y Villalta), *El gobierno español en sus relaciones con la Santa Sede* (Madrid, 1856), pp. 132–3.   [3] Wallis, *Spain*, p. 203.
[4] V. Bertrán de Lis, *Los gobiernos y los intereses materiales* (Madrid, 1851), p. 29.
[5] Sisto Saenz de la Cámara (usually known as Sixto Cámara), *Espíritu moderno* (Madrid, 1848), p. 44.
[6] J. Frexas, *El socialismo y la teocracia* (Barcelona, 1852–5), vol. i, p. 135, vol. iii, p. 726.

adopted the brave motto: 'More liberal today than yesterday, more liberal tomorrow than today'; it only scandalized the older men. Alcalá Galiano thought it time to recognize that the common people had many bad as well as some good instincts, and that once more the tree of knowledge was bearing the fruit of death.[1]

Much stir was being made by the writings of Donoso Cortés, an ex-Liberal preaching a combination of religion with bayonets to save order and property; and by those of the Catalan priest Balmes, one of the originators of Christian Socialism, who had been acutely aware of the strife of capital and labour in his native province. For Liberals in office religion as the most facile way of escape from the social problem clearly had attractions, and soon after the return of the Moderados to power there were symptoms of a more conciliatory attitude towards the clergy. After the *grande peur* of 1848 these multiplied. The penal code was severe against any public dissent from Catholic faith. In 1851 a Concordat halted sales of the property of the secular clergy, which had begun to go the same way as that of the monks; it also restored to the clergy much of their control over education, and encouraged a revival of priestly pretensions galling to all anti-clericals. Already, in short, there was a drift towards the morganatic alliance of *bourgeoisie* and Church soon to be known as neo-Catholicism.

Whether Liberals out of office could give Liberalism a new lease of life remained to be seen. Progresistas had been in the wilderness long enough to wrangle themselves into complete confusion. So far as they had any acknowledged leader it was Espartero, even though many of them had turned against him in 1843; the party still felt helpless without a military figurehead. Espartero was allowed to return home after five years' exile in England, and since then had been vegetating in his garden at Logroño on the upper Ebro. He was understood to be keeping his eye on events and reserving himself for some great moment, but was doing nothing to rally his straggling followers.

The green branch of Liberalism was the Democratic movement, which put out a first manifesto in 1849.[2] Its early doings were

---

[1] A. M. Alcalá Galiano, *Breves reflexiones sobre la índole de la crisis* (Madrid, 1848), pp. 46–47, 49–50.
[2] Part of the text is given in E. López, *Antología de las Cortes de 1846 á 1854* (Madrid, 1912), pp. 548 ff. Cf. J. Ordas de Avecilla (usually known as Ordax Avecilla), *La política en España* (Madrid, 1853), pp. 41–48.

shrouded in the conspiratorial secrecy, or sometimes mystification, that both police meddling and force of habit induced in Spanish politics. It had contacts with Freemasonry, which about 1850 was making some efforts to reorganize, and with secret societies. One of these, 'Young Spain', headed by a Grand Planet, sought influence among the students[1]—without much effect, for the student body does not figure among the active political forces of this period; though writers often talked vaguely of 'Youth' as a progressive force, as happens in all uneasy communities where class lines have not yet been clearly drawn. There was much misconception of what Democracy stood for. One of its adherents was disconcerted when he came to Madrid to find a notion prevalent that its intention, on gaining power, was to authorize three days of free-for-all looting; whereas, he protested, it signified simply 'government of the people by the people and for the people'.[2] What this catch-phrase meant in practice was faith in thoroughgoing radical Liberalism: universal suffrage, local self-government verging on federalism, and, increasingly, republicanism.

The Democrats were a mixed lot by origin. Next to Orense the nobleman,[3] the best known was Rivero, a short swarthy Andalusian who began life in 1815 as a foundling. But fairly characteristic of Democrats, and marking some of them off from other Liberals more clearly than their formal tenets, was a vein of sympathy with the poor, a concern for social amelioration. One day the working-man would vindicate his right to citizenship, declared Ordax Avecilla, in spite of selfish *bourgeois* obstruction.[4] This turn of thought was more prominent in some of the younger recruits: Sixto Cámara, ten years junior to Rivero, and still more Garrido, who picked up Fourierism in exile and became its leading exponent in Spain.

Ideas about the social problem suffered from lurking contradictions. Ordax Avecilla, classed by some as a socialist, believed that private enterprise and capital, once set free from all clogs, would

[1] V. Mage, *Les Isabelle* (Clermont-Ferrand, 1861), pp. 52–53.
[2] *Diario de las Sesiones de las Cortes Constituyentes . . . de 1854, 1855 y 1856* (Madrid, 1856) (cited below as 'D.S.'), pp. 3,699–3,701.
[3] His *Qué hará en el poder el partido Progresista?* (Madrid, 1847) is a good summary of his tenets. He and his friends were inclined to admire the Basque provinces, under home rule, as a model for the rest of Spain; cf. his *Los fueros* (Madrid,1859).
[4] Ordax Avecilla, pp. 57–58, 60.

revivify the national economy and thereby deliver the poor from pauperism. Even among the younger men 'socialism' hardly got beyond a hazy concept of 'association', or something like a co-operative movement. Garrido developed little interest in the nature of capitalism. Democrats stood for a broadening and completion of the *bourgeois* revolution: the dilemma they were never sufficiently to comprehend was that a *bourgeoisie* so weak and wavering could only be made to do its own work by mass pressures, and that these could only be mobilized round economic demands. So far they had virtually no contact with the peasantry; with the urban workers some, though too little. A Malaga carpenter named Miralpeix was one of their most enthusiastic agitators. Cervera starved himself to buy candles for evening classes of Madrid working-men;[1] but the idea of learning lessons from the working class and its conditions, as well as teaching it, had scarcely dawned.

In the stalemate of old things and new, another competitor was about to take a hand. Pushed into the background for many years by the advance of Liberalism and by Isabel's minority, the throne ought to have had no chance of ever recovering a real share of power. But for it as for the Church the now deepening 'crisis of the ruling classes'[2] opened up fresh prospects. It too would be hailed as a useful barrier against anarchy or socialism; under cover of this recommendation the *palaciegos* would be free to play their own game.

---

[1] F. Garrido, *Historia del reinado del último Borbon de España* (Barcelona, 1868–9) (cited below as Garrido, *Historia*), vol. iii, pp. 190–1, 213–14.

[2] M. Fernández Almagro, *Cánovas. Su vida y su política* (Madrid, 1951), p. 63.

II

THE ATTACK ON THE CONSTITUTION

The Palace Ministries, 1851–3

IN 1850 Isabel II was in her twentieth year. One English traveller thought she looked forty already.[1] Another, more indulgent, thought not more than twenty-five, 'a prettyish, ladylike woman', the nose bad certainly but not quite so bulbous as it appeared on her coins.[2] Amiable and good-hearted when allowed to do just as she pleased, she was besides very *Madrileña* in mannerism and gesture and in her idiomatic Spanish. All this went a long way with her subjects. Four years earlier she had been wretchedly married, amid intrigues that convulsed European diplomacy, to her reputedly impotent cousin Francisco de Asís, a clever, timid, superstitious, meddlesome young fellow encumbered with a disreputable old father, a jealous brother, and a bevy of sisters. Adapting herself phlegmatically like her mother before her to the exigencies of their profession, Isabel found consolation in a fund of naïve piety or credulity, and in a long series of liaisons. Both promoted a good understanding between palace and Church; a royal sinner who repents on Sundays makes an ideal subject for clerical manipulation.

By now she was acquiring a taste for political power also. Her grand design was to rule Spain through a *camarilla* of her own intimates, much as her father Ferdinand had done. Many threads linked the palace with the landed aristocracy, the Church, everything backward-looking; but also with newer men and ideas, those of the Stock Exchange. Cristina the Queen Mother was a link with both. Once free of her repulsive first marriage, she had made a happier second one with a humble guardsman named Muñoz, and had a fresh brood of children, as well as costly tastes, to provide for. She and her husband, now Duke of Riánsares, were

---

[1] Baxter, vol. i, p. 215.
[2] G. J. Cayley, *Las alforjas (or, the bridle-roads of Spain)* (London, 1853), vol. ii, p. 130.

dabbling in the latest methods of get-rich-quick finance, in partnership with Spain's would-be railway king, Salamanca.

An epoch ended when Narváez quitted office in January 1851. His domineering nature had irked his own party as well as the opposition. It irked also the Court in whose name he ruled, and his departure was an unmistakable dropping of the pilot. Paradoxically, it made constitutional government more, not less, insecure. He and his fellow generals were content with the measure of parliamentarianism that existed, and they were less easily thrown into panic than some were by fear of the people and of anarchy: the hysterical reactionaries were civilians like Donoso Cortés. But by depriving parliamentarianism of real vitality, and ruling through the royal prerogative instead, they had opened the way for the palace to circumvent them and their Constitution of 1845 at once.

To Isabel and her fellow schemers any Constitution at all was an encumbrance; they wanted, for instance, to remove the budget from public scrutiny. To timorous conservatives who heard tumbrils hurrying near, this Constitution of 1845 was still not a close enough strait-waistcoat to confine the nation's limbs. Among them was Juan Bravo Murillo, Narváez's Minister of Finance and then his successor, who was exactly the respectable figure needed to smooth the way for *camarilla* rule. Encouraged by the *coup d'état* of December 1851 in Paris and the revival of absolutism in France, and with a pretext furnished by a madman's attempt on the Queen's life in February 1852, he and his Cabinet applied themselves to a project of constitutional 'reform', in a highly restrictive sense.[1] A vociferous opposition soon arose against it. Despite a new and stiffer press law,[2] a united front of newspapers in defence of the Constitution ranged from the radical *Novedades*, owned and edited by Fernández de los Ríos, to the staidly Progresista *Nación*, run by Rua Figueroa, and the conservative *Diario Español*.[3] Among the politicians the lead was taken

---

[1] The 'reform' plan is explained and defended, and its text printed, in Bravo Murillo, *Opúsculos*, vol. iv, and in Marqués de Miraflores (one of his ministers), *La Reforma en 1852* (Madrid, 1852). See also L. Sánchez Agesta, *Historia del constitucionalismo español* (Madrid, 1955), pp. 270–2.

[2] On the press law of 2 Apr. 1852 see J. E. de Eguizábal, *Apuntes para una historia de la legislación española sobre imprenta* (Madrid, 1879), pp. 198 ff.

[3] On this newspaper campaign see C. Martos, *La revolución de julio en 1854* (Madrid, 1855), pp. 29–33; cf. Silvela, p. 239.

by Moderados, or those among them not yet seduced by offers of government posts. They were not demoralized as Progresistas were by a decade in the wilderness, and their military men were very ready to despise Bravo Murillo as a civilian. Narváez got himself ordered out of the country before the end of 1852. José, one of the three powerful brothers Gutiérrez de la Concha, was dismissed from the captain-generalship of Cuba. Leopoldo O'Donnell, Conde de Lucena, threw up his post of director-general of infantry in a huff at seeing a junior, Lersundi, promoted over his head to the War ministry—a post always held by an army man.

These malcontents had seats in the Senate, and there, whatever their private motives and grudges, they voiced genuinely the indignation of both *bourgeoisie* and populace against jobbery, waste, and rule by 'the hidden power'. When Bravo Murillo re-opened the Cortes on 1 December 1852 he suffered an immediate defeat, and next day dissolved it. Rumours of an impending *coup d'état* were rife; but on the 13th ministers lost their nerve and resigned. Still obstinate, Isabel replaced Bravo Murillo with Roncali, Conde de Alcoy, an undistinguished soldier. Elections were held in February 1853, and the opposition in spite of official pressure on voters got a quarter of the seats. In the session that opened on 1 March there was much denunciation of fraudu-lent railway contracts: the senior Concha—Manuel, Marqués del Duero and a prominent general—hinted broadly at connexions between Salamanca and Cristina's husband.

On 6 April one more Addled Parliament was abruptly pro-rogued, and on the 14th Roncali was dropped, just as uncere-moniously, by the *camarilla*. Discontent was curdling by now into talk of plots and risings, and mutterings could be heard even about a change of dynasty.[1] Isabel had never inspired the old instinctive loyalty in the peasantry, and she had forfeited the esteem of the urban classes; she was making things worse by being horribly indiscreet with her current lover, a young officer named Arana, most odious of all the profiteers. In Galicia a fright-ful famine was raging; the British Minister, Lord Howden, thought things as bad there as they had ever been in Ireland,[2] and

[1] Baron A. du Jardin, Belgian Minister at Madrid, to H.-M.-J.-G. de Brouckère, Minister for Foreign Affairs, no. 53, 10 Apr. 1853; *Espagne*, vol. 7 (2), in Foreign Ministry archives, Brussels.

[2] Howden to Clarendon, no. 82, 20 Apr. 1853, F.O. 72. 822.

the French Ambassador, the Marquis de Turgot, wrote of whole villages literally perishing.[1]

Roncali was replaced by a similar second-rate general, Lersundi, whose Cabinet represented another fragment broken off from the Moderado party. The crowning service expected of him by his employers was legitimation of the railway concessions they had got by hook or by crook; one above all that rival interests had wrestled over for years, for a 'Northern Railway' from Madrid to the French frontier. Unluckily the minister responsible, Claudio Moyano, was the least pliable of Lersundi's colleagues, and his conscience got the better of him.[2] He was replaced at the department of *Fomento* (Development) by the more accommodating A. Esteban Collantes, and on 7 August a decree validated all the concessions—which, the opposition maintained, required parliamentary sanction.

With this, the idea of removing Isabel from the throne took a more positive turn. It came naturally to its sponsors to begin by sounding foreign governments, those at any rate of France and England. These two countries bulked far the largest in Spain's foreign relations, political and commercial alike, and the lack of ballast in her internal politics gave them a good deal of influence there too. Between them there was chronic jealousy and jockeying. French ties were traditionally with Moderado circles, English with Progresista. Howden and Turgot were both men who threw themselves heartily into the game. The former had been in Madrid since 1850, and was an old friend of Lord Clarendon, who became Foreign Secretary early in 1853; Turgot was appointed in April 1853, after having preceded Drouyn de Lhuys as Foreign Minister. During 1853, however, the two countries were being drawn together by their common enmity to Russia over the Eastern question, and some mutual recognition of interests was growing up between them. England's recurrent anxiety in these years was the thought of reaction in Spain backed, as in 1823, by armed French intervention. Napoleon III, insecure at home, was equally sensitive to any risk of a swing towards democracy in his neighbourhood; his Spanish nightmare was a 'red republic'. There was

---

[1] Turgot to É. Drouyn de Lhuys, Minister for Foreign Affairs, no. 8, 13 June 1853; *Espagne*, vol. 842, in Foreign Ministry archives, Paris.

[2] See C. Moyano, *Memoria sobre las concesiones hechas de ferro-carriles* (Madrid, 1854).

no Russian agent at Madrid to play on their differences, since Isabel had never been recognized by Nicholas I.

The longer Isabel was allowed to go on, the more real the danger of a popular revolution became. If she was to be removed, a successor must be held in readiness, for a republic was a prospect as frightening to most Spaniards as to Napoleon. Her only child, the Princess of Asturias, was a sickly infant, to say nothing of her debatable paternity. Her sister María Luisa, while intensely respectable, was insignificant; moreover she was married to the Duke of Montpensier, who was only too willing to replace Don Francisco as King-Consort, but was unacceptable to England as a Frenchman and to France as a son of Louis Philippe. Looking then abroad, it was natural to think of borrowing a new ruler from Portugal, especially because a sentiment had been spreading for some years in favour of an 'Iberian union' between the two nations.[1]

England's paramountcy at Lisbon was well understood; and late in August, when Howden was on holiday in Paris, his assistant Otway was visited by General Infante, an old Progresista 'esteemed for his prudence and judgement'—anything but a firebrand. He broached the whole problem, and said that a revolt would have started already were it not for the difficulty of whom to put in Isabel's place.[2] A few weeks later Otway had another visitor on the same errand, the third of the Concha brothers, Juan. He and his Moderado friends, comprehending English objections to a Braganza and a possible union, were thinking as a second best of the Duke of Genoa, brother to the King of Sardinia.[3] Similar overtures were made to the French. But England and France each feared that any change of dynasty might be prejudicial to their own interests and perilous to their new-fledged alliance. They agreed that the least of possible evils was for Isabel to be kept on the throne as long as might be; a consensus which was to exert an appreciable influence on events in Spain.

A financial scandal helped to capsize Lersundi's unsteady Cabinet. Once more the opposition argued that it was Isabel's duty to choose new men who enjoyed the confidence of the public;

---

[1] S. de Mas, in *La Iberia* (3rd ed., Madrid, 1854), was one of its chief proponents. See also J. del Nido y Segalerva, *La unión ibérica* (Madrid, 1914).
[2] Otway to Clarendon, no. 75, Secret & Conf., 27 Aug. 1853, F.O. 72. 824.
[3] Otway to Clarendon, no. 89, Conf., 20 Sept. 1853, F.O. 72. 825.

she might indeed have answered that this was something no Spanish ministry of any hue was ever likely to enjoy. At the announcement on 19 September of the next premier's name, Howden expressed the general view when he summed him up as 'a man of great talents, but great political immorality'.[1] Luis José Sartorius, first Count of San Luis, was a parvenu, a southerner who had risen by journalism and served as Minister of the Interior, an obediently unscrupulous one, under Narváez. He collected about him his own faction of *Polacos*; he collected also a fortune, and displayed, Otway wrote, 'an Asiatic luxury, and the pomp and splendour of a most wealthy capitalist'.[2] Lately he had been currying favour with the palace and toadying to Arana. Like many another with a bad conscience, his government would be strong on justification by public works. His newspaper, the *Heraldo*, always preached the gospel of material progress as the one thing needful, and as a diplomat was to remark, San Luis's Cabinet always affected to be maturing economic plans of the most far-reaching importance, though when one tried to discover what they were one could get only the vaguest replies.[3]

San Luis took the Interior himself; a practised hand would be required there. At the War Department he had Anselmo Blaser, a general too inconspicuous to overawe the military men of the opposition. The two most significant appointments were those of Domenech, a Catalan lawyer who had ratted on his Progresista friends, for Finance, and Esteban Collantes who retained the portfolio of Development.[4] As a sop to the army San Luis authorized the return to Spain of his old patron Narváez, though the two were no longer friends, and he conferred the highest army posts on men who had been loud in opposition, Juan de la Concha and Ros de Olano and Fernández de Córdova.[5] Most

---

[1] Howden to Lord John Russell, then Foreign Secretary, no. 6, 10 Jan. 1853, F.O. 72. 821. Cf. a severe character-sketch by J. Rico y Amat, in *El libro de los Diputados y Senadores* (Madrid, 1862–6), vol. iii, pp. 223–34.

[2] Otway to Clarendon, no. 95, Conf., 29 Sept. 1853, F.O. 72. 825.

[3] Comte A. van der Straten-Ponthoz (Du Jardin's successor) to Brouckère, no. 22, 7 Feb. 1854; *Espagne*, vol. 8 (1).

[4] Calderón de la Barca, Foreign Minister, and the Marqués de Molíns, at the Navy, were aristocratic ciphers. The best man in the new Cabinet was the Marqués de Gerona, who before resigning from the Ministry of Justice produced some useful reforms in judicial procedure.

[5] Concha and Ros de Olano accepted their appointments with a show of reluctance, or under protest; see F. Fernández de Córdova, *Memoria . . . sobre los sucesos políticos . . . de julio de 1854* (Madrid, 1855), pp. 18–19.

ingratiating of all, he promised that the Cortes should soon meet again. But he had against him, besides his own unsavoury reputation, the conviction that the real government was the *camarilla*. Conscious of this, when the Cortes met on 29 November he offered, in effect, a bargain: he would withdraw the famous plan of constitutional reform in return for ratification of all the railway concessions. His enemies were in no mood for compromise, and floods of eloquence were soon washing over the benches.[1] On 9 December came the dramatic scene, one of those that may go far, if history is propitious, to cement a genuine parliamentary tradition, when the Senate divided on the railway contracts, and the best-known men in Spain stood up to be counted. San Luis was beaten by 105 to 69; next day he prorogued the session.

He had no choice now but to show himself in his true colours. Reprisals, following an often-repeated pattern, were taken against place-holders who had defied the government. José de la Concha and Ros de Olano were among those dismissed. They and their confederates argued heatedly that the Cabinet ought to have resigned instead of closing the Cortes.[2] A private meeting on the 11th agreed on a protest to the Queen, drafted by one of the least unprincipled Moderados, Ríos Rosas. Editors of the anti-reform group of newspapers drew up a manifesto of their own, which was widely circulated in spite of official menaces.[3] As 1854 opened everything seemed ready for an upheaval. All Spain, it could be said, was conspiring.[4] A rumour got afloat of a plot against Isabel's life instigated by the new American Minister among foreign refugees in Madrid.[5] He was the soon notorious Pierre Soulé, whose object was by fair means or foul to obtain Cuba, and who had just commenced his operations by shooting the French

---

[1] On these debates see, for example, Marqués de Miraflores, *Continuación de las memorias políticas para escribir la historia del reinado de Isabel II* (Madrid, 1873), vol. i, pp. 439-40.

[2] e.g. *Clamor Público*, 4 Jan. 1854, 1st leader; cf. *Memorias de Buenaventura Vivó, ministro de Méjico en España durante los años 1853, 1854 y 1855* (Madrid, 1856), p. 38.

[3] J. del Nido y Segalerva, *Historia política y parlamentaria del Excmo. Sr. D. Antonio de los Ríos y Rosas* (Madrid, 1913), pp. 349, 350-4, with text. Cf. A. Fernández de los Ríos, *Estudio histórico de las luchas políticas en la España del siglo XIX* (2nd ed., Madrid, 1879-80), vol. ii, pp. 303-4, 309; and a leaflet reproduced in Anon. (Señora Calderón de la Barca, a Scotswoman), *The Attaché in Madrid* (New York, 1856), pp. 122-3.

[4] M. Angelón, *Isabel II: historia de la reina de España* (Madrid and Barcelona, 1860), p. 360; cf. M. Villalba Hervás, *Recuerdos de cinco lustros (1843-68)* (Madrid, 1896), p. 146.

[5] French police reports from London in *Espagne*, vol. 843, pp. 129-30.

Ambassador through the knee in a duel on the Prado.[1] Another complication lay in Isabel's approaching confinement: the birth of a prince might embolden the Court to strike its long-meditated blow and alter the Constitution by a *coup d'état*.

With civil war on the horizon, the more responsible men of the opposition had to face the possibility that any upheaval, if not carefully guided, might turn into the 'red revolution' so much talked of since 1848. A diplomat newly arrived, the Belgian Minister, Count van der Straten-Ponthoz, was impressed by the extent to which political feeling had by this time penetrated the masses. The highest matters of state, no longer sacred from them, were being canvassed in street and market.[2] Moreover, the European war about to break out was expected on all hands to have repercussions in Spain. Allied victory, it was assumed, would stimulate Liberalism there, Russian victory would benefit Carlism, but a long-drawn-out conflict might open the gates for another 1848 all over the Continent. A Spanish revolution would be no joke, Howden observed, if the politicians were to lose control and 'the People were stubbornly to take the bit between their teeth, instead of allowing it to be put into their mouths'.[3]

In face of such hazards the opposition chiefs were growing more anxious to keep the situation in their own hands. There was a ready model for them to follow in the carefully restricted *coup*, the revolution of limited liabilities, which brought to power in 1851 the soldier now governing Portugal, the liberal-conservative Duke of Saldanha. One of them was to say after it was all over that their prime object was to forestall a dangerous popular rising.[4] To achieve this might well prove impossible without the removal of Isabel. They were agreed by now that only a Braganza would do in her place; and they realized that to have any chance of winning Britain's consent they must rule out any 'Iberian union'. On 4 January, accordingly, Howden was visited by the Marqués

[1] Strained relations with the U.S., chiefly over U.S. designs on Cuba, were a chronic embarrassment to every Spanish government of this period. On Soulé see A. A. Ettinger, *The Mission to Spain of Pierre Soulé (1853–1855)* (Yale, 1932).

[2] Straten-Ponthoz to Brouckère, no. 203, 31 Dec. 1853; *Espagne*, vol. 7 (2).

[3] Howden to Clarendon, no. 31, Conf., 18 Jan. 1854, F.O. 72. 842.

[4] This was General Dulce, speaking to the French consul-general at Barcelona: Baradère to Drouyn de Lhuys, no. 130, 7 Sept. 1854, in *Espagne*, Consular, vol. 51. O'Donnell's admirers represented things in this light later on; see M. Ibo Alfaro, *Apuntes para la historia de D. Leopoldo O-Donnell* (Madrid, 1868), vol. i, pp. 8–9, and C. Navarro y Rodrigo, *O'Donnell y su tiempo* (Madrid, 1869), p. 96.

del Duero, who, with Narváez back in Spain but only sulking in his tent down in the south, could be considered 'the active and recognized head of the Moderado opposition'. He wasted no time beating about the bush, but said 'that it was absolutely necessary for the prosperity and tranquillity of Spain to do away completely with the Bourbon dynasty'. His proposal was that young Pedro V, who had just succeeded his mother, Maria II, should become King of Spain, leaving the Portuguese throne to his brother Luiz.[1] Two days later General Infante came to pledge Progresista support to the arrangement.[2] Howden made himself its warm advocate with his government, which, however, could not be induced to countenance it, while France, too, reiterated a firm preference for the *status quo*.[3] It is a pity that they were so inelastic, and still more that the cautious men at Madrid set so much store by their approval instead of forcing their hands by acting without it. A change of dynasty at this stage would have represented a real, if limited, step forward.

Isabel's child was born on 5 January. On one side there was keen disappointment at its not being a boy—this was 'evidently regarded as another ministerial blunder', said a wit[4]—while the opposition newspapers pointedly ignored it. On the 8th it expired. Meanwhile big meetings of politicians were being held; on 13 January two hundred senators and deputies at Duero's house approved an address to the Queen which demanded reopening of the Cortes, and warned her that any attempt at a *coup d'état* would put the throne in jeopardy.[5] In the inner ring of the opposition preparations were being made for action.[6] Four army men in particular were coming together in a distinct group: O'Donnell, Messina, León y Medina, and Serrano y Domínguez, who had been Isabel's first lover. León y Medina was soon on his way to Saragossa to feel the pulse of his friend Dulce, captain-general of Aragon, and from there down to Loja to see what could be made of Narváez, whose neutrality, if not more, would be essential.

---

[1] Howden to Clarendon, no. 12, Conf., 4 Jan. 1854, F.O. 72. 842.

[2] Howden to Clarendon, no. 15, Conf., 6 Jan. 1854, F.O. 72. 842.

[3] Clarendon to Howden, no. 6, 14 Jan. 1854, F.O. 72. 840; Drouyn de Lhuys to Turgot, no. 1, 10 Jan. 1854; *Espagne*, vol. 843.

[4] *The Attaché in Madrid*, p. 169.

[5] Text in Ribot y Fontseré, *La revolución*, pp. 46–50, and Navarro y Rodrigo, pp. 66–71.

[6] See A. Pirala, *Historia contemporánea* (Madrid, 1875–9), vol. ii, pp. 175–6; G. Borao, *Historia del alzamiento de Zaragoza en 1854* (Saragossa, 1855), pp. 14–15.

San Luis broke in rudely on these plottings. That some treasonable approaches had been made to foreign Powers was already leaking out, as everything did in Spain, and gave him all the pretext he needed. Any officer on the army list could be directed to reside in any prescribed place: it was a virtual right of banishing trouble-makers, often utilized. On 17 January Duero and O'Donnell were abruptly ordered off to the Canary Islands, José de la Concha and Infante to Majorca. Infante and Duero tamely allowed themselves to be escorted off. José de la Concha took a middle course by going as far as Barcelona and then absconding into France.[1] Only O'Donnell defied the order outright, by going into hiding in Madrid, at first in the house of a young admirer, the Marqués de la Vega de Armijo, and then in a corner of the offices of the *Novedades*, where he could sleep safely among bales of newsprint.[2] San Luis had got in the first blow, and a telling one. Neither army nor country was willing to rise merely because a number of generals were being sent out of the way. Their elimination was followed by that of other prominent officers; and on 5 February the police made a sudden swoop on the central committee of the Democrats, in session at Becerra's house in the Calle de Jardines. A dozen were laid by the heels, including most of the top men not in exile—Rivero, Sixto Cámara, Ordax Avecilla— and lodged in the Saladero jail.[3]

Jealousies between Progresista and Moderado, neither wanting to be the other's catspaw, were always liable to break out afresh; while both parties lacked credit with the public, which had seen too many desertions and suspected that those who sounded the most patriotic were only waiting their turn to be offered a plum. Some newspapers kept up the struggle as best they could under a bludgeoning of fines and confiscations, but, as several of them confessed, with diminishing effect. The revolutionary mood was in danger of fizzling out. 'The Government inspires no sympathy

[1] Frederick Hardman, newly arrived as *The Times* correspondent, thought him 'by far the cleverer of the two brothers' ('The Insurrection in Spain', *Blackwood's Magazine*, Aug. 1854, p. 152).
[2] Fernández de los Ríos, *Luchas políticas*, vol. ii, pp. 332–4. All accounts of the period of hiding derive from this work or from the author's briefer narrative, *Cinco meses de ocultación del general O'Donnell*. This appeared anonymously in *La Ilustración* (Madrid), no. 286, 21 Aug. 1854, but its authorship is clear from *Luchas políticas*, vol. ii, pp. 313–15.
[3] *Nación*, 7 Feb. 1854, 1/4 (i.e. p. 1, col. 4), protesting at the arrests; cf. Rodríguez-Solís, vol. ii, pp. 470–1. All but one were released on bail on 13 May.

anywhere', wrote Howden impartially, 'the opposition no sympathy, and the Throne no sympathy.'[1]

A first attempt to turn the tables was made at Saragossa. A plot
there parallel or related to O'Donnell's at Madrid was impeded by
the transfer of Dulce to the capital: he was given, presumably to
keep him quiet, the post of director-general of cavalry. A Brigadier Hore took over the lead; not much light was ever shed on
his plans.[2] When on 20 February he led his men of the Cordoba
regiment out on to the streets, some three hundred citizens joined,
including a group of republicans or Democrats headed by the
university teacher E. Ruiz Pons. In the old town's narrow crooked
alleys a brief fight took place; Hore was among the few killed.
Most of his followers gained the French frontier, where they were
interned.[3] The *Heraldo* affected to treat the rising as a contemp-
tible triviality; but a state of emergency was proclaimed over the
whole country.[4] A miscellaneous batch of well-known men were
arrested as a precaution, and a fresh platoon of unreliable generals,
including Serrano, was expelled from Madrid. On the night of the
22nd there was a regular round-up of opposition journalists.
Fernández de los Ríos of the *Novedades* was among those wanted,
and he and O'Donnell had to evade capture by clambering through
a trap-door into a draughty loft and shivering till dawn in the
north wind.[5]

Though resistance now seemed quelled, repression was steadily
intensified; in the capital the harsh and despotic governor, Count
Xavier de Quinto, ruled with a rod of iron. Thus sheltered, the
reigning faction made haste to enjoy the golden time of graft and

---

[1] Howden to Clarendon, no. 58, 18 Feb. 1854, F.O. 72. 842.

[2] Fernández de los Ríos (*Luchas políticas*, vol. ii, p. 338) and Martos (p. 56) both
confessed that they could not discover the real facts. M. Ibo Alfaro, *La Corona de
Laurel* (Madrid, 1860), vol. i, p. 106, is positive that Hore acted under O'Donnell's
instructions. Howden reported, as if sure of the fact: 'Had the insurrection at
Zaragoza succeeded, Espartero intended to present himself' (Howden to Clarendon,
no. 66, 25 Feb. 1854, F.O. 72. 842).

[3] See F. Pi y Margall and F. Pi y Arsuaga, *Las grandes conmociones políticas del siglo
XIX en España* (Barcelona, 1933), cited below as Pi, *Conmociones*: vol. i, pp. 372-3;
E. Escalera and M. González Llana, *La España del siglo XIX* (Madrid, 1864-6),
vol. iii, chap. 42; Martos, pp. 71-77; official reports in I. Bermejo, *Alzamiento popular
de 1854* (Madrid, 1854), pp. 9-12.

[4] R.O. (*Real Orden*, or decree) of 22 Feb. 1854; *Colección Legislativa de España*—
cited below as C.L.—vol. lxi, p. 264.

[5] Fernández de los Ríos, *Cinco meses*, p. 327, and *Luchas políticas*, vol. ii, pp. 339-
42; on the round-up cf. *Nación*, 24 Feb. 1854, 1/2.

jobbery. Cristina was the presiding genius, and fiestas glittered one after the other in her ornate mansion, where all who were lucky enough to have the entrée flocked in quest of entertainment and Stock Exchange tips. All this cost money, and San Luis was haunted by the shadow of approaching bankruptcy, though the unvoted budget was being enforced by decree. 'The financial affairs of this country', Howden wrote to Clarendon in February, 'are in a most lamentable state. . . . Your Lordship will probably say that you never knew them otherwise, which is perfectly true; there are, however, degrees in the shame and misery of this unfortunate Treasury.'[1] In April it suffered a still more acute spasm of distress, and ministerial papers accused a rancorous opposition of trying to engineer a run on the bank.

One serious consequence was that money could not be found for carrying on the public works which helped to lessen unemployment, and at a time when economic hardship was severe. Howden thought with alarm of the probable effect on 'that most dangerous population who live in the suburbs'.[2] An expensive concession had to be made to the hunger-pinched masses in another way, by a reduction in the price of State salt.[3] Trade was dismally depressed, food prices were going up, and not until late in April did enough rain fall to allay fears of a catastrophic harvest. 'At no period since the civil war', *The Times* reported in May, 'have there existed greater penury, misery, and discontent.'[4] An old friend of Clarendon, the Progresista leader Olózaga—a close friend also of General Dulce—was writing to him that if the long-foretold upheaval did come there would be a revolution graver than any that modern Spain had seen.[5] Most formidable of all was the unrest in the turbulent Catalan towns, where the rising cost of living in the spring combined with unemployment caused by new machinery to bring on a bitter strife of capital and labour. At Barcelona the French consul-general, Baradère, expressed alarm at the growing strength of the workers' organizations,[6] and to make things worse there were reports from Catalonia and the

---

[1] Howden to Clarendon, no. 42, 1 Feb. 1854, F.O. 72. 842.
[2] Howden to Clarendon, no. 81, 15 Mar. 1854, F.O. 72. 843.
[3] Decree of 21 Apr. 1854; C.L., vol. lxi, pp. 535–8.
[4] 29 May 1854, 10/2.
[5] S. de Olózaga to Clarendon, Madrid, 31 May 1854; Clarendon Papers (private papers of 4th Earl of Clarendon, Bodleian Library, Oxford), vol. c. 20.
[6] Baradère to Drouyn de Lhuys, no. 100, 2 Apr. 1854; *Espagne*, Consular, vol. 51.

Basque provinces of clerical or Carlist agitation, primed with foreign money.

A monarchical *coup d'état* would enable the government to get its itching hands on more of the taxpayers' money. Isabel was believed to be pressing for action, and sundry hints reached San Luis that if he hung back too long he might find himself thrown over as unceremoniously as his predecessors. He had his private interests to think of, and wanted to cling to office for the benefit of his own purse. Hesitating on the brink, he felt constrained, just as the army conspirators had felt, to reckon with England and France. He made approaches to both Howden and Turgot, saying that no government had ever been more conciliatory than his, but factious obstruction was making things impossible.[1] To all intents he was asking for an assurance that no objections would be raised if he proceeded to demolish the Constitution. Clarendon's refusal cannot have surprised him, but the French response also was very cool.[2] At war now with Russia, the two countries could not afford to disagree.

San Luis fell back on a search for one more makeshift. On 20 May a decree came out ordering the collection in advance of six months' tax dues, as an interest-bearing loan to the government.[3] This would mean serious hardship to many poorer tax-payers; politically it made for a momentary relaxation of tension, being seen as a substitute for the famous *coup d'état*. Ministers themselves heaved a sigh of relief, and a week later ordered themselves in another decree to carry sticks with gold tops and tassels as badges of their high office.[4] A few weeks more and they would be glad to pass unnoticed and escape from Madrid in disguise.

---

[1] Howden to Clarendon, no. 81, 15 Mar. 1854, F.O. 72. 843; Turgot to Drouyn de Lhuys, no. 67, Conf., 28 Mar. 1854; *Espagne*, vol. 834. Howden told San Luis that even under Ferdinand VII there had never been 'a state of more complete despotism, of more thorough indifference to personal security'.

[2] Clarendon to Howden, no. 58, 5 May 1854, F.O. 72. 840; Drouyn de Lhuys to Turgot, no. 13, 10 Apr. 1854; *Espagne*, vol. 844.

[3] Decree of 19 May 1854; C.L., vol. lxii, pp. 58–63. See on it J. Sánchez Ocaña, *Reseña histórica sobre el estado de la Hacienda* (Madrid, 1855), p. 350.

[4] R.O. of 24 May 1854; C.L., vol. lxii, p. 77.

III

CONSERVATIVE RESISTANCE

O'Donnell and the Army Rising, June 1854

AFTER the police raid of 22 February, and some dodging to and fro, O'Donnell and Fernández de los Ríos came to rest in a house in the Ballesta passage midway between the Puerta del Sol and the northern limit of the city. Here from then on was the headquarters of the conspiracy. Hagiographers were to delight in tales of further hairbreadth escapes from discovery, only not incredible because the prevailing corruption clearly extended to the police as to all else. Fernández de los Ríos had plenty of time to scrutinize his strange companion while day after day the general read newspapers, smoked cigarettes, paced his small room, or sat speechless over the fire. Extremely tall and bulky, he looked too heavy for his long thin legs; his ruling trait was a sang-froid that compatriots fondly credited to his remote Irish ancestry.

In these five months he was serving a hard apprenticeship. He had not expected to be left so nearly alone, and he talked bitterly of the craven submission of the other plotters;[1] at the same time their withdrawal did him a service by leaving the leadership to him. No doubt at the outset he was counting on an early attempt by San Luis at a *coup d'état*, and he must have gone on praying for this. All he could do in the meantime was to try to pick up more support. He had been detached from party feuds by his long Cuban absence, and the idea gradually forming in his mind was of a new party of his own, built out of the debris of the old ones now visibly crumbling.

Few at present from any of the parties were prepared to give him more than sympathy. Among Moderados, many looked to Narváez. That great personage was still wrapping himself in a cloud, and waiting for the emergency that would make the country turn to him as its saviour and arbiter. Espartero was doing much the same at the other end of Spain, and it was towards him that Progresistas were looking. He was the sole leader whom

[1] Fernández de los Ríos, *Luchas políticas*, vol. ii, p. 316.

the party could recognize, proclaimed the *Clamor Público*; the hour had struck for him to come forward again, echoed the *Nación*.[1] True, the events that led to his fall in 1843 had demonstrated that his talents were as slender as his vanity was swollen. But there had been time to forget this, and the very fact of his fall and his exile helped to stamp him as the man of the people, whose martyrdom he somehow symbolized. His reviving popularity might bridge the chasm between the classes, and stand moderate Progresistas in good stead against revolutionary excess as well as against Court reaction.[2]

Democrats were less inclined to put their faith in him or sit waiting for him, and at Saragossa they had proved willing to join an army movement. But evidently they were disagreed about such tactics, as well as hampered by the arrest of their leaders; for two of these issued a statement from prison condemning support for any plan of rebellion without guarantees as to its political principles.[3] O'Donnell could offer nothing of the sort. He had no constructive programme, no vision of national reform; and although he may have been quite as ready as some believed to contemplate a change of sovereign as well as of ministry,[4] he had to leave this to be decided by circumstances. Promises of help came from Freemasons,[5] but their organization, to which a great many of the older sort of public men still nominally belonged, had grown too shadowy a thing to count. Altogether O'Donnell could gather in no more than a handful of civilians, and among these, apart from Fernández de los Ríos, the only one of any public standing was Ríos Rosas. Cánovas del Castillo was only a brilliant young law-student and journalist,[6] destined to spend

---

[1] *Clamor Público*, 1 Feb. 1854, 1st leader; *Nación*, 28 Mar., 1/1.

[2] 'There is no doubt that the lower orders of Madrid, Saragossa, and in most of the principal towns, are Esparteristas. . . . Like Napoleon in France, his portrait is universal in the huts of the poor, and his alone' (Howden to Clarendon, no. 52, Conf., 10 Feb. 1854, F.O. 72. 842).

[3] Open letter by M. Becerra and A. del Riego, reprinted in *Heraldo*, 2 Mar. 1854, 1/3–4. They added that no junta was authorized to speak for the Democrat party.

[4] Howden assured Clarendon some months later that O'Donnell had intended to dethrone Isabel (no. 182, Conf., 22 Aug. 1854, F.O. 72. 845). At Brussels a similar impression was formed: Brouckère to Straten-Ponthoz, Très conf., 25 June 1854; *Espagne*, vol. 8 (1).

[5] N. Díaz y Pérez, *La francmasonería española* (Madrid, 1894), pp. 471–2; cf. M. Tirado y Rojas, *La masonería en España* (Madrid, 1892–3), vol. ii, pp. 146–7.

[6] On his motives see V. C. Creux, *Antonio Cánovas del Castillo* (Paris, 1897), pp. 3 ff., and A. M. Fabié, *Cánovas del Castillo* (Barcelona, 1928), p. 25.

many years as a Conservative Prime Minister living down his political wild oats of 1854. A limited supply of money for buying arms seems to have been subscribed by some of the bankers, especially the mildly liberal Collado and the tough conservative Sevillano. Parasites as these capitalists were, they yet had some vested interest in constitutional government.

Practically it all remained at the level of an army plot, when the experience of Saragossa had already shown a military *coup* to be futile: the day of the old-style *pronunciamiento* was passing. Even in the army the plotters held only one ace, the cavalry of the Madrid garrison which was more or less at the disposal of Dulce as inspector-general.[1] A man with whom conspiracy was second nature, Dulce let it be understood among his intimates, who of course let it be known among theirs, that he had accepted his new post merely in order to be in a better position to work against the government. O'Donnell's friend Ros de Olano came in late, bringing no more than his own sword. Among the rest of the garrison forces only a sparse harvest of recruits was being won. Some junior officers undertook to work on the still worse paid and more discontented N.C.O.s, but their seniors, the men O'Donnell really wanted, were sitting on the fence.[2]

Want of support made for long hesitations and delays. One postponement followed another until the whole business was in danger of growing ridiculous. Confinement was telling on O'Donnell, and still more on Ríos Rosas, who began to suffer delusions, and after April was quite out of action. As though to fill in an awkward pause, there began coming out a satirical sheet, the *Murciélago* or Bat.[3] Its target was racketeering in high places, and one of its witticisms, over which the cafés hugged themselves, was to print Salamanca's name as that of its editor. More and more with each number its claws fastened on the royal family itself. But summer was at hand, and O'Donnell's little circle perceived that they must strike soon or never: 2 June was chosen, then

---

[1] For biographical detail on him and other officers see P. Chamorro y Baquerizo, *Estado mayor general del ejército español* (2nd ed., Madrid, 1851–8), and Ibo Alfaro, *La Corona de Laurel*.

[2] Fernández de los Ríos, *Luchas políticas*, vol. ii, pp. 337, 344.

[3] Who produced it was never discovered. For various conjectures see ibid., vol. ii, p. 344; Fabié, p. 23; A. Pons y Umbert, *Cánovas del Castillo* (Madrid, 1901), p. 100. Long extracts are printed in Martos, pp. 82–97, and J. Ruiz de Morales, *Historia de la milicia nacional* (Madrid, 1855), pp. 624–36.

13 June. On that day O'Donnell slipped out of town and waited in vain for six or seven hours, which must have passed as slowly for him as any in this half-year, for the others to join him. With astonishing luck he stole back undiscovered to his lair.[1] There were hot recriminations, and then Wednesday 28 June was fixed on for the final throw.

Early on the 26th the Court removed to the Escorial, whither San Luis had gone the day before. At 3.30 a.m. on the 28th the rebel forces, Dulce's eleven cavalry squadrons and a solitary infantry battalion belonging to Brigadier Echagüe, marched out of barracks, ostensibly for an early review on the Campo de Guardias, a parade-ground in the northern suburb of Chamberí.[2] At 4.30 a.m. O'Donnell left the Ballesta in Vega de Armijo's mule-coach, driven by its noble owner in disguise, and the little army set off. At Canillejas, the first hamlet on the highroad to Alcalá, there was an harangue by O'Donnell in the established phraseology. Only one or two officers declined to go further. About 3 p.m. they reached Alcalá, fifteen miles north-east of Madrid, where Dulce had been working on the garrison; it was waiting to join them and bring up their strength to something over two thousand.

Behind the march lay a decision to rely on a military demonstration outside the capital to intimidate San Luis into surrendering, or the Queen into dismissing him. An alternative plan for a rising inside Madrid had been rejected. Cavalry would be at a disadvantage in the streets; besides, these gold-braided rebels had no desire to call on the population for more than a few shots and a lot of shouts to help to scare the authorities. Manifestoes left behind for distribution were, as Fernández de los Ríos had laboured to convince O'Donnell,[3] far too trite and colourless.[4] A disillusioned public was being invited to trust the rebels with a blank cheque; and as one of the few radicals among them observed, the public was 'invincibly distrustful of the army, which it looked upon as

---

[1] On the events of 13 June see Fernández de los Ríos, *Cinco meses*; Hardman, in *The Times*, 26 June 1854, 9/6, and *Blackwood's*, Aug. 1854, p. 156; Ibo Alfaro, *La Corona de Laurel*, vol. i, p. 342, and *O'Donnell*, p. 844.

[2] On the events of 28 June see Fernández de los Ríos, *Cinco meses*, and *Luchas políticas*, vol. ii, pp. 362–4; Martos, p. 116. Martos, a young radical with a political future, had been connected with the plot in its later stages.

[3] *Luchas políticas*, vol. ii, pp. 361–2.

[4] Texts: ibid., pp. 377–81, and Ribot y Fontseré, *La revolución*, pp. 59–65.

its natural enemy'.[1] Everyone rejoiced to see the hated government brought to bay, but few felt inclined to lend a hand.

San Luis was not a man to be put down so easily. At the Escorial it was decided to bring Isabel back to Madrid at once. She entered about 10 p.m. and drove through the town to the palace. The *Heraldo* heard continuous applause as her cortège passed; the Belgian Minister heard none.[2] Next day martial law was proclaimed over the whole country; the bankers Collado and Moreno were among those arrested, and Sevillano had to lie low. In the evening a grand review was held on the Prado, the object being to test the reliability of the troops.[3] Both Otway (Howden was on holiday) and Hardman of *The Times* were among the onlookers and were struck by the 'deep and ominous silence' of soldiery and crowd.[4] Still, the troops were obeying orders, and early next day, Friday the 30th, with the rebels moving tentatively back towards the city, the government made up its mind to risk a battle outside the walls.

Some 4,500 infantry with 500 horse and 20 guns took position on a low ridge fronting the hamlet of Vicálvaro, a league to the east. They were under Juan de Lara as captain-general, and Blaser, who as War Minister was also commander-in-chief. At the palace the Queen's carriages were kept ready for flight.[5] It seems to have been anticipated that when the two sides got within musket-shot one of them would go over to the other without serious fighting, as happened a few miles away at Torrejón when Narváez beat Espartero's forces in 1843. But the military machine had hardened, and there were no desertions. O'Donnell cheered his rank and file by promising a deduction of two years from each conscript's term of service. His plan was to draw his opponents out on to open ground and then, with his superior mobility, get between them and the walls. Dulce spoiled this by the impatient gallantry with which he delivered a series of cavalry charges against the batteries, which were protected by a gully. To continue

[1] Martos, pp. 127–8.

[2] *Heraldo*, 29 June 1854, 1/1; Straten-Ponthoz to Brouckère, no. 101, 29 June; *Espagne*, vol. 9 (1).

[3] F. Fernández de Córdova, *Mis memorias íntimas* (Madrid, 1886–9), vol. iii, p. 363.

[4] Otway to Clarendon, no. 26, 30 June 1854, F.O. 72. 844; Hardman, *Blackwood's*, Aug. 1854, p. 158. Cf. F. Díaz-Plaja, *La historia de España en sus documentos. El siglo XIX* (Madrid, 1954), p. 292.

[5] Otway to Clarendon, private, 1 July 1854; Clarendon Papers, c. 20.

the fighting to the point of heavy bloodshed would alienate the
army as a whole, and might strain the loyalty of O'Donnell's
men too far. With honours about equal he broke off the action
when it had lasted from two o'clock to five. Casualties were a mere
sixty killed or wounded on the rebel side, fewer on the other.[1]

Both claimed victory; the rebel chiefs—henceforth the *Vicalvaristas*—kept their position that night, but their hope of seeing
the government collapse was gone. They had now to face a longer
campaign than they had bargained for, under the Castilian sun of
July and very slenderly supplied with cash. One proposal was to
draw off towards Saragossa. In that direction popular support
could without doubt be enlisted; only, however, at the price of
a liberal programme and, very likely, the emergence of Espartero
to supplant them. They decided to turn south instead of east,
towards feudal Andalusia instead of progressive Aragon. Next
morning they set off, making use of the newly built railway to
Aranjuez, thirty miles south of the capital.

So far so good for San Luis, but his employers might still con-
clude at any moment that they would be safer without him. His
newspaper argued lengthily that the revolt was against queen and
dynasty as well as ministry; others, among them two conservative
elder statesmen, Martínez de la Rosa and the Marqués de Miraflores, were trying to convince her that it was aimed solely at her
ministers.[2] On 2 July she dispatched a private messenger to the
rebels at Aranjuez, and on his return a special cabal was called
together.[3] Fernández de Córdova, the director-general of infantry,
urged San Luis's dismissal; there were strong palace influences
against this, and Cristina above all was 'the soul of the policy of
resistance'.[4] It seemed to be succeeding, for by 4 July O'Donnell's
little column was on the move further southward, and on the 7th
Blaser left Madrid to organize a pursuit. He had to take part of
the garrison away with him, leaving the forces of law and order
thin, but reinforcements were being brought up from other points.

[1] On the battle see Lara's report, in the *Gazette* on 1 July 1854; Bermejo, *Alzamiento popular*, p. 35; Anon., *Asamblea constituyente de 1854!* (Madrid, 1855), pp. 162–3;
A. Borrego, *España y la revolución* (Madrid, 1856), p. 220; I. Calonge y Pérez, *El
pabellón español* (Madrid, 1855–6), article 'Vicálvaro'.
[2] *The Times*, 10 July 1854 (Madrid, 3 July), 10/6.
[3] Córdova relates this discussion with some discrepancies in his *Memoria* of 1855,
pp. 30–32, and in his much later *Mis memorias*, vol. iii, pp. 368–9.
[4] Otway to Clarendon, no. 44, 10 July 1854, F.O. 72. 844.

O'Donnell was drifting now, hoping for something to turn up. Everywhere he found the population not at all unfriendly, but not at all eager to join him. His tiny committee in Madrid had urged on him the necessity of a more rousing programme, and now Cánovas was deputed to make a final attempt. At Manzanares on the 7th the 'Constitutional Army' was joined by Serrano, fresh from unavailing efforts to rally support in his southern province of Jaén; he backed up Cánovas and, it seems, threw in the crucial proposal for restoration of the national militia.[1] This before its suppression in 1843 had been the embodiment of militant radicalism, and its revival was ardently desired by the urban masses, though unwanted of late years by right-wing Progresistas as well as by all Moderados. Debate ended in the celebrated 'manifesto of Manzanares', in which the rebels came out in favour of a list of reforms, including tax reductions, with restoration of the militia to set the seal on all the rest, and invited the nation to express its will freely through juntas and through the Cortes.[2] They were committed at last; whether too late, as well as reluctantly, was still to be seen. By the time they had pushed through the Sierra Morena and turned eastward towards Cordoba they were unmistakably in flight towards the Portuguese border.[3]

Within a few weeks it would be repeated and believed by all sorts of people that the situation was suddenly transformed, the country electrified, by the manifesto of Manzanares. There was a good deal of illusion here. Where it became known it was read with lively interest, but chiefly because Spain was already moving forward towards revolution. Vicálvaro had provided the spark of excitement that long-gathering discontents needed to set them off. One incident after another kept ministerial nerves on edge. On 5 July there was a small outbreak at Alcira near Valencia, described as republican rather than O'Donnellite. On the 9th a band of volunteers seized Cuenca, under the lead of M. Buceta del Villar, a veteran of 1848. On the 13th a detachment of the Montesa

---

[1] See Martos, pp. 180–3; Miraflores, *Continuación*, vol. i, p. 474; Marqués de Villa-Urrutia, *El general Serrano, Duque de la Torre* (Madrid, 1929), p. 95; Marques de Lema, *Cánovas o el hombre de estado* (Madrid, 1931), p. 38.

[2] A constituent assembly was not explicitly referred to. The text has been often reprinted; it may be found conveniently in P. Zabala y Lera's continuation (vol. v) of R. Altamira's *Historia de España*, part i, p. 458.

[3] On the way O'Donnell made overtures to Narváez, who, he was to assert later, had promised support, but who now drew back. See A. Borrego, *Historia de la vida militar y política de Don Francisco Serrano y Domínguez* (Madrid, 1892), p. 30.

cavalry regiment mutinied within a few miles of Madrid. Every kind of rumour was rife in the capital, all the more because the opposition papers had been silenced.

Cánovas's copy of the manifesto, brought to Madrid on a tiny bit of paper rolled up inside a cigarette, began circulating there not before the 14th.[1] Already four days before this, Turgot was reporting that everyone from high to low was against San Luis, and that only an iron hand could prevent another 1848.[2] A rapid series of outbreaks was in fact about to take place. They did not begin at the capital, and they followed different patterns according to local circumstances. In a number of places the O'Donnellites got a fresh chance. Scattered far and wide as they had been by San Luis, they escaped being all involved together in the retreat to the south; and with the public mood portending a cataclysm, it seemed to many officers the part of common sense to come out with them against the régime before it was, for themselves or for the social order, too late.

Barcelona was the first town to rise. As always, its fever-fit grew out of its private distempers of capital and labour; these were not without an effect even on the troops stationed there. Popular ferment was intensified by the news of O'Donnell's rising, with which both the military authorities and the soldiery, as well as the public, were thought to be in sympathy from the start. A climax of excitement was reached on 14 July. Workers began forcibly closing mills and going on strike, and between 7 and 8 p.m. soldiers at some barracks declared against the government, and troops and people fraternized.[3] Ramón de la Rocha, the captain-general, made up his mind promptly. By about midnight he was at the Town Hall, haranguing the crowd and presenting himself as a convert to the revolution. The night then passed off quietly, except that 'some ill-intentioned persons', as Consul Baker denominated them, murdered a mill-owner along with his son and foreman and burned down his mill.[4] All the propertied

[1] Fernández de los Ríos, *Luchas políticas*, vol. ii, pp. 383-5; he and the others at Madrid took it upon themselves to alter and strengthen the wording. See also V. Barrantes, *Páginas ilustradas de la revolución*, pp. 305-6; this young journalist had been connected with the O'Donnell group. His narrative appeared in *La Ilustración*, Nos. 282, 284, 286, July–Aug. 1854.

[2] Turgot to Drouyn de Lhuys, no. 98, 10 July 1854; *Espagne*, vol. 844.

[3] See on these events Carrera Pujal, vol. iv, pp. 238 ff.

[4] Baker to Clarendon, no. 18, 15 July 1854, F.O 72. 851.

classes were left deeply apprehensive, but it was accepted that La Rocha had taken the most judicious course open to him. There was much the same story at Valencia, another city with a tradition of social unrest, when the news from Barcelona arrived on 16 July by the steamer *Elba*.[1] The mass of the people rose at once, and the city 'pronounced', so overwhelmingly that resistance was out of the question. Captain-general Blanco made haste to join the movement, in the hope of being able, along with other sound men, to keep control of the junta that was to be set up.

Another important provincial centre had just struck its independent blow. Valladolid was a smaller place, though beginning lately to grow and to stir in its Old Castilian sleep. The garrison had been weakened by the drawing off of two regiments to reinforce Madrid; on the 15th the rest of the force pronounced.[2] General Nogueras was the leading spirit. Like Serrano and Dulce he had mildly Liberal antecedents, and he had been banished here by San Luis in February. He seems to have belonged to a circle of plotters which may have had contacts with O'Donnell. Prominent citizens, and the town council, lent the garrison chiefs their moral support, and a junta was set up; a proclamation extolled the Vicalvaristas for having acted to arrest the nation's drift towards ruin, and before long it was decided that Nogueras should lead out the troops and make a demonstration towards Madrid. Further north meanwhile, at San Sebastian, events followed still more closely the sequence O'Donnell had designed for the whole country: action by the army, applause by the public. At 5 a.m. on the 17th the small garrison rose, to the tune of *vivas* for O'Donnell and the Queen. It was a district where the government was highly unpopular, but the British vice-consul noticed that the citizens continued to go quietly about their affairs and left the rebellion to the soldiers, who, it was humorously remarked, were paid for rebelling.[3] Before anything else could happen, Zabala, another general packed off in February, slipped across the frontier from Bayonne and took command.

[1] See Bermejo, *Alzamiento popular*, p. 60.

[2] Ibid., pp. 53, 56–58; Borao, *Historia del alzamiento*, p. 21; F. Pi y Margall and F. Pi y Arsuaga, *Historia de España en el siglo XIX* (Barcelona, 1902; cited below as Pi, *Historia*), vol. iv, p. 65.

[3] Vice-consul March to Clarendon, no. 1, 17 July 1854, F.O. 72. 849; the next seven dispatches contain further news, copies of proclamations, &c., from northern Spain.

At Saragossa a different pattern was developing. A compact Liberal middle class played a more significant part, and although military men figured too, they were distinctively Esparterista rather than O'Donnellite. Ever since 1843 Saragossa had smarted under the rule of arbitrary officials, and as soon as O'Donnell rose, a faithful old Esparterista, General Gurrea, made his way secretly from Bilbao to try to incite disaffected elements in the garrison to a fresh effort. He found shelter with Juan Bruil, a wealthy banker and, as bankers go, a Liberal. On the night of 16 July, a few hours in advance of the public, Rivero, the captain-general of Aragon, got the news of Barcelona's rising and decided unwillingly but without delay to copy the example of La Rocha. He drew up a suitable proclamation; the civil governor and his minions went into hiding, the police evaporated; next morning a junta came into being, not elected but self-chosen or nominated. Of its dozen members the majority were old Liberals and men of property, and Gurrea and Bruil could expect to keep the lead in their own prudent hands. Rivero's attitude was grudging, and he clearly had no mind to be elbowed aside: the junta's first thought was not to arm the people against him but to send for Espartero, under cover of whose prestige its path would be easy. At 9.30 on this morning of the 17th an urgent summons went out to him at Logroño, a hundred miles to the north-west.[1]

[1] On events at Saragossa see Borao, pp. 23–33.

IV

POPULAR RESISTANCE

The Revolution, July 1854

IN Madrid alone of all the cities an armed struggle between the
people and their rulers was to take place; it was scarcely open to
Isabel and her cronies to save themselves by swimming with the
tide, like their representatives in the provinces. Amid feverish
excitement, as reports and rumours poured in from the provinces,
the *Heraldo* on 16 July declared in what was to be its very last
issue that the news everywhere was of perfect tranquillity. Tidings
of Valladolid's defection spread through the streets on this day;[1]
next morning the crushing news from Barcelona fell on the
ministers; by midday they were assembling at the palace to resign
before they could be dismissed. A soldier was bound to be thought
of as San Luis's successor, and two men were sent for in haste:
Lara, captain-general and a former War Minister, and Fernández
de Córdova, director-general of infantry. Lara declined the offered
premiership.[2] Córdova showed a more robust self-confidence, and
at 12.30 was commissioned to form a new Cabinet.

Few Spaniards judged Fernando Fernández de Córdova as
indulgently as he did himself, though he was undeniably well
built, well dressed, and a descendant of the Great Captain. He had
been suspected lately of currying favour with the camarilla.[3]
Certainly he had political ambitions, aspiring much like O'Donnell
to head a new moderate party.[4] An absolutist, though not a
Carlist, in earlier days, he was still considered very much a man
of the Right, and to the public any ministry led by him was bound

---

[1] Martos, p. 198. San Luis in desperation telegraphed a circular to the army
promising rewards for even passive loyalty (Córdova, *Mis memorias*, vol. iii, p. 373).

[2] J. de Lara, *Aclaraciones . . . sobre los acontecimientos militares de Madrid en los días 17
y 18 de julio de 1854* (Madrid, 1855), p. 6.

[3] Hardman, 'The Spanish Revolution', *Blackwood's*, Sept. 1854, p. 356; Ribot y
Fontseré, *La revolución*, p. 99; *The Times*, 26 July 1854 (Paris, 24 July), 10/1.

[4] Córdova, *Memoria*, p. 80. He had been trying to enlist a faction of his own in
the army, and had proposed to join forces with O'Donnell, who declined (Fernández
de los Ríos, *Luchas políticas*, vol. ii, pp. 351–2).

to look merely a fresh disguise for palace rule. This could not make his task of cabinet-building easy. From some of the Moderados he approached, all mildly associated with the opposition of the past year or two, he met with refusals. One who accepted was the 63-year-old Duke of Rivas, dilettante poet, playwright, and diplomat, and Liberal of bygone days; another was Mayáns, a reputable former Minister of Justice. The man both Córdova and Rivas were most anxious to bring in was Ríos Rosas, who had sufficient connexion with O'Donnell to give him a claim on the public, not enough to make the Court reject him. He had to be ferreted out of his place of concealment, and then only very hesitantly gave his consent.[1] Some of his associates felt that he was shamefully deserting them by agreeing to serve the Queen without insisting on the terms of the Manzanares manifesto.

Córdova wanted something that would look like a coalition government: Progresistas as well as Moderados were being sounded, and a number of them assembled at Cantero the banker's house for a hurried confabulation. Here too there was much wavering, which ended in a decision to join if three of them were given places: Miguel de Roda, Pedro Gómez de Laserna, and Cantero.[2] All these were men of the old school, Progresistas of very sober hue. To many in their party their willingness to serve would, like that of Ríos Rosas, seem precipitate. But apart from personal motives they were strongly influenced by the fear of social upheaval that had been deepening in these last weeks. He and his friends took office, Roda was to declare in his apologia, in defence of society and order against anarchism.[3]

While the politicians spun their spider-webs for Demos, Demos was enjoying himself at his Monday afternoon bullfight in the arena outside the Alcalá gate. Before long it was turning into a political demonstration. Special editions of newspapers were hawked about, spectators began to raise shouts of Liberty, and the band was made to strike up the Hymn of Riego, Spain's Marseillaise. Jubilant and tumultuous, the crowd poured out of the arena and along the broad acacia-lined Calle de Alcalá towards

[1] Fernández de los Ríos, *Luchas políticas*, vol. ii, p. 396. Cf. a narrative in L. de Taxonera, *La revolución del 1854* (Madrid, 1931), pp. 125–9, whose authority, however, is only vaguely indicated.
[2] Pirala, vol. ii, pp. 193–4; Córdova, *Memoria*, pp. 39–40.
[3] See his speech during the Cortes debate on these events in Dec. 1854: D.S., pp. 382–5.

Madrid's forum, the Puerta del Sol.[1] All police had vanished, no soldiers had been called out, though there were plenty of them in barracks, besides a contingent of the Civil Guard or gendarmerie which had been brought into Madrid.[2] There was anger at the news that began to percolate of what sort of ministry was being planned; anger fully shared doubtless by the multitude of *cesantes*, half-pay government servants wild to get back their jobs. As night settled over the ill-lit town batches of demonstrators were truculently on the move. Some made their way unresisted into the public buildings in the vicinity, including the Casa de Villa or Town Hall. Further away another throng broke into the Saladero prison and released its inmates, among them Rivero the Democrat. The fiercest whirlpool was outside the Principal, the grandiose edifice at the south-west corner of the Puerta del Sol that housed the Ministry of the Interior and was also the military command-post of the capital; the next best thing to a Bastille in a city which, unlike Barcelona and many others, had no regular fortress to overawe it. Sentries left without orders were unwilling to shoot, and soon after 9 p.m. the rioters were inside.

Lara, who was equally without orders and had expressed a wish to resign, was shut up in the War Office,[3] in the Buenavista mansion at the corner of the Calle de Alcalá and the Prado, about a mile away from the palace on the opposite, eastern fringe of the old town. Córdova was still engrossed in his political combinations; all his prospective colleagues except Rivas were showing signs of backing out. At about 8 p.m. he was summoned to the palace by the nervously impatient Isabel, and was alarmed by the sight of crowds streaming towards the building. He sent for troops to clear the precincts, though he forbade firing as yet, and sent urgently to Rivas and the others to come at once.[4]

On their side too the people were trying to improvise a leader-ship. Once inside the Town Hall it came naturally to them to set up a junta there. Popular figures were being asked to come and join it: chief among them General Evaristo San Miguel, one of the

---

[1] Martos, pp. 234–6. This belongs to part 2 of his work, added by a separate hand, 'Un hijo del pueblo', which is cited below by its own title: *Las jornadas de julio*.

[2] M. Gistau Ferrando, *La Guardia Civil* (Madrid, 1907), p. 349.

[3] Lara, pp. 7–9. He and Córdova blamed each other later for the failure to take any action until the city had got out of control (Lara, pp. 9–10, 12; Córdova, *Memoria*, pp. 50–51, 58–60).

[4] Córdova, *Memoria*, pp. 41–42; *Mis memorias*, vol. iii, pp. 379–80.

old guard of Liberalism, a small wizened man with the nickname 'Monkey-face', terribly deaf, but a spry stirring body still. He had been advising his Progresista friends against accepting office, but he wanted to give them time now to show what they could do;[1] and his aim when he reached the Town Hall and was promptly voted president of the junta was to let popular passion expend itself in noise. Corradi, editor of the *Clamor Público*, was fetched from his office,[2] and was to claim credit for the only practical idea that emerged at the Town Hall amidst tumult and hubbub: a warning to the Queen that none but a genuinely popular government would be accepted by the country. An address was hastily drawn up, while San Miguel kept the show going with declamation from the balcony.[3] It was to be carried to the palace only by a small deputation, Corradi and two others. They set off about midnight.

San Miguel soon went home to bed; things were beginning to go much too far for his taste. A new cry was sweeping the squares and thoroughfares in the city centre—'To the ministers' houses!' One mass of people, women as well as men, were chanting a doggerel chorus of 'Death to Cristina', to the tune, much in vogue, of 'La donna è mobile'. That lady's experienced nose had scented danger in good time, and she had slipped away by a side door of her mansion to the palace. San Luis too had taken sanctuary there. Houses suffered for the sins of absent owners. San Luis's grand residence on the Prado, as well as the office of his *Heraldo*, was completely gutted; three huge bonfires blazed outside it, on to which his collection of pictures, furniture, and books was hurled pell-mell. Meanwhile Isabel, who had much faith in the power of affable nothings and fine eyes to soften disagreeable situations, insisted in spite of Córdova on seeing the delegates, and professed much anxiety to avoid bloodshed. Corradi behaved

---

[1] Pirala, vol. ii, p. 194.

[2] *Clamor Público*, 20 July 1854; and see the speeches by Gómez de la Mata and Corradi in D.S., pp. 385–7 (12 Dec. 1854) and 329–31 (7 Dec.) There are numerous difficulties about the exact time-table of this week's events, and particularly of this Monday night. The Madrid newspapers had scanty resources or leisure, when they reappeared after the revolution, for sifting the flood of accounts from readers of happenings in odd streets or districts. The *Diario Español* (22 July, 2/1–5) printed a more consecutive narrative from 27 June. Hardman, in *The Times* and *Blackwood's*, is invaluable.

[3] Corradi, as above; Bermejo, *Alzamiento popular*, p. 67; Pirala, vol. ii, p. 196, n. 2. Text of the remonstrance in Díaz-Plaja, pp. 292–3.

correctly, perhaps a little too correctly.[1] Córdova was seeing them off, amicably enough, on the Plaza de Armas, and it may have been about 1.30 a.m., when a new actor rushed on the scene, 'raging like a famished hyena'.[2] This was Joaquín de la Gándara, come to say that mobs were attacking Salamanca's house, where he was a guest. Gándara was an old Progresista,[3] but he and Córdova were involved in a railway deal together,[4] and both had connexions with Salamanca.

Hitherto Córdova had undoubtedly been hoping to get his ministry started without bullets, but under stress of noise, fatigue, and alarmist reports he was growing flustered, and convinced that social war was breaking out.[5] His first move was to dispatch a column to clear the Town Hall; he had formed a quite delusive notion of the junta there as a dangerous revolutionary caucus. In point of fact the delegates on their return with Isabel's vague assurances had just been recommending the crowd to go quietly home, when it was exasperated afresh by the sound of musketry close by in the Calle Mayor. Who fired these first shots was never known for certain. But Córdova's next stroke was quite certain to mean bloodshed. He entrusted two companies to Gándara—an officer, but not on service or in uniform—with orders to clear away the rioters from the houses under attack, beginning with Cristina's as the nearest.

It stood close by the English Legation, conspicuous for an entrance vestibule hung with gaudy glass lustres, Cristina's special pride and joy.[6] As elsewhere the crowd seething in front of this stately pleasure-dome of the new plutocracy was a mixture of all ranks. Only after the firing in the Calle Mayor did the real assault begin. Then a storming-party, having hunted in vain for the proprietress, started hurling everything movable out onto the plaza, where a great bonfire was soon blazing. In the midst of this

[1] Corradi, as above; Córdova, *Memoria*, pp. 52–53, 56–57, and *Mis memorias*, vol. iii, pp. 381–2; Miraflores, *Continuación*, vol. i, pp. 493–5.

[2] Ribot y Fontseré, *La revolución*, p. 100.

[3] Gándara later pretended that, being fresh from abroad, he thought it was a counter-revolution he was coping with; see his *Manifiesto . . . al pueblo español* (Madrid, 1854), pp. 3–13, 15–23.

[4] *Nación*, 26 May 1854, 1/1. The received opinion came to be that all three men were mixed up in shady speculations together.

[5] Córdova, *Memoria*, pp. 100–1; *Mis memorias*, vol. iii, p. 386.

[6] It is described in Mesonero Romanos, *Nuevo manual*, pp. 390–1, and there are pictures in Barrantes, *Páginas*, p. 308, and Ribot y Fontseré, *La revolución*, p. 73.

Gándara arrived, and immediately fired a series of volleys into the dense throng, which scattered at once; 'a tolerable number' of dead and wounded, women among them, were left on the ground.[1] It was this massacre that roused the hottest feeling against Córdova's *ministerio metralla*, or 'grapeshot ministry'. Its perpetrator hurried on to Salamanca's house, dispersed the assailants, and phlegmatically went to bed.

Patriots were beginning to find arms, and Fernández de los Ríos and Vega de Armijo distributed the small stock of muskets the conspirators had laid by.[2] One band posted itself in the vast Plaza Mayor, south of the Puerta del Sol, and there was prolonged fighting or sniping before a detachment of troops got in through the archways,[3] led by Mata y Alós, an officer who was to display more zeal than most.[4] Quesada, the military governor, had an easier task in recovering the Principal and the Puerta del Sol. Briefly before dawn a 'sepulchral silence' descended.[5] Madrid was not asleep: insurgents were coming together in small fighting groups, and a new weapon was being got ready, the barricade.

Of Córdova's Cabinet recruits Ríos Rosas, it seems, was the last to arrive, after commissioning Cánovas to go back to O'Donnell in the south and urge him to support the new government— and then presently take it over.[6] By the time Córdova was free to join them, towards 3 a.m., these oldish gentlemen were probably in a frame of mind to agree with him that a united front against anarchy was imperative. Still, the three Progresistas could see that his name, now that things had gone so far, would stick in the public's throat. He made no difficulty about contenting himself with the Ministry of War, which was enough to give him the whip hand, and proposed the easy-going duke for premier. This arrangement was adopted, and about 3.30 a.m. they went up to see Isabel and be sworn in, and then groped their way downstairs again to the ground floor offices to plunge into disjointed

[1] Hardman, *Blackwood's*, Sept. 1854, p. 359; he gives an eyewitness account here and in *The Times*, 25 July, 10/5–6 to 11/1.

[2] Fernández de los Ríos, *Luchas políticas*, vol. ii, pp. 397–8.

[3] Eyewitness account in *Clamor Público*, 29 July 1854, 1/1–2; Gistau Ferrando, p. 355.

[4] Mata y Alós was an old friend of Córdova. See his long letter in *Clamor Público*, 28 July 1854, 2/1–3, denying having ordered any firing unnecessarily.

[5] F. Pi y Margall, *La reacción y la revolución* (Madrid, 1854), p. 15.

[6] Fernández Almagro, pp. 76–77.

consultation.[1] It was speedily agreed that Blaser should be recalled, and O'Donnell invited, with all haste to Madrid.[2] None of the staid Liberals suggested Espartero, to say nothing of a constituent assembly. They agreed to annul the press law of 1852, cancel San Luis's forced loan, and make one or two appointments that they hoped would go down well, such as that of the Marqués de Perales as civil governor. An officer named Garrigó, captured at Vicálvaro and reprieved by Isabel after numerous appeals in his favour, was promoted brigadier. At 6 a.m. the Cabinet was formally inaugurated. Its reception was not encouraging; everyone saw it as no more than a stopgap, Otway commented.[3] Perales, venturing forth to take up his duties, had to beat a hasty retreat into the palace.

From early dawn groups of insurgents had been opening a steady fire against Córdova's outposts. His total strength he afterwards gave as 2,300 or so, which must be an understatement;[4] it is true that he had to keep a great part of his forces strung out in small detachments. His rank and file proved dependable; the commanders less so, for anyone near the top of the army always had his political future to think of, and in the course of the day a brisk competition sprang up to avoid being last off the ship. Quesada, like Lara, wanted to resign, and Córdova was reduced finally to the very unsavoury choice as military governor of José Pons, not long since a Carlist chief notorious for his ferocity under the nickname of *Pep del Oli*, or Pepe the oil-seller.

The one constructive idea produced by the three Progresista ministers was to send Garrigó about the streets, as the hero of the hour, to convince the citizens of their new government's bona fides. The others were obliged to fall in with this, and Garrigó was given a horse and sent off. He met with a boisterous welcome from a peaceful crowd when he rode through the Puerta del Sol,

---

[1] Córdova, *Memoria*, pp. 41–42, 55–57, and *Mis memorias*, vol. iii, pp. 384 ff.; cf. Taxonera, pp. 129–35.

[2] Cf. Otway to Clarendon, private, 23 July 1854; Clarendon Papers, c. 20: 'Cordovas intention during his brief reign was to have made "coute que coute" a transaction with O'Donnel [*sic*] . . .'

[3] Otway to Clarendon, no. 51, 18 July 1854, F.O. 72. 844. Cf. J. H. García de Quevedo, *Apuntes para la historia de las jornadas de julio* (Madrid, 1854), in *Obras*, vol. ii, p. 534.

[4] Córdova, *Memoria*, pp. 72–78; *Mis memorias*, vol. iii, pp. 395–6. Figures given in *Las jornadas de julio*, pp. 296–7, and Ruiz de Morales, p. 682, indicate that he had about 5,700 infantry.

about 11 a.m., to the Principal, a dried-up little veteran who had lost an eye in one of his campaigns. Presently he reappeared on the balcony, and commenced a speech tending to goodwill and harmony. Applause was interrupted by shouts for the Civil Guards to be disarmed. He moved on next, escorted by a large concourse, to the Plaza de Santo Domingo, to arrange a truce which was soon broken. About 3 p.m. he reached the Plaza Mayor, which was held by Civil Guards; here again the exchange of shots died down, and then abruptly started afresh. Each side accused the other of treachery, and a cry of 'Death to the Guards' ran across Madrid.[1]

Elsewhere fighting had been continuous, most of it in the form of sharp-shooting. In the southern, mainly working-class area the Plaza de la Cebada formed the rebel rallying-point, and its champion, Pucheta the bullfighter, crossed the Toledo bridge with a band of daring spirits to raid the powder-magazine.[2] Córdova's object was to link up his two strongholds, the palace and the Buenavista, by means of thrusts from both sides, and thus cut the city and the main mass of insurgents in two. Mata y Alós was sent to the Buenavista to start a two-pronged attack from the line of the Prado. He entrusted one column to Gándara, while he himself led the other in a northward sweep and then down the Montera and across the Puerta del Sol to the palace. He had only cleared the path momentarily, and Gándara could not get through at all. Setting off about 3 p.m. with some 250 men and a few field-guns, he seems to have bludgeoned his way through the maze of streets as far west as the Plaza de Santa Ana, and turned south on to one of the town's chief arteries, the Calle de Atocha.[3] Near the Plaza de Antón Martín he was brought to a halt by assailants swarming and buzzing round him from every nook and corner. He was accused of using his cannon vindictively, bombarding houses at random, until at nightfall he was ready to give up and draw his men back to the Prado. By this time Córdova too was reduced to the defensive, and by 10 p.m. the silence was complete.

[1] On Garrigó's movements see *Las jornadas de julio*, pp. 260 ff.; Gistau Ferrando, pp. 357, 362–3; Bermejo, *Alzamiento popular*, p. 72.
[2] Calonge y Pérez, article 'Madrid, 1854'. A long letter in *Clamor Público*, 29 July 1854, 1/3, recounts Pucheta's services in the fighting.
[3] It is impossible to reconcile the varied accounts of Gándara's route. Compare, e.g., Córdova, *Mis memorias*, vol. iii, p. 400; Barrantes, *Páginas*, p. 312, and ibid., p. 321. Gándara himself (p. 27) passes lightly over this afternoon.

So was the darkness, for no lamps or windows were lit, and there was no moon.

Local juntas had begun to spring up; one in particular on the Calle de Toledo was claiming or being given the title of 'Junta del Sur', implying a right to speak for the whole southern half of the town, where shouts for Espartero, even for a republic, were heard.[1] The longer the battle raged the more extremism would spread, and it was clearly time for men of foresight to look for means of averting this. San Miguel was now to undertake from the rear of the revolt the soothing operation that his friends in the ministry had attempted in vain from the front.

On Wednesday morning, while shots were already being exchanged close to the palace, he was early astir, bustling about his own neighbourhood—he lived near the Plaza de Santo Domingo —in full uniform, accosting patriots and soldiers alike as brothers. Others joined him, and soon a cheering crowd gathered, under the impression that San Miguel was coming to lead the people to victory.[2] Sevillano the banker threw open his house in the Jacometrezo street, and by about 7 a.m. a rough-and-ready committee was taking shape. Doubtless it was not quite such an impromptu affair as the public was allowed to suppose. One or two of its original members may have shared the illusions of the citizens cheering outside, militants like Ordax Avecilla, the Democrat, or Fernández de los Ríos. Most of the dozen were old-fashioned Progresistas like Escalante, or General Iriarte. Vega de Armijo represented O'Donnellism. Sevillano could speak for the capitalists. Tabuérniga, a third marquis, once very radical, lately touting his services as a journalist on the side of absolutism,[3] could speak for anyone. Altogether the amalgam differed little from that represented by the Rivas ministry. Its purpose was not to hasten the revolution, but to put a surreptitious brake on it.

As a first step San Miguel was deputed to go with some others to the palace and urge ministers to suspend hostilities.[4] He was received with great coldness by his friends, who, shut up inside the palace since Monday night, could not comprehend why such

[1] Barrantes, *Páginas*, p. 322.
[2] Ibid., pp. 322–5, and speeches by San Miguel (12 Dec. 1854) and Escalante (7 Dec.): D.S., pp. 396–9, 333–5.
[3] See Otway to Clarendon, no. 22, Conf., 22 June 1853, F.O. 72. 823.
[4] Speeches of Escalante and San Miguel, as above, and of Ríos Rosas (D.S., pp. 399–400).

deserving men as they knew themselves to be should be treated so scurvily by the public. Thus rebuffed, the new committee voted itself the sonorous title of 'Junta de Salvación, Armamento, y Defensa', and set to work getting out proclamations. One of these fatuously 'instructed' patriots not to fire unless attacked, and 'hoped' the soldiers would imitate them.[1] It fell perfectly flat. Córdova was still dogged, bent on holding his ground until reinforcements could arrive. None were in fact likely, for most of Spain was in a state of revolt by now. Isabel was frightened, and there was talk of her slipping out of Madrid to some safer place.[2] Only one other course was left, and some in the palace as well as the new Junta's emissaries must have been pressing her to take it. Suddenly her ministers were called upstairs and informed by the Queen, much to their mortification, that she was sending for Espartero to take their place.

The Junta, whose sole claim to attention was that it could appear to be negotiating with the palace on behalf of the people, was quick to exploit its 'success' and to busy itself with arrangements for a cease-fire. Even now firing died down only slowly and fitfully. San Miguel had to keep on showing himself about the streets in his role of pacificator until past midnight. His associates were perturbed by the growing influence of the rival Junta del Sur, and in the small hours the indefatigable old man was off again to the Cebada. There he gained at least tacit recognition of his own committee as Madrid's mouthpiece; and the radical Salmerón, one of Corradi's fellow delegates of Monday, agreed to come over to the new body.[3] With morning, on the other hand— it was Thursday the 20th—Córdova was unpleasantly surprised and the Junta probably little less so to find barricades still going up instead of being dismantled. Soldiers cut off in the Principal for twenty-four hours were famishing, but the patriots even after a balcony appeal by San Miguel would allow no food to reach them until they handed over their weapons.[4] Last to submit were the iron men of the Civil Guard.[5] In the history of this picked corps

[1] Texts in Barrantes, Páginas, pp. 322–3, and Las jornadas de julio, pp. 291–2. All this day and the next San Miguel went on offering the ministers his services: see his speech, above.

[2] Hardman, Blackwood's, Sept. 1854, p. 362; Pi, Historia, vol. iv, p. 73.

[3] The Junta del Sur seems to have treated earlier approaches by its rival with contempt; see Las jornadas de julio, pp. 304–5.

[4] Ibid., p. 300; Novedades, 21 July 1854; Clamor Público, 26 July, 1/3–4.

[5] Hardman (Blackwood's, Sept. 1854, p. 360) speaks of the Civil Guards as 'in some

1854 completed its transformation from protector of the people against brigandage into protector of the established order against the people.

It would not be easy to calm feeling down so long as Córdova was there to inflame it, and the Junta wanted Isabel to transfer authority, pending Espartero's arrival, to San Miguel. When she demurred it felt called on to make a spirited gesture by resolving to occupy the Principal, where it could assume more of the air of a provisional government. No more than a gesture was required; the Cabinet, Córdova still dissenting, advised Isabel to call in San Miguel, and by 6.30 p.m. he was being summoned to the palace. Both the English and French representatives, who had been asked to go there because the Court was badly in need of moral support, tried to impress on the Queen the necessity of making friends with Espartero. Turgot took the occasion also to warn her emphatically against leaving Madrid: 'en de telles circonstances une fuite était souvent une abdication.'[1]

There was remarkably little hue and cry after the dismissed ministers. Rivas sheltered for a day or two with Turgot, an old friend. Even Córdova, after a few days' hiding in the King's apartments, was able to leave Madrid quietly and go abroad. His last recollection of this evening of 20 July was of looking down from a palace balcony and seeing a cart go by laden with dead bodies of soldiers. The exhausted general thought of their futile sacrifice and of his own blasted future, and burst into tears. Two years later, when he was going to be given his old post in the army again, Isabel refused to have him, because at some moment during the fighting, when she kept asking inanely when would the revolution be over, he made some impatient answer.[2] Poetic justice saw to it that Fernández de Córdova should live to serve, however half-heartedly, the first Republic.

sort the Swiss Guards of the Madrid July revolution—equally firm in duty and discipline, and almost equally odious to the people'.

[1] Otway to Clarendon, no. 58, 21 July 1854, F.O. 72. 845, and Turgot to Drouyn de Lhuys, no. 109, 21 July 1854; *Espagne*, vol. 845.

[2] Córdova, *Mis memorias*, vol. iii, pp. 406, 413–15.

V

THE REVOLUTION HALTED

Espartero's Return to Power, July 1854

BLOODSHED had been by Parisian standards trivial. Incomplete municipal records listed 74 civilians killed, 279 wounded.[1] This was a high proportion all the same of the total number active on the rebel side, not more than five hundred or so, an observer thought, even towards the end.[2] Córdova, whose losses were somewhat lower, was not overwhelmed as many supposed by numbers.[3] But the insurgents were backed by far more numerous casual helpers and barricade defenders, and by the sympathy of the population as a whole; and Hardman noted how well adapted to insurrection was the labyrinthine heart of 'this most irregularly built capital'.[4]

Twenty years before, on 17 July, a frantic mob was rushing from the Puerta del Sol to the Calle de Toledo to massacre Jesuits accused of poisoning wells; and Lord Clarendon, then Mr. Villiers, was writing from Madrid to Lord Howden, then Colonel Caradoc, about 'the wholly unrestrained fury of the worst canaille in Europe'.[5] Nothing more startlingly showed how far Spain had moved since 1834 than the behaviour of the Madrileños during these four days of July 1854. 'There is no account', the wondering Otway reported, 'of any grave excess having been committed.'[6] Hardman did not see 'a single instance of misconduct, of theft, outrage, or drunkenness'.[7] Various other spectators, both Spaniards and foreigners, put on record similar tributes.[8] What

[1] *Clamor Público*, 18 July 1855, 3/3.

[2] *Las jornadas de julio*, p. 297.

[3] Córdova (*Memoria*, p. 134) gives his losses as 2 officers and 21 men killed, 10 and 82 wounded. Miraflores (*Continuación*, vol. i, p. 514) says 31 killed, 109 wounded.

[4] *Blackwood's*, Sept. 1854, p. 360.

[5] F.O. 323. 3. It was accepted belief that Madrid mobs were pre-eminently dangerous; cf. 'Trelawney Tomkinson, Esq.', *The Inquisitor; a view of many things* (London, 1846), p. 209.

[6] Otway to Clarendon, no. 61, 22 July 1854, F.O. 72. 845.

[7] *The Times*, 27 July 1854, 10/3–5; cf. *Blackwood's*, Sept., p. 362.

[8] Córdova himself (*Memoria*, p. 117) admitted the people's generosity and

astounded them most of all was that there was no looting. Barricades bore the warning *Pena de muerte al ladrón*, 'Death for theft'.

These men of July were a motley band. Some were foreign refugees, chiefly Frenchmen who provided instruction in barricade-building with the latest technical improvements. Middle-class individuals took part, but it seems clear that the lion's share of the fighting was done by the working class, including artisans. Most of the snipers and skirmishers were described as ill-armed and scantily supplied with powder and shot, to buy which many of them spent the wretched coins they needed for their children's food.[1] They were of the race that Pérez Galdós in his portrayal of the July revolution typifies in the artisan Gamoneda and his son, half-starved creatures kept alive by naïve and splendid dreams.[2] For such humble rebels days like these, tragic in prodigality of sacrifice and meagreness of reward, were their own best recompense.

Thus if the working class at Barcelona gave the signal for this revolution, working-men at Madrid brought it to its triumphant conclusion. Córdova was not altogether wrong in thinking that social revolt, class conflict, had broken out; the men who defeated him were not in arms against a ministry but against the whole miserable condition of their lives. But when the battle was over the question was whether their turbid flood of revolt could find some clear channel before it ebbed away. They were far less accustomed to organized action than their fellows at Barcelona, and had no leadership of their own. They also had no funds, and could not survive many more days without work and wages.

San Miguel misfired completely with his first allocution as acting head of the government, on the 21st, which told the

self-restraint. Cf. *The Attaché in Madrid*, p. 367; Vivó, p. 49; M. Torrente, *Política ultramarina* (Madrid, 1854), p. 401; A. Bravo y Tudela, *La religión y el trono* (Madrid, 1855), p. 15; Villalba Hervás, p. 153; J. Nombela, *Impresiones y recuerdos* (Madrid, 1909–12), vol. ii, p. 36; and an anecdote from an English witness in O. C. D. Ross, *Spain and the War with Morocco* (London, 1860), pp. 30–33.

[1] They were mostly 'artisans, small tradesmen and the like', Hardman wrote to Blackwood (*Blackwood Papers*, vol. 4,105, pp. 121–2). Cf. an eloquent tribute to them in Fernández de los Ríos, *Luchas políticas*, vol. ii, p. 315 n.

[2] *La revolución de julio* ('Episodios Nacionales'). Cf. *The Times*, 27 July 1854 (Madrid, 19 July, 3 p.m.), 10/3–5: 'This is no ordinary Spanish *pronunciamiento*, beginning with noise and ending in smoke. It has all the earnestness and fierceness of a Parisian revolution.'

patriots in laudatory phrases that they might now go quietly home.[1] 'The People must work its own salvation', declared as if in answer a district junta's manifesto.[2] How to do so was less easily said. Some of these juntas thrown up in the fighting kept together for weeks, serving as mouthpieces for street-level opinion. Only the 'Junta del Sur' stood out sufficiently to be capable of pressing the revolution further forward, as many were expecting it to do; in fact it showed little inclination to give a lead. Its membership was mixed, but middle-class Progresistas set the tone, one of them, Huerta, acting as chairman.[3] Those further Left seem to have felt that the best course was to try and influence the San Miguel junta, as the most important, and besides the radical Salmerón, Becerra the Democrat migrated from the Cebada to the Principal. They and others who followed them put themselves in a somewhat equivocal position, and did not pass uncensured.[4]

Democrats especially might have been expected to act more independently. In the rising Rivero's house in the Calle de Atocha had been a rebel stronghold and suffered heavy damage; Chao was at the barricades, 'a musket in his hands, a pen between his teeth', until he was captured by the enemy; Sixto Cámara and Ordax Avecilla and Cervera endeavoured in every way to unfurl the Democrat banner over the struggle.[5] This revolution would be looked upon as the coming of age of their party in Spain. But its forces were still few and scattered, the chief leader Orense still in exile. Moreover, the state of discredit of all the older parties meant that the very conception of party was tarnished, and that any political group could be disparaged as a selfish faction. Their worst handicap, however, was lack of a programme with sufficient social objectives to attach the aroused workers and the rest of the poorer classes firmly to their cause. Except as republicans they did not stand out saliently from the more radical Progresistas, whose papers were now advocating quite advanced political, but no social, demands.

---

[1] Text in *Las jornadas de julio*, pp. 300–1; Barrantes, *Páginas*, p. 323.

[2] Text in *Clamor Público*, 22 July 1854, 1/1.

[3] Pi y Margall (*La reacción y la revolución*, pp. 21–24) describes his disappointment at finding the Junta del Sur so little different from San Miguel's.

[4] See Garrido, *Obras escogidas* (Barcelona, 1859–60), vol. i, pp. 400–1.

[5] On Chao see M. Curros Enríquez, *Eduardo Chao* (Madrid, 1893), p. 63; on the others Garrido, *Obras escogidas*, vol. i, p. 400, and *Historia*, vol. iii, pp. 221 ff.

One of the few Democrats who saw or glimpsed the need was Pi y Margall, one of their youngest recruits, and as such, and as a Catalan, sensitive to the newer ideas stirring in Europe: he was much under the influence of Proudhon. He was one of those who thought the party ought to be grasping opportunity, and on 21 July he produced what was intended to be the first number of a propaganda sheet, *El Eco de la Revolución*.[1] It called on the people not to lay down their arms until such reforms were won as would stop the parasitic rich from putting all the burdens on the poor through indirect taxes, exorbitant rents, conscription, exploitation of labour. To many readers all this sounded alarmingly 'socialistic'—though socialism in Marx's sense was completely alien to Pi y Margall's thinking. He was even taken into custody for some hours, and his *Eco* came out no more.

While politicians and parties failed to lend clarity to the Cebada's confused thoughts, it was left to others to find a vent for its passions. Several bullfighters, idols of the slums, had come to the front in the fighting, and one of these, José Muñoz, or Pucheta,[2] was loath to quit the limelight; to remain in it he would give the kind of lead that his imagination could reach to. San Luis and his confederates had found safe hiding-places: San Luis at first like Rivas in the French embassy. They left a worthy scapegoat in Francisco Chico, lately chief of police and a man accused of every crime,[3] who had retired with his ill-gotten gains to a luxurious residence in the Plaza de los Mostenses. Early on the 23rd a passer-by found all the neighbours and street-vendors gaping at one house, no. 19. Presently he saw four of Pucheta's men come out, with Chico, old and ill, perhaps already dying, on a mattress laid over an improvised stretcher.[4] Ten thousand townspeople swelled the concourse that moved southward, pelting Chico with dirt and stones and abuse, until at last it reached the Cebada and the firing-squad. The wretch went to his death a Spaniard, stoically.

[1] Reprinted in his *La reacción y la revolución*, App., pp. 411–17, and Bermejo, *Alzamiento popular*, pp. 118–22.

[2] For an account of 'Pucheta', and portrait, see J. M. de Cossío, *Los toros* (Madrid, 1945), vol. iii, pp. 657–8, who describes him as unskilful but courageous in the arena.

[3] For stories of Chico see T. M. Hughes, *An Overland Journey to Lisbon* (London, 1847), vol. ii, pp. 71–72; Comte A. d'Antioche, *Deux diplomates. Le comte Raczynski et Donoso Cortés* (Paris, 1880), pp. 203–5; Nombela, vol. i, pp. 256–7.

[4] Nombela, vol. ii, pp. 22 ff.; see also *The Attaché in Madrid*, pp. 325 ff., and P. de Répide, *Isabel II, reina de España* (Bilbao, 1932), p. 172.

San Miguel displayed once more both courage and shrewdness. He hurried to the scene and, hoisted up on a chair, delivered a homily which reduced some hearers, like scolded schoolboys, to tears.[1] That Chico richly deserved his fate no one in Madrid questioned, but the wild justice done on him alarmed the middle classes and helped to rally them round San Miguel. He and his friends were leaving nothing undone to bring the situation under cooling restraint before Espartero's advent. Critics were disarmed by being co-opted to the Junta; sundry newspapermen were included. Reforming decrees were being brought out, and dust made to fly impressively.[2] The unpopular town council was dissolved and the councillors of 1843 recalled. Above all the revival of the national militia, already ordered on the 21st, was being pushed on. A bogy hitherto to all but radicals, this wore a different aspect now that an armed working class had entered the scene: in Madrid after all a militia would be largely, even predominantly, middle-class in composition. On the 26th San Miguel, who was to be inspector-general, held a first big review, and the jackets and blouses of the 'people' contrasted strikingly with the black coats and yellow gloves of the respectable;[3] a presage of dissensions still to show themselves.

In all the Junta's utterances the Queen figured as an estimable, inexperienced young sovereign rescued from bad advisers, not a culprit awaiting trial. To keep her on the throne was the best way to damp down 'extremism'; but the task looked no easy one. Public feeling had worked itself up, as it usually does, more in terms of personalities than of abstract principles. It could be fairly argued too that no genuine constitutional life was possible while such a woman with such hangers-on occupied the throne. During the discussions of the past year or so the practical alternatives to Isabel had boiled down to a single one: adoption of a new monarch from Portugal. The idea of bringing King Pedro from Lisbon to Madrid had been gathering support, and was, Otway wrote, 'extremely popular and general'.[4]

Unfortunately its more conservative advocates had been put off, first by the Anglo-French veto and now by the mass revolt

[1] Barrantes, *Páginas*, p. 326.
[2] The Junta's enactments, ten in all, are in C.L., vol. lxii, pp. 371–5.
[3] *Nación*, 28 July 1854, 1/2; *The Times*, 3 Aug., 7/2; Ruiz de Morales, p. 671.
[4] Otway to Clarendon, no. 52, 19 July 1854, F.O. 72. 845.

they had previously hoped to avert. There was no party to mobilize opinion in favour of a new dynasty. Democrats could not do it, because most of them were bent on getting rid of all crowned heads. Monarchy was dead, its carcass stinking, the time come to bury it, exclaimed Fernando Garrido, returning hot-foot from exile, in a fiery pamphlet.[1] Many Democrats were inclined to fix on the mere proclaiming of a republic the same exorbitant hopes that the populace was fixing on the mere advent of Espartero. This meant in addition gambling on Espartero's willingness to sponsor a republic. And even if he proved willing, republicanism was alien to all Spanish feeling and tradition. There could be no republic without republicans, the Catalan radical Ribot y Fontseré pointed out: it would be at best a frail bark 'launched by surprise, beating against wind and tide'.[2] Proclaimed in any of the big towns it might easily frighten the countryside back towards Carlism, given the fact that nobody was ready with agrarian reforms to lend meaning to it. Even in the poorer quarters of Madrid its preachers, Turgot was soon comfortably convinced, were losing touch with the feeling of the streets.

A chance remained of a fresh impetus coming to the revolution from somewhere else in the country. In these July days Madrid had greatly strengthened its claim to be a fully-fledged capital, but it was still much less so than Paris, and less in danger therefore of isolation from the country at large. All the towns were in an exalted mood. Everywhere local interests, grievances, feuds, were apt however to engross attention; and in the south, as in some northern towns, it was O'Donnell who, somewhat fortuitously, was coming out on top. Andalusia did not wait passively this month to be liberated by others: news of the fall of San Luis, as it leaped southward with the aid of the 'optical telegraph', sufficed to set off pronouncements in one centre after another. But with O'Donnell close at hand it was natural for them, while further news came pouring in from Madrid, to bestow their plaudits on the man who had been first to draw the sword, and who was now in addition the man of Manzanares, pledged to serious reform. It was equally natural for the local authorities to welcome his proximity,

---

[1] *Propaganda democrática. El pueblo y el trono* (reprint, Tarragona, 1855), pp. 5, 9.
[2] *La revolución*, p. 126. Cf. Pi, *Historia*, vol. iv, pp. 107–8: 'La República, para el pueblo, sobre todo para el de los campos, era algo espantable, algo fuera de lo natural, invención seguramente de *espíritus malignos*.'

once they decided that resistance was hopeless; by hastening to give their adhesion to O'Donnell they could hope to forestall demands for Espartero, or for worse yet.

Badajoz, in one of the areas where social tensions were to come into the open before long, was restless even before the first Madrid news arrived. Demonstrations then broke out, and the authorities made very little of a stand. Ciudad Real followed. Further south Cordoba too rose at the first news of San Luis's fall; its junta immediately, on 19 July, sent greetings to O'Donnell. At Cadiz next day while the band was giving its Thursday evening concert the crowd forced it to strike up the Hymn of Riego. On the 21st at 5 p.m. the senior officer duly pledged himself to the movement, the crowd was duly harangued, and a junta duly set up, which, like many others, set to work by dismissing the town council and recalling that of 1843.[1] At Granada to the east there was a day or two of uncertainty before the troops were allowed to fraternize with the people.

Seville, the city that claimed primacy over Andalusia,[2] was the seat of a captain-general, F. Alcalá Galiano, who had appeared outstandingly loyal to the government. When it became known that at Madrid the régime was collapsing there was a small disturbance; on the 21st Alcalá Galiano fell into step with the march of events by declaring for O'Donnell, and next day the 'Constitutional Army' was being welcomed into the city. O'Donnell proved quite as determined as the captain-general can have hoped to shepherd the revolution along a safe road; he appointed a junta himself, with no nonsense about elections. He was revealing at Seville how he would have treated Spain if Vicálvaro had been a victory. Cánovas del Castillo was soon at his elbow, on a very different errand this time, to warn him of the perilous state of Madrid; and he seems to have started planning to march back to the capital and put down extremism.[3] Next came word of the Queen's invitation to Espartero. It was mortifying indeed to him and all the Vicalvarists to think of this rival stepping coolly in to

[1] Bermejo, *Alzamiento popular*, pp. 106 ff. See *Clamor Público*, 22 July 1854, p. 2, for a set of typical proclamations by provincial juntas.

[2] For a description of Seville ten years earlier see Wallis, *Glimpses of Spain*, chaps. 14–22. The trade report by Consul Williams in *Parliamentary Papers*, 1857, vol. xxxviii, dwells on the considerable manufactures of silk, linen, and soap. On events there now see J. Guichot, *Historia de la ciudad de Sevilla* (Seville, 1875–86), vol. v, pp. 34 ff.

[3] Fernández Almagro, p. 78; cf. Córdova, *Mis memorias*, vol. iii, pp. 392–3.

reap the reward of their labours,[1] and he was suspected of thinking for a bitter moment of making a fight.[2] But the manifesto of Manzanares cut him off from the conservative support he might have appealed to; and the southern provinces now applauding him would not follow him against Espartero and Madrid.

Malaga with its smoking factory chimneys was an exception to the general southern pattern. It rose in response to events at Barcelona and Valencia, and had more in common with them. The authorities, who had few troops at their disposal, were making nocturnal efforts to put the fort in readiness for a defence when on 19 July rumours from up the coast started a ferment. That evening demonstrators set the cathedral bells ringing, houses were illuminated, and by ten o'clock the civil and military governors deemed it prudent to join in the rejoicings. This make-believe conversion was treated with contempt; the people took up arms, there was a clash with the police, and before the night was over both governors boarded ship and weighed anchor.[3]

Tomás Domínguez, a wealthy proprietor and uncle of General Serrano, headed a provisional junta chosen next day, and on the 21st, on the news of the royal capitulation at Madrid, the troops came over to it. In Malaga things could not so easily be halted; there was a cry for a new, elected junta, and this, it was agreed after delicate discussions, was to be chosen by universal and direct vote. On the 23rd voters thronged into the bull-ring. Esparteristas, or so conservative critics alleged, posted themselves at the entrance and rival lists of candidates were torn up. At any rate the new body was mostly made up of radical Progresistas, though Domínguez was again president and all the others belonged to the business or professional classes. A few days later a new town council was elected:[4] again, Malaga was not content like many other towns merely to recall the men of 1843 to office. Very soon

---

[1] Later O'Donnell asserted that before starting his movement he signified willingness to accept Espartero's leadership (speech of 19 Jan. 1856; D.S., pp. 6,287–9).

[2] Pi y Margall, *La reacción y la revolución*, p. 12.

[3] Detailed accounts in the reports of the French consul, Vicomte du Bouzet, no. 16, 10 July 1854, and no. 18, 20 July; *Espagne*, Consular, vol. lvi. Also Acting-consul J. A. Mark to Sir R. Gardiner, Governor of Gibraltar, 20 July 1854, in C.O. (Colonial Office records, P.R.O.) 91. 216.

[4] Bouzet, no. 19, 21 July 1854; no. 20, 22 July; no. 21, 24 July 1854, and no. 23, 5 Aug., ibid. On Malaga's turbulence cf. J. L. Adolphus, *Letters from Spain in 1856 and 1857* (London, 1858), pp. 130, 155.

a further contest was under way, as workers in various trades
stopped work, forced others to stop, and demanded higher wages,
which employers were obliged to concede. In the junta, too,
divisions were soon acute. Because of this very effervescence
Malaga remained somewhat detached, shut up with its own
problems and quarrels.

On a larger scale the same was the case with Barcelona, where
industrial strife continued to rage, labour now on the attack in
spite of the execution by court martial of a number of agitators.
Wrecking of machines and building of trade unions went on
briskly,[1] but had little connexion with any political programme;
while by terrifying the propertied classes, among whom there
was a mass exodus from the city, they deterred local liberalism
from launching plans of national reform. Manuel de la Concha,
who left his place of banishment in the Canaries and reached
Barcelona by way of France on 27 July, was welcomed with open
arms by the harassed provisional junta of Catalonia, functioning
since 17 July, which made him its president, and by the captain-
general who turned over to him the military command. La Rocha
was being compelled to temporize with the workers, listen to their
deputations and grievances, and prohibit the hated 'self-acting'
machines. The old city walls which for years now had constricted
Barcelona's growth were to be demolished, providing jobs for
labourers and building land for sale. In early August mill-hands
were returning to work, many of them after being on strike for
three weeks.

All this was not enough to save La Rocha. Concha felt obliged
to sacrifice him because the troops could not be relied on,[2] and on
5 August he sought refuge in the house of the British consul, who
helped him to escape by sea.[3] On the same day the junta was
compelled to order all employers who had closed their mills to
have them open again by the 7th. Concha's difficulties with his
soldiers came to a head when two regiments particularly infected
with democratic ideas were picked for colonial service, in order,
it must be surmised, to be got rid of. They replied by mutinying
and killing two of their officers. It was the only serious act of

[1] Bermejo, *Alzamiento popular*, pp. 59–60; Castillo, pp. 66–67; Carrera Pujal,
vol. iv, pp. 239 ff.
[2] Baradère to Drouyn de Lhuys, no. 123, 8 Aug. 1854; *Espagne*, Consular, vol. 51.
[3] Baker to Clarendon, no. 25, 6 Aug. 1854, F.O. 72. 851.

defiance by the army rank and file in this whole period, and in
Concha's eyes one that must be dealt with firmly at all hazards.
Four soldiers were shot; both regiments were disbanded, and all
the men scattered among other units or sent overseas for a double
spell of service.

Alone of all the juntas springing up in the provinces Saragossa's
felt qualified to rise to the height of the national situation, and to
take an equal tone with Madrid. With a population of 60,000 or so
Saragossa stood only ninth among the cities. But not long since
as Spain measures time it had been the capital of an independent
kingdom. One of the junta's manifestoes indeed hinted at revival
of a separate monarchy of eastern Spain.[1] This year Saragossa
could boast of having blown the first trumpet-blast, with the Hore
rising, and it was the sanctuary of pure Liberalism: Borao declared with pride that his city was struggling for Liberty alone,
not like Barcelona adulterating the sacred cause with grosser ends
and aims.[2] There was at any rate no big industrial working class
to alarm the middle classes, and they had a prime cause for self-
confidence in the proximity of Espartero. Saragossa, the junta
boasted, was his pole star.[3]

Its summons came to him after years of hopeful scanning of the
horizon. Even before receiving it on 18 July he was more or less
aware of the efforts his friends were making at Saragossa, and now
he set out at once. It might have been well for him and for Spain
if events had compelled him to take part in an open struggle
against the Queen's government. But though he was drawing the
sword, he was in no hurry to throw away the scabbard. His desire
was to be accepted as the nation's unquestioned arbiter and
saviour, and when word reached him on the way that the junta at
Saragossa was not firmly in control, he showed irritation, and
called a halt. Rivero, the captain-general, was proving recalci-
trant; but popular pressure and Gurrea's successful appeals to the
troops, coupled with the news from Valladolid and elsewhere,
compelled him to climb down, and on the 19th he resigned.

All Aragon was responding to the example of its capital; and
over the rest of northern Spain rebellion was spreading while the
struggle at Madrid was still being fought out. Oviedo pronounced

[1] Howden to Clarendon, no. 149, 2 Aug. 1854, F.O. 72. 845. Some such idea was
to crop up again occasionally in the next two years.
[2] *Historia del alzamiento*, p. 47.   [3] Ibid., App. 25.

and threw up a junta on the 18th; so did Burgos, where a militia was immediately set on foot; Bilbao quickly followed.[1] By the time Espartero reached Saragossa the revolution was an accomplished fact. It was early on the 20th when the hero entered the city, by the gate of Santa Engracia, amidst deafening rejoicings of the multitude and the local poets; a short thick-set man with friendly manners and a certain acquired dignity of bearing. He acknowledged the welcome in the spare, lapidary style of one who reserves himself for deeds instead of words, with a phrase he was to repeat on all occasions: 'Cúmplase la voluntad nacional', let the will of the nation be fulfilled. The junta designated him its president, and, more sweepingly, Generalissimo of the National Armies. On the 23rd it 'lifted its powerful voice, to let it resound through the country', in a manifesto embodying the aspirations of middle-class liberalism.[2]

Espartero hung about at Saragossa for a whole week. The citizenry were clamorous against his going away to Madrid and giving the palace a chance to weave snares round him. To many, including undoubtedly Isabel, it seemed that he was waiting in the hope that developments would topple the crown from her head. 'L'Espagne semble marcher fatalement au renversement du trône d'Isabelle II', Baradère at Barcelona was writing.[3] If she fell Espartero could be regent again to another child-queen, Isabel's daughter; or king-maker; or his daydreams might soar still higher. In France a less reputable parvenu had just picked up the sceptre dropped by a less disreputable Bourbon. When the Duke of Victory paid his respects to the shrine of the Virgin he was led by cathedral dignitaries up the altar steps, a privilege of royalty. On the other hand, compared with what he had been in his regency the Espartero of 1854 was a mellower personage, with an unmistakable touch of old fogy about him. He was sixty-two; six titles and twenty-four decorations had allayed the cravings of ambition; and he was not hemmed in so closely by a bevy of hungry partisans egging him on to the 'everything or nothing', *o todo o nada*, of 1841. Cristina, again, was his old enemy, but Isabel was too young in 1843 to have any part in his ruin. He had won fame and fortune as

---

[1] There is an account of developments at Bilbao in the French consul's report, no. 24, 21 July 1854; *Espagne*, Consular, vol. 58.

[2] Borao, *Historia del alzamiento*, App. 35. It called for a new Constitution, new laws on the press and elections, opening of careers to merit.

[3] Baradère to Drouyn de Lhuys, no. 122, 1 Aug. 1854; *Espagne*, Consular, vol. 51.

her knight-errant, and still perhaps saw in her sentimentally a frightened innocent clinging to his martial hand. In some moods he could be, as Marx said, her Don Quixote, she his Dulcinea del Toboso.[1] He too hailed from La Mancha.

He put off decision by sending to Madrid a trusted henchman, the well-to-do Basque officer and progressive Allende Salazar: not to consult with the party of which Espartero was titular chief, but to confront the Court with a sort of ambiguous ultimatum. He arrived by midday on the 24th. Madrid was in a mood 'gloomy, menacing and obscure', Otway wrote, and Isabel a prey to agonizing doubts about Espartero's intentions.[2] Allende Salazar conferred briefly with the Junta, and delivered his terms at the palace in the blunt fashion that he cultivated. Pending a constituent assembly the insurrectionary juntas were to remain in being:[3] in other words the royal authority was to be suspended with no assurance of ever being revived. When he left, hysterical argument raged, in the heat of which, if rumour spoke truth, high words were bandied to and fro, Cristina losing her Italian temper and the King brandishing a sword at her husband.[4] San Miguel was there about 8, and doubtless gave the same counsel as Turgot, who told Isabel that as she had no force at her back she must take what terms were offered.[5] At 10 p.m. Allende Salazar was called to receive her submission, and set out for Aragon.

'If Espartero desires to push on the revolution', a left-wing member of the Junta had just said to Hardman, 'we are ready to second him, and to begin this very day'.[6] San Miguel and the Junta majority probably found means of making it plain to Allende Salazar that they wanted no more revolutionism. If necessary they would appeal to the army, so largely refashioned by Narváez since the days when Espartero led it. He could appeal against them

---

[1] K. Marx and F. Engels, *Revolution in Spain* (collected articles; London, 1939), pp. 108–9.

[2] Otway to Clarendon, no. 64, 24 July 1854, F.O. 72. 845.

[3] Otway to Clarendon, no. 66, 25 July 1854, F.O. 72. 845. M. A. S. Hume, *Modern Spain, 1788–1898* (London, 1899), pp. 421–2, alleges that Allende Salazar taxed Isabel rudely with levity and immorality.

[4] Hardman, *Blackwood's*, Sept. 1854, p. 363.

[5] Isabel gave way with a protestation, repeated next day to others, that she would consider any agreement as made under duress and not binding. See Turgot to Drouyn de Lhuys, no. 113, Très conf. (sent in cypher), 25 July 1854; *Espagne*, vol. 845.

[6] *The Times*, 31 July 1854, 9/2–5. The first move against the palace would have been to cut off its water.

to the people, and at first he had, it appears, some idea of doing so, for instance of stirring up Barcelona against Concha. If so he may have dropped it, as some there surmised, because he shrank from a trial of strength with the army.[1] He had besides no desire to find himself a mob leader, allied with a new-hatched Democracy. A grateful, docile Isabel, visibly owing everything to him, might after all suit him best. And while the man of destiny scratched his head the men of order went on working hard to bring about a state of affairs that would leave him no choice. San Miguel was imploring him to come at once:[2] he was also privately urging O'Donnell to do the same.[3] He was employing all his arts to reconcile the public to Isabel; he did not neglect to win the good graces of Pucheta.[4] On 26 July the *Gazette* carried a manifesto in a very wheedling tone in the Queen's own name, which began by regretting—the words attained celebrity, like some of her father's on similar occasions—'a series of deplorable misunderstandings' between nation and throne.[5]

Few leaders and few days have ever been more rapturously awaited than the Duke of Victory and his day of judgement. Otway saw his portraits in the streets 'surrounded with flowers and lamps, as would be that of the Madonna'.[6] The apocalyptic sound of his name was the measure of Spain's immense, inarticulate longing for change. Not many could have said what he had done to deserve such faith; but in his long retirement he had grown into the symbol of a confused radicalism. His features as a flesh-and-blood politician were as indistinct in memory as in the crude daubs that were being stuck up all over Spain. Where little was known, everything could be hoped. It is the fatal habit of revolutions, Marx wrote as he contemplated the spectacle, to succumb when on the point of fruition to illusions of bygone years.[7]

---

[1] Baradère to Drouyn de Lhuys, unnumbered, 17 Mar. 1855; *Espagne*, Consular, vol. 52. He had this from a General Lemery, who said Espartero had been dreaming of a regency, or even the throne, and tried to make use of him. Cf. *Annuaire des Deux Mondes*, 1854–5, p. 255; F. Melgar, *O'Donnell* (Madrid, 1946), p. 81.

[2] Fernández de los Ríos, *Luchas políticas*, vol. ii, p. 406 n. and 427.

[3] Baradère to Drouyn de Lhuys, no. 130, 7 Sept. 1854; *Espagne*, Consular, vol. 51, with information from Dulce.

[4] See G. Borao, *Historia de España* (by J. Cortada) *adicionada y continuada hasta 1868* (Barcelona, 1872–3), vol. ii, pp. 274–5. E. García Ruiz says that San Miguel pacified the *barrios* by offering jobs to the noisiest brawlers: *Historias* (Madrid, 1876–8), vol. ii, p. 563.   [5] Text in C.L., vol. lxii, pp. 191–2.

[6] Otway to Clarendon, no. 61, 22 July 1854, F.O. 72. 845.

[7] Marx, p. 102; cf. p. 107.

On the 28th Madrid scarcely went to bed; crowds sang all night in the streets. Espartero was at Alcalá. Next morning, Saturday, he was on the road early. Town council and Junta were coming half a league out from the walls with an address of welcome by San Miguel, speeches, *vivas* for Liberty, Espartero, Isabel, and everything else. His reply, as at Saragossa, was laconic and monumental: he placed at the service of freedom the legendary sword of Luchana with which he defeated the Carlists in 1836, and vowed with it, should freedom ever again be in peril, to show his Spaniards the path of glory. Then in a splendid carriage he drove through the Alcalá gate, the garrison forces drawn up on one side and the militia on the other, every bell in the city pealing—everywhere delirious thousands, draped balconies, thronged windows and even rooftops, and the hero on his feet, waving a handkerchief with which from time to time he brushed tears from his eyes, or shaking hands with the citizens who pressed closest. He had been deprived for too long of these intoxicating draughts. As he entered the Puerta del Sol, doves bedecked with green ribbons were set loose; along the Calle Mayor it seemed as if the carriage would be buried under a rain of flowers.[1]

The Calle Mayor led towards the palace. No one, Espartero perhaps least, knew what he was going there to do. But tactful men of the Junta were at his elbow. He was conducted to the Queen's apartments; and when after a long interval he reappeared to the expectant sea of faces the royal pair were adroit enough to be on the balcony above the Plaza de Armas, waving to him. He returned through the sounding streets to the house of an old friend, Matheu, where he was to lodge, in the Calle de Espoz y Mina off the Puerta del Sol, and it was long before the dizzy crowds left him free to sit down and think. And by this time another hero was at hand. O'Donnell had set out from Seville on the 23rd, judiciously leaving his troops behind. He declined a joint entry, shrewdly aware that he would be eclipsed; instead he arrived by the railway between 5 and 6 on this Saturday evening, was received at the Atocha station by San Miguel and all the other dignitaries, and, coming thus modestly, was able to reap a fair aftermath of enthusiasm as he progressed towards Matheu's house.

[1] On Espartero's entry see press accounts next day; also *The Times*, 5 Aug. 1854, 9/3; *Blackwood's*, Sept., p. 365; Anon., *Asamblea Constituyente de 1854!*, pp. 137–8; Anon., *Spaniens Verfassungskampf* (Leipzig, 1854), p. 54.

The Junta was thrusting on Espartero a magnanimous role he could scarcely evade. Another balcony scene followed as the victors of Luchana and Lucena sealed their alliance with a politic embrace.

'Scarcely were the rebels in possession of the field of battle than the spirit of reaction began to set in.'[1] So San Miguel had written of the France of February 1848, unwittingly prophesying of the Spain of 1854. It was his own turn now to be the rebel of one epoch stultifying the rebellion of the next; his reward was to be made field-marshal and, next year, duke, peer of the first class, commander of the royal halberdiers, and to be petted by Isabel like a good old mastiff by the fireside, while misrule and oppression resumed their easy sway.

[1] E. San Miguel, *La cuestión española. Nueva era* (Madrid, 1850), p. 10.

VI

THE NEW POLITICAL PATTERN

Coalition Government and Democrat Opposition
August 1854

ON the night of his arrival Espartero was sworn in as president of
the council. By thus condescending to accept office as the Queen's
minister he was already appearing to accept her as well. He was not
proposing to hold a departmental portfolio, as premiers usually did,
and this would help somewhat to mark him out as occupying an
exceptional position. At the same time it left open the Ministry of
War, the one customarily taken by a premier who was also a
general and the one that all O'Donnell's hopes centred on. He
was unpleasantly isolated, and his claim to any place in the
Cabinet precarious. But friends of order, even if they mistrusted
him after Manzanares, wanted him in as a brake on radicalism;
and to leave him out, after he had risked so much and laboured
so long, would look indecent even to the more progressive. As
head of the army, on the other hand, he might become a formidable power. Espartero wanted his faithful Allende Salazar to
have the place, and offered O'Donnell instead Foreign Affairs, or
Cuba.[1] O'Donnell would have the army or nothing; and Espartero gave way, as he was often to do with this man. He may have
consoled himself with the thought that it was only a stopgap
Cabinet which could be altered after the Cortes met. O'Donnell
moved promptly into the Buenavista, and set himself to stick
there like a limpet.

The rest of the new Cabinet was whipped together in no time.
Pacheco, one of those who had added themselves opportunely
to the Junta, stepped up from it into the Foreign Ministry.[2] He
was a distinguished jurist, and briefly in 1847 a liberal-conservative

---

[1] Otway to Clarendon, no. 73, 30 July 1854, F.O. 72. 845; O'Donnell, speech of
18 May 1857, cited by Navarro y Rodrigo, p. 117.

[2] J. F. Pacheco had been Foreign Minister (as well as Premier) in 1847, and was
so again in 1864. In Pi, *Historia*, vol. iv, p. 93, he is referred to as 'the only states-
man in this cabinet'.

premier. The rest were Progresistas of the old school. Allende Salazar, the most radical of them, only got the Navy, a post regarded as little more than nominal. Luxán at the Ministry of Development stood closer to O'Donnell. Neither he nor Francisco Santa Cruz, the well-to-do proprietor from Teruel who took the Interior,[1] was much known to the public. Alonso, Minister of Justice, had held the same office long before, and was known chiefly as an anti-clerical. Finance went to one of the platoon of financiers on or behind the political stage, the tepidly liberal Collado. In quality this was a distinctly mediocre Cabinet. One of the ablest Progresistas, Olózaga, obnoxious to Espartero as a ringleader of the party mutiny of 1843, was being given the Paris legation instead of a seat. In outlook, nothing less like a government born of revolution could well be imagined, and the *Diario Español*, chief voice of the right wing of 'Liberal Union', was able to give it a warm welcome.[2]

In the ministerial politics of the whole 'Bienio', the two-year period now opening, Espartero and the much younger and more alert O'Donnell would represent the fixed digits, all the rest a perpetual coming and going of ciphers: three at Foreign Affairs, four at Justice, five at Finance.[3] Meanwhile the relative weight of the 'two Consuls', as they were soon christened, would undergo a steady shift. Far too much of Espartero's time was given up from the first to parades, fiestas, plaudits. He kept a small staff of intimates about him, headed by his secretary Venancio Gurrea whose brother Ignacio was appointed captain-general of Aragon; but he neither directed them effectively nor allowed them to direct him. Similarly he had no notion either of rebuilding and reorienting the Progresista party himself, or of making room for anyone else to do it. He had no inclination to bring forward its Democrat element, by way of new blood;[4] he could never comprehend what need the country could have of anyone more progressive than himself.

Espartero's recreation was gambling at cards; O'Donnell's was chess. Having no party of his own as yet, he was taking care

[1] On F. Santa Cruz's career, especially during the Bienio, see an article in *Escenas Contemporáneas* (Madrid), vol. ii (1857), pp. 512–54.
[2] 1 Aug. 1854, 1/1.
[3] For lists of ministerial names and changes see Muro Martínez, vol. i, p. 222.
[4] Rodríguez-Solís says, however, that the Ministry of Development was offered first to Ordax Avecilla, but declined (vol. ii, p. 539).

to call himself neither Progresista nor Moderado, but plain Liberal. He wanted progressives to think him one of them; he wanted friends of order to believe that he was joining a Progresista government to rescue Spain from anarchy, not from selfish motives.[1] Meanwhile the constituency he had to nurse was the army, which alone could provide him with solid backing and especially with a counterpoise to the militia. In return he made an excellent spokesman for all his fellow officers, sorely in need of a defender against the cry for economies. As Fernández de los Ríos had noticed during their days in hiding, O'Donnell instinctively looked at everything from a professional point of view; he came of a military family, the camp bed was his cradle.[2] His group of Vicalvarists were being moved into the key posts. Other gratifications came their way too; along with some sense of what they owed their country these military men had a very high sense of what their country owed them. O'Donnell himself immediately became a field-marshal, Dulce and Messina rose to lieutenant-general. But the whole army was strongly in the mood for rewards, refreshers, and consolation prizes. O'Donnell had promised promotion to all officers in his rebel band, as well as two years' reduction of service for conscripts, and to prevent jealousies this had to be granted all round.[3]

Outside the army a similar voracity reigned. In one of its heterogeneous aspects 1854 was a revolution of half-pay civil servants wanting to be back on full pay, itself slender enough. All over the country a frenzy of job-hunting raged, and every junta was besieged by applicants. It was worst at Madrid, where the moment fighting ended opportunists began pushing themselves forward for a share in the coming distribution of *turrón*, or nougat, as loaves and fishes were known in political cant. Thousands boasted of the deeds that a few hundred nameless men had performed, as though, it was remarked, they had all outdone Leonidas.[4] Many an old reactionary was trumpeting the most advanced sentiments, the *Nación* complained.[5] Freemasonry was treated as a passport to

---

[1] This view of O'Donnell's conduct was endorsed by J. Cancio Mena, *El pasado y el presente de la política española* (2nd ed., Madrid, 1865), p. 20. A. Borrego, in *La revolución de julio de 1854* (Madrid, 1855), pp. 123–7, condemned his taking office.
[2] *Luchas políticas*, vol. ii, p. 375.
[3] Decree of 11 Aug. 1854; C.L., vol. lxii, pp. 226–8.
[4] H. del Busto, *Los partidos en cueros* (Madrid, 1856), p. 42.
[5] 3 Aug. 1854, 1/1–2.

a job: a lodge was farcically formed in the palace itself, the versatile Don Francisco presiding.[1] It was a greasy atmosphere in which Espartero, who unlike Narváez and divers others was admitted to be personally disinterested so far as money went, was commencing his second tenure of power. His anteroom was crammed with suitors, his desk deluged with petitions, from morning to night.[2] An opportunity to break away from the *empleomanía*, the obsession with government jobs that all recognized as a national disease, was being lost.

Spain now had a coalition whose supporters were demanding from it quite opposite things. From one side it was told that its duty was to bring the country back to 'normality': a bad ministry had been got rid of, the work of the revolution was finished. The counter-view was that its real work was only just beginning. Many juntas up and down the country had been counting on Espartero to rule through them, and exercise what Sixto Cámara called in a broadsheet this month 'a grand popular revolutionary dictatorship',[3] hammering out great reforms at once. This after all was what his ultimatum to Isabel from Saragossa had implied. To the masses his name made a far more potent appeal than any Cortes could do, for centuries of monarchy had left a blank which only the image of an individual could fill; and parliamentary methods so far had benefited only the élite. But with his lack of ideas and his indolence he preferred to conceive his mandate as merely to prevent the obstruction of the national will. 'I am only a soldier', he would tell visitors complacently when asked for his proposals.

Liberal purists chimed in by arguing that it would be reprehensible to forestall the constituent assembly in any way, and ministers accepting this comfortable self-denying ordinance could logically impose it on others too. A decree of 1 August thanked the juntas and reduced them to simple consultative bodies.[4] Saragossa protested that this left the old régime still in being in the shape of a corrupt or reactionary bureaucracy.[5] At Saragossa,

[1] Díaz y Pérez, p. 473; cf. Tirado y Rojas, vol. ii, p. 149.
[2] F. Hardman, 'Spanish Politics and Cuban Perils', in *Blackwood's*, Oct. 1854, p. 490.
[3] *La revolución*; copy with Howden to Clarendon, no. 194, 29 Aug. 1854, F.O. 72. 845. Cf. V. García de la Torre, *Reformas económicas que deben plantearse en España* (Madrid, 1854), pp. 8–9, 13, and É. de Girardin, *Questions de mon temps* (Paris, 1858 ff.), vol. viii, p. 854 (4 Aug. 1854).   [4] C.L., vol. lxii, pp. 196–7.
[5] 5 Aug. 1854; text in Borao, *Historia del alzamiento*, App. 54.

however, the junta was itself busy suppressing all the minor ones in the province, and itself being heckled by more advanced critics who wanted to knock out some of its members.

Another decree recalled to their posts all provincial councillors of 1843.[1] Not many of these were likely to be in the van of progress in 1854, and frequent complaints reached the press that their return, and that of former town councillors, was putting power in the hands of some very undesirable characters. Old laws as well as old faces were being exhumed. Of the Moderado administrative system built up in the past decade some parts were oppressive, nearly all unpopular, and pending its reconstruction by the Cortes there was all too conveniently at hand a mass of statutes of earlier Liberal epochs that could be revived. On 7 August the local government law of February 1823 was restored; next month the militia law of June 1822 with its later additions.[2] These provisional revivals dragged on into permanency, and, as everyone acknowledged, the old legislation was by now in many ways obsolete. Here was a prolific source of trouble, and the whole record of the Bienio in administration and local government was to be painfully open to criticism as confused and inefficient.

To a marked degree the popular risings in the country had been a revolt against the tax-collector. Nearly all juntas swept away the salt monopoly, and over wide areas collection of the *puertas* and *consumos*, the hated excise duties, was paralysed. Aragon was one such area, and there was a riot at Saragossa while Espartero was still there when the junta tried to collect the half-share of the *consumos* that went to local revenue.[3] But San Luis had left behind him a swollen floating debt as well as an empty treasury. The conservative press thundered against the folly of indiscriminate tax remissions, and ministers saw in the imminent prospect of bankruptcy the grand argument for discarding Utopian fancies. They were scarcely in office before they were flying in the face of the national will by declaring null and void everything done by the juntas to alter or abolish any tax.[4] How quickly they would be

---

[1] 7 Aug. 1854; C.L., vol. lxii, p. 210.

[2] C.L., vol. lxii, pp. 207-8, and vol. lxiii, pp. 74-77.

[3] Borao, *Historia del alzamiento*, pp. 81-82. The *consumos* were collected in a variety of ways, but most districts made up their quota by imposing a local levy—virtually a direct tax. See R. Santillán, *Memoria histórica de las reformas hechas en el sistema general de impuestos . . . desde 1845 hasta 1854* (Madrid, 1888), pp. 174-5.

[4] Decree of 1 Aug. 1854; C.L., vol. lxii, pp. 197-9.

able to enforce this decision remained to be seen; but it marked already a deep crack opening between government and public. The revolution was being taken neatly out of the people's hands. Espartero's magic name prevented his dazzled admirers from seeing very clearly what was happening, but there were grumblings at so much being promised, so little given. One service rendered by the militia, a cynic remarked, was that its brass bands helped to drown these mutterings.[1] To prevent a relapse into bureaucratic inertia was the new task facing the Democrats. What was required was that an anaemic and lagging *bourgeoisie* should be prodded on towards more complete elimination of feudal remnants, fuller creation of conditions for economic and intellectual expansion. Democrats could keep up the necessary pressure only if they gained the confidence of the ordinary people; they could do this only by putting forward realistic demands on their behalf. No such plan of campaign had been worked out, though the party was very ready at least to back up popular feeling about taxation. And it is the chronic dilemma of radicals under half-heartedly progressive governments that if these are left to carry out reforms at their own speed, they drop quietly off to sleep: if pressure is put on them too forcibly, they take fright and may easily bolt to the rear.

Even at this early stage Democrats were not seeing eye to eye about their tactics. Sixto Cámara was all for action; Rivero, who was to be the moderate of the party, accepted though only temporarily an offer of the governorship of Valladolid. In the absence of a real party machine a sort of headquarters was provided by a 'Union Club', or *Círculo de la Unión Progresista*, set up in Madrid after the fighting as a forum for radical opinion, whose debates reminded Howden and many others of the Jacobin Club. It met in the 'Basilios', an old monastery of St. Basil now serving as theatre and café, a little north of the Puerta del Sol. Espartero was offered and declined the presidency, which was bestowed instead on Orense, free at last to return from long banishment. A programme or manifesto which appeared in the press on 19 August ran mostly on familiar radical lines, free enterprise and retrenchment and decentralization. It took a small step forward by including a phrase about 'amelioration for the proletarian

---

[1] F. M. Morales Sánchez, *Páginas de sangre. Historia del Saladero* (Madrid, 1870), vol. ii, p. 802.

classes'.[1] But Democrats were still resting heavily on the republicanism that was their own most emotional conviction. In another uncompromising pamphlet, which speedily sold two editions of many thousand copies and landed its author in the dock, Garrido urged the sweeping away of the entire Bourbon race of 'ingrates and traitors', and rejection of any other dynasty in their stead.[2]

In the Press the dynastic question continued under hot debate. '*Nobody* believes that the Queen will be three months on her throne after the meeting of the Cortes', wrote Howden on 10 August.[3] All who thought themselves in the running were canvassing vigorously, including her sister's husband Montpensier and the flamboyant Don Enrique, the King's liberal or mountebank brother; the fact, however, that a ruler from Portugal would be far the most acceptable was so evident that Napoleon III toyed with the idea of sponsoring an Iberian union, only to be held back by his British ally.[4] What would be decisive for the monarchy, as for all reform prospects, was the character of the coming Cortes. There was press controversy about whether this ought to include a Senate, and disagreement also within the Cabinet. O'Donnell was very much on Isabel's side; her fall would mean a regency or something very like it for Espartero, and, too probably, his own political extinction. He was proposing a bargain: a unicameral Cortes, with debate on queen or dynasty prohibited.[5]

Espartero acquiesced, and on the 12th the eagerly awaited decree on the summoning of the Cortes came out, with a preamble breathing loyalty.[6] Liberal opinion was outraged, and Espartero must have realized how egregiously he had let himself be overreached. He gave a promise to a delegation on the 13th that the Cabinet would consider the matter again, and the prohibition was soon being treated as a dead letter. On this same day a great Press banquet was taking place in the Teatro del Oriente;

[1] Text in F. Garrido, *Espartero y la revolución* (Madrid, 1854), pp. 30–31.

[2] See title-page of 3rd ed. (1854) as to its sales. It belonged to a series, 'Propaganda Democrática'.

[3] Howden to Clarendon, private, 10 Aug. 1854; Clarendon Papers, vol. c. 20.

[4] See T. Martin, *The Life of His Royal Highness the Prince Consort* (London, 1875–80), vol. iii, pp. 118–19.

[5] Howden to Clarendon, no. 164, 10 Aug. 1854, F.O. 72. 845. Hardman heard that all ministers except Allende Salazar threatened to resign if the compromise were rejected (*The Times*, 21 Aug. 1854, 7/5).

[6] Text, often reprinted, in C.L., vol. lxii, pp. 230–3.

long bruised and mauled, the press was bursting out with a giant's noise and was credited with a giant's strength. Espartero gave the toast of Liberty. O'Donnell, seizing the chance to mark his position firmly, followed with 'Queen Isabel and the Constitution'.[1]

Three days later when she at last ventured out for a drive her smiles fell upon stony silence.[2] But the virulence of feeling was much less against her than against her mother. All the outcry against the country's late oppressors, some of whom had escaped and none of whom had been brought to book, was converging on Cristina, that Circe whose evil arts reduced men to grovelling beasts, and at whose door unarmed folk were shot down on the night of 17 July. By identifying themselves with the cry for her to be put on trial the Democrats were undoubtedly taking a popular line. What was more, they were catching at the best available means to compel Isabel's abdication. For Espartero, with his tremulosities of purpose, here lay another dilemma. He had no reason in the world to love Cristina; and whatever dreams of grandeur he cherished would be vastly aided by her public prosecution.[3] There were many on the other hand to warn him that a further plunge into uncharted waters might end in social war. The government as a whole, Pi y Margall observed with insight, shrank from putting Cristina on trial for fear of 1854 turning into 1789.[4]

How to smuggle Cristina out of Spain and out of the public mind became the anxious preoccupation of all who judged it prudent to keep the throne untouched. Plans for her removal in the first days of the new government were frustrated partly by bands of armed patriots at the city gates and bridges. On 5 August the Junta felt constrained to endorse a declaration by all the Madrid districts against letting her go. Espartero called a Cabinet, and late that night a pledge was given—or so it was understood— that Cristina would not be allowed to leave. But a fortnight later a decree politely put an end to all the small fry of juntas surviving

[1] *Clamor Público*, 15 Aug. 1854, 1/2–2/2; *Diario Español*, 15 Aug., 1/1–2/4.

[2] *The Times*, 25 Aug. 1854, 8/2.

[3] Dulce told Baradère that Espartero wanted Cristina put on trial in order to compel Isabel to abdicate, but that he and O'Donnell quashed the scheme (Baradère to Drouyn de Lhuys, no. 130, 7 Sept. 1854; *Espagne*, Consular, vol. 51). Cf. Melgar, p. 82.

[4] *La reacción y la revolución*, pp. 45–46.

from July, those of the Madrid districts for example; only juntas representing provinces, as a rule the most moderate, were excepted.[1] Soon there was a fresh slither in the same conservative direction, this time under stress of the urgent need for a loan. On 26 August Espartero presided over a meeting of capitalists. He invoked their patriotism, and, more realistically, gave them an assurance that order would be maintained and the country rebuilt on liberal but monarchical foundations; and they felt public-spirited enough to promise half a million pounds on the security of the colonial tribute that still formed part of Spain's revenue.[2]

On the same day a fresh statement about Cristina was being drawn up by a meeting of militia commandants, who, elected by their men,[3] could act or at times might be compelled to act as tribunes of the people. Forced to decide, the Cabinet in two long sittings screwed itself up to letting Cristina go, on terms that it was hoped the public could be got to swallow. Her lavish pension was cut off and all her properties in Spain sequestrated, and she was to be 'expelled' from the country and never allowed to return. At 7 a.m. on the 28th ministers were at the palace to witness her departure. She was cool and self-possessed as she got into a big travelling coach with her dejected husband to begin a week-long drive to the Portuguese frontier.

At the same hour a *Gazette* was announcing her expulsion. To Madrid this meant her escape, and a broken pledge; and a deep though obscure feeling welled up that it meant also the revolution frustrated. By mid morning an indignant crowd was surging outside Espartero's temporary residence in the Conde de Barrajas square. If the situation was a ticklish one for him, it was so equally for the Democrats, and in particular for Orense[4] who had only had a week or two in Spain to get his bearings. They could

---

[1] R.O. of 23 Aug. 1854; C.L., vol. lxii, pp. 294–5. The decision seems to have been inspired by Duero, fresh from his wrestlings with refractory Barcelona: Straten-Ponthoz to Brouckère, no. 133, 25 Aug. 1854; *Espagne*, vol. 8 (1).

[2] Turgot to Drouyn de Lhuys, no. 131, 27 Aug. 1854; *Espagne*, vol. 845. Cf. *The Times*, 31 Aug. 1854 (Paris, 30 Aug.), 7/1, and brief accounts in *Clamor Público* and *Diario Español*, 27 Aug., 1/4; *Nación*, 30 Aug., 2/1.

[3] Under the provisional decree of 15 Sept. all officers below the 'planes mayores' or provincial staffs were elected. On this meeting see *The Times*, 2 Sept. 1854, 10/4.

[4] Orense was on the spot; by his own later statement he had been sent for by Espartero, and only addressed the crowd to try to calm it (speech of 31 Dec. 1855; D.S., pp. 5,423–4). Press accounts of this day's events are not informative; several newspapers appeared next day as single sheets, and explained that their staff had been called away by militia duties.

see the risk of a head-on collision with Espartero, and the best they could hope was that he might have second thoughts when he saw what a storm he had raised, and be induced to drop some of his more retrograde colleagues. Beset by excited deputations, one of them led by Orense from the Union Club, which had gone into permanent session, Espartero fumbled, as he was apt to when there was no one at his elbow to stiffen him, and promised to call an immediate conference of representative bodies, Junta and town council and militia commandants.[1]

But his vanity was having a rude upset, and he seems to have arrived at the Principal for the conference in a vinegary mood.[2] Orense put the case against the government's action, with, he maintained afterwards, studious moderation. O'Donnell spoke forcibly, and Espartero had only to echo him. None of the listeners cared to defy his still resplendent reputation; and the only outcome was a leaflet designed to mollify the public. Outside the building Howden watched a handwritten poster being fixed up on the wall, 'calling upon the inhabitants in the name of the Sovereign People to again raise their barricades, and punish the treason of the Government'.[3] When San Miguel sallied out to reason with demonstrators he had to retire crestfallen. At this critical moment everything depended on the militia, whose presence allowed the regular troops to be kept discreetly out of sight. Its strength stood at about 20,000, only half of them as yet equipped with muskets. In composition it was more plebeian than Madrid as a whole: there must have been some substance in Straten-Ponthoz's lament that the 'bonne bourgeoisie' was not joining, and was letting the force be overrun by extremists.[4] But these were Espartero's warmest admirers. Up to this point a great many citizens were firmly convinced that Cristina's escape had been managed by trickery against their idol's wishes. Most of those who were getting ready to fight wanted to fight for Espartero, not against him. There was nothing for it, once his attitude became clear, but to shrug Cristina off.

Militiamen might look 'sulky and dissatisfied',[5] and there were

[1] Text of the agreement in Ribot y Fontseré, *La revolución*, pp. 152–3, and Ruiz de Morales, pp. 688–9.
[2] Turgot to Drouyn de Lhuys, no. 134, 30 Aug. 1854; *Espagne*, vol. 845.
[3] Howden to Clarendon, no. 193, 28 Aug. 1854, F.O. 72. 845.
[4] Straten-Ponthoz to Brouckère, no. 130, 23 Aug. 1854; *Espagne*, vol. 8 (1).
[5] Hardman, *Blackwood's*, Oct. 1854, pp. 479–80.

some shouts for the resignation of all the other ministers; but by 8 p.m. the authorities felt strong enough to order the streets to be cleared. Many flimsy barricades were quickly dismantled. One small area remained firmly fenced off, round the Basilios, where a knot of Democrats were struggling with their awkward predicament. They could not hope now for any victory, yet they could not very well call the agitation off. That they were preparing a summons to Isabel to abdicate was one of a variety of charges brought against them subsequently. A graphic if malicious sketch of the scene was made by Hardman, who found his way into the building about 11 p.m. or later. 'At a low table, surrounded by a tumultuous throng, sat Orense, Marquis of Albaida, and mad democrat *par excellence*—a stout, heavy-looking man, about 50 years of age. He was dictating to a secretary who wrote, with remarkably dirty fingers, by the light of a single candle.' That guttering candle made no bad symbol of a new age struggling fitfully into life in the mephitic atmosphere of Spain. At the Principal, where Hardman arrived about midnight, he found better illumination. Colonels and generals bustled about, and Pucheta dropped in, 'a wiry, active man, with a very quick, lively eye' and scarred nose, to be lionized for his sterling work in keeping the *barrios bajos* quiet.[1] In the streets the hubbub was dwindling away. Before dawn most of the malcontents went home, many leaving their weapons behind at deserted barricades; about a hundred who failed to retire in time were arrested in the early morning.

A British officer in Spanish service rejoiced that the affair had compelled Espartero to 'break at last openly with socialism and anarchy'.[2] A few foodshops broken into after nightfall served as text for press diatribes about the perils confronting society. Liberal editors who did not care to discuss the rights and wrongs of Cristina's escape accused reactionary agents of being at work to stir up mob violence. Another whipping-boy was the American Minister Soulé, who left hastily for France on 31 August under a shower of newspaper abuse.[3] Whether as alleged there was any

---

[1] *The Times*, 5 Sept. 1854 (Madrid, 29 Aug.), 8/5–6.

[2] Sir R. Le Saussage to Clarendon, private, Madrid, 10 Sept. 1854; Clarendon Papers, vol. c. 20.

[3] See Ettinger, pp. 303–6. Cf. Hardman to Blackwood, 14 Sept. 1854: 'There is no doubt of his participation . . . the strongest evidence has been obtained' (*Blackwood Papers*, vol. 4,105, pp. 125–6).

understanding between him and any Democrats is doubtful;[1] though certainly in those far-off days Democrats looked as naturally to the U.S.A. as Progresistas to England, Moderados to France, or Carlists to Russia. At all events the party's enemies seized their chance to fix on it the odium of an attempted rising and the ignominy of a fiasco. Republicanism had collapsed, Straten-Ponthoz wrote with much satisfaction.[2] The twenty-eighth of August was at least a tremendous set-back for the cause, Garrido was to admit later.[3] It did duty for years as proof that Democrats were both irresponsible and ineffective.

Sixto Cámara was arrested once more, and Orense wrote to the newspapers complaining that he was being forced to leave the country again.[4] In the upshot he only had to withdraw to Palencia, where he was standing for the Cortes. The government could not afford to make martyrs of men who after all had said what most of Spain thought. Fifty of those arrested were tactfully released on the Queen's birthday on 10 October, the rest soon afterwards. But the day after the tumult citizens not in the militia were ordered to surrender firearms within twenty-four hours. Next day all political societies, among them of course the Union Club, were suppressed, and all but purely electoral meetings banned, on the pretext that they were being infiltrated by secret enemies of liberty, and that freedom of the press and the right of petition were all the public required.[5]

This would seriously hinder development of political life, and the *Clamor Público* felt compelled to protest;[6] the *Nación*, regarded as Espartero's mouthpiece, offered no comment. Stormy protests about the decree and about Cristina's escape were feared at Barcelona, but the cholera epidemic helped to damp them down. Salamanca expressed disgust by deposing its governor. This was

[1] Soulé contradicted the allegation in a statement in *La Soberanía Nacional* (Madrid), 16 Dec. 1854.
[2] Straten-Ponthoz to Brouckère, no. 140, 3 Sept. 1854; *Espagne*, vol. 8 (1).
[3] *Obras escogidas*, vol. i, pp. 401–2, and *Historia*, vol. 3, pp. 236–8. O'Donnell's brother Enrique could represent Aug. 28 as the Democrats' single, and damning, attempt at force during the Bienio: *La democracia española* (Madrid, 1858), p. 10; cf. N. Fernández Cuesta's reply, *Vindicación de la democracia española* (Madrid, 1858), pp. 25–26.
[4] *Clamor Público*, 5 Sept. 1854, 1/2–3, and 8 Sept., 1/1.
[5] Decree dated 29 Aug. 1854; C.L., vol. lxii, pp. 363–4.
[6] 31 Aug. 1854, 1/4–2/1; cf. a long protest by Castelar in *Iberia*, reprinted in M. Morayta, *Juventud de Castelar* (Madrid, 1901), pp. 36–44.

the town whose junta was said to have artlessly abolished taxation and sent to Valladolid for money; troops now came from there instead to reinstate the deposed dignitary. The Madrid Junta was probably acting on a hint from above when it treated itself to a farewell banquet on 7 September and disbanded. At Segovia, Valladolid, and elsewhere its example was followed; also, with a bad grace, at Saragossa. Juntas at Lugo, Corunna, and some other places that continued to meet were dissolved by government order. In the capital the governor Sagasti suspended all periodicals that had failed to comply with the regulations, including payment of a substantial deposit. His action would snuff out a great many of the struggling left-wing journals that had mushroomed—'the thousand blackguard papers which infest the streets' as Howden called them.[1]

Safe in Portugal Cristina composed a vindictive manifesto which made it clear that she was looking forward to a counter-revolution.[2] From Lisbon she made her way to Bayonne, always the city of refuge of Spanish politicians. San Luis had got there, with his fair hair dyed black, not long before her.[3] It had been a strong argument for locking Cristina up that it would be folly to let her go and plot abroad as she did in her former exile; she plunged now into the thick of the intrigues with which Bayonne was humming. At Spain's request she was removed before long to Paris,[4] only to settle down at her property of Malmaison to the concoction of further mischief.

---

[1] Howden to Clarendon, private, 25 Aug. 1854; Clarendon Papers, vol. c. 20, with a copy of *El Grito de las Barricadas*, 20 Aug.

[2] Text in Miraflores, *Continuación*, vol. i, pp. 604 ff. R. Sencourt, *Spain's Uncertain Crown* (London, 1932), p. 222, refers to Cristina's 'vigorous correspondence' with Isabel after her flight.

[3] *The Times*, 16 Sept. 1854, 10/6. Olózaga at Paris was drawing his government's attention to the exorbitant number of Spanish generals on leave in France: Olózaga to Pacheco, no. 638, 26 Sept. 1854; *Francia*, 1854, in archive of the Foreign Ministry, Madrid.   [4] Papers in *Espagne*, vol. 845.

VII

PARTIES AND PROGRAMMES

The Elections to the Constituent Assembly September–October 1854

ELECTIONEERING was now the grand political business; but only a minority of Spaniards could have any direct concern in it. Under the decree of 11 August the franchise was regulated by the law of 20 July 1837, which gave the vote to men from the age of 25 possessing any of various professional or property qualifications, the basic test being payment of at least 200 reals a year in direct taxation. More generous than the law of 1846, which prescribed 400 reals,[1] this fell far short of the universal manhood suffrage for which Democrats were agitating. If payment of about £2 seems a modest price for a vote, the vast majority of Spanish incomes were much less than modest. In fact the total number qualified to vote turned out to be 695,110, less than 1 in 20 of the population though more than five times as many as in the election of 1851.[2] It was less in this narrow arena than in agitation outside that hopes and excitements stirred up by the revolution found vent during the autumn months.

Progresistas often declared that they had no objection to universal suffrage except the danger of its working to the advantage of Carlism. Pacheco told Howden, who quite agreed, that with universal suffrage half the votes would go to Carlism and a quarter or more to 'socialism, division of property, and all sorts of wild and impracticable theories'.[3] To a Pacheco this second prospect may have looked the more alarming of the two. To Pi y Margall it appeared that the poor, the men who overthrew the last régime, were being allowed no other means of expressing

---

[1] The electoral laws of 1837 and 1846 are in C.L., vol. xxiii, pp. 46–68, and vol. xxxvi, pp. 474–87.

[2] See figures of recent elections compiled by P. Madoz, in *Novedades*, 9 Feb. 1856, 1/1–6.

[3] Howden to Clarendon, no. 211, 13 Sept. 1854, F.O. 72. 846.

their opinions than further insurrection.[1] In Madrid itself
working-class dissatisfaction was very obvious. Some men were
arrested for trying to organize a strike of road and building
labour. There was a cry against machinery: the printers asserted
in a leaflet that it would take all their jobs away just as it was doing
in England.[2] In the provinces there was widespread clamour
against high food prices. Rioters at Burgos, demonstrators at
Saragossa, demanded a stop to export of food and wine to France.[3]
At Malaga agitation for wage increases continued in spite of the
efforts of O'Donnell's brother Enrique, who served as civil
governor till the end of the year, to bring things back to normal.
Northward from there, at Antequera, the big baize industry was
in a turmoil over some new 'mulgenny' spinning-machines, and
a strike broke out on 11 September. Other fearful symptoms
were reported in the press from Valencia and Catalonia, and most
of all from the great cockpit of capital and labour at Barcelona.

In an effort to soothe passions here Pascual Madoz, eminent
lawyer, encyclopaedist, and Progresista, was appointed governor
of Barcelona, and took up his post on 11 August. Duero was
replaced as captain-general by Dulce, who began by lifting the
state of siege. Prostration of trade was threatening a fresh labour
crisis: conservatives were alarmed, believing that the officers
chosen in the first militia elections, some of them wage-earners,
were all extremists. Madoz collected funds for poor relief, visited
cholera hospitals, and listened patiently to the workers' grievances, which some critics thought highly improper: they objected
most strongly to a tentative scheme that he drew up for giving
labour a legal right to organize. Between the workers and their
very well-organized employers his position was uncomfortable;
he confessed privately that his efforts were futile,[4] and before
long he was glad to abandon them and betake himself to electioneering. Before leaving on 20 October he got an agreement
patched up that the mills should continue as before until the
Cortes could go into the whole matter. But before the end of the
year Spain's first labour federation, the *Unión de Clases*,[5] with

[1] *La reacción y la revolución*, p. 37.
[2] Text, and disapproving comment, in *Clamor Público*, 24 Aug. 1854, 3/1–2.
[3] *The Times*, 7 Oct. 1854, 7/3; cf. V. Gebhardt, *Historia general de España y de sus Indias* (Madrid, 1861–4), vol. vi, p. 1,080.
[4] Baradère no. 130 (above), and no. 137, 12 Oct. 1854; *Espagne*, Consular, vol. 51.
[5] The name did not denote class harmony, but the combination of workers from

headquarters at Barcelona, was coming together out of the small illegal unions that had sprung up all over the province.

Still more perturbing was the unrest showing itself, especially in the deep south, among the peasants, whose stock of resignation had always been supposed inexhaustible. In Badajoz they were said to be refusing taxes, burning olive-trees and vineyards, and dividing lands among themselves. An economist, Cabanillas, lamented that private property was being denounced, and that wild ideas had been engendered by the revolution, barbarous throwbacks to the Jacqueries or to Anabaptism.[1] Probably some of the 'excesses' talked of were invented or inflated by conservatives hoping to scare timid voters, or by mischief-makers at Bayonne. But the Liberal press was far too ready to fancy that there was no real reason for discontent, whether agrarian or industrial. Rua Figueroa, editor of the *Nación* and a member of the Junta, wrote to Otway with much satisfaction about a workers' meeting in Madrid being dispersed by the militia: they had been set on and paid, he was convinced, by Soulé.[2] His paper could not believe that the 'incendiaries' infesting Catalonia could be genuine Spanish workmen. In the same vein the *Clamor Público* put all the trouble down to intriguers with motives of their own, and declared fatuously: 'Exploitation of man by man does not exist in this generous Christian nation.'[3]

Here once more it rested on the Democrats to break a vicious circle. Their ill-wishers blamed them for any tumults or threatening moods in the country: having failed in Madrid on 28 August, it was argued, they were transferring their subversive activities to the provinces. In reality most Democrats shrank from anything like a class appeal to the poor. The People, one of them said revealingly, is always under age, always a minor in need of a wise guardian's care.[4] They were least well qualified to supply an agrarian programme. Some of them could see well enough on the technical level what was required for better agriculture, but how

different branches of the textiles industry. On the working agreement, announced on 4 Nov., see Carrera Pujal, vol. iv, pp. 259–60. It soon broke down.
  [1] Cabanillas, vol. i, p. 129 (3 Dec. 1854). Cf. *The Times*, 13 Sept. 1854, 8/3; and 14 Sept., 9/4, on Malaga and Caceres.
  [2] Rua Figueroa to Otway, Madrid, 19 Aug. 1854, enclosed with Otway to Clarendon, private, Biarritz, 22 Aug.; Clarendon Papers, vol. c. 20.
  [3] 17 Sept. 1854, 1/4–2/1; cf. 26 Sept., 1/4–2/1.
  [4] Salmerón, speech of 7 Dec. 1854; D.S., pp. 337–9.

to overcome the social and political obstacles lay beyond their ken. Yet in 1854 the revolution, penned up inside its urban bases, could consolidate itself only by breaking out into the countryside with a message of hope and an offer of alliance.

Until this happened there would be a perennial risk of the peasant with his native suspicion of the Liberal being drawn in behind reactionary forces dangerous to both alike, and Carlism being given a new lease of life. Liberals often overestimated its resources, partly from timidity and partly for the sake of an excuse for not being too liberal, particularly with votes. The Carlism of this period has been credited by its historian with a monolithic integrity,[1] and such was the face it sought to show to the world: its real condition was as fissiparous as that of any party. Its hopes had been dashed by its last failure of 1846–9. Its top men, mostly in exile and out of touch with Spanish currents, were divided as to tactics, and Montemolín in Naples made a woefully drab Pretender. But inside rural Spain and among the old-conservative classes Carlist sentiment undoubtedly lingered on; and the party was beginning to look for means of profiting by this new situation.

Among the small-scale disorders of the election period those at Palencia, Burgos, Aranjuez, and elsewhere were ascribed to Carlist instigation. Carlists as well as Democrats could take up the cry against dear food, and both were against Isabel; now as in 1848, and as often during the Bienio, these opposites were accused of collusion. Rumours were getting into the press of Carlist preparations for action of a more ambitious kind. The émigré leadership, however, preferred to see first how much it could achieve by means of propaganda. It rested its chief hopes on the nervousness of the propertied classes; if they became sufficiently scared they might turn back towards Carlism as the only force capable of protecting them. At the same time it had some inkling of the need to make the party look a little less antediluvian, and in certain émigré circles it was even being suggested that Montemolín might abdicate in favour of his brother Juan,[2] who lived in London, the Carlist counterpart of Isabel's sansculotte brother-in-law Don Enrique. Montemolín was not prepared for this; but he made his appearance in the election with a manifesto

---

[1] M. Ferrer, *Historia del tradicionalismo español* (Seville, 1941–), vol. xx, p. 69.

[2] There is an account of D. Juan's career, with some judicious omission, in F. de P. Oller, *Album de personajes carlistas* (Barcelona, 1887–90), vol. iii, pp. 177–93.

announcing that he would be seen before long in Spain, not as conqueror but as benevolent father of his people. It summoned Spain back to the safe anchorage of national tradition, but it had something to say also of mild reform, and declared that not all change was anathema.[1] Its progressive phrases, whatever pangs they may have cost its authors, fell flat. Newspapers printed the manifesto and dismissed it with contempt.

Carlist hopes were strongly encouraged by the quarrel the new régime was drifting into with the Church; a quarrel likely, if not inescapable, from the first moment of the revolution. Spain had lived for too many centuries by the fitful glimmer of candle and faggot for any political upheaval to take place without a religious accompaniment. July abruptly cut short the Moderado drift towards the Church, continued and accelerated by Isabel and San Luis. At Cadiz the junta came out against the Concordat; at Valladolid religious properties were taken over; at Burgos the Jesuits were denounced and their college suppressed.[2] Espartero's advent rubbed salt into these wounds. He was personally a sincere Catholic, which O'Donnell was not,[3] but as head of a reform party he had as a matter of course when in power been at loggerheads with the clergy.

Liberalism inherited from the old monarchy a rooted Erastianism, and Alonso at the Ministry of Justice was a noted *regalista*, an upholder of the suzerainty of State over Church. The traditional relationship could not offer adequate guidance to a nineteeth-century government, even if this one had possessed much more of the courage of its convictions. Some steps were taken without delay. Expulsion of Jesuits belonged to the routine of revolution, and it was common prudence to remove them from their headquarters at Loyola, in the heart of a Carlist recruiting-ground, to Majorca. Where more constructive measures were required the Cabinet was less equal to its task. It failed above all to strike while the iron was hot by getting rid of the Concordat of 1851. Liberal principles demanded this, and the radical press was calling for abrogation or at least revision. At first it appeared to be the government's firm intention

[1] Text in Miraflores, *Continuación*, vol. i, pp. 670–5, and Ferrer, vol. xx, pp. 201–4. The latter stresses (pp. 120–1) the derivation of its ideas from Balmes.
[2] For a Catholic view of the revolution as anti-Catholic see F. de A. Aguilar, *El libro de la Unidad Católica* (Madrid, 1877), pp. 704–5.
[3] Fernández de los Ríos, *Luchas políticas*, vol. ii, pp. 375, 426.

to act. It began by nominating Infante as its representative at Rome, and Infante was one of those Progresistas with whom anti-clericalism made up nine parts of their progressiveness. Then as in so many things it was too ill-knit and too irresolute to get any further. Infante did not go to Rome, and for several months no one else was sent either. Nor was the simple experiment tried of an improvement in the village curé's beggarly and irregular stipend, to wean him away from his hankerings after the good old days.

Churchmen in later years would never cease to shudder at the memory of the *infausto bienio*, the *ominoso bienio*,[1] as a time of tribulation for good Catholics when atheism, Freemasonry, Methodism were all permitted for a season to show themselves in the market-place. In sober truth no serious ill-usage of the Church can be imputed to the Liberalism of 1854–6, whatever may be said of other periods. Catholicism was only in a rhetorical sense persecuted, except in being hindered from persecuting others. Its own zealots were at least as prompt to attack as to defend. They were men like Pedro de la Hoz,[2] Carlist editor of the widely circulated *Esperanza*; or Costa y Borrás, the truculent Bishop of Barcelona who had even before the revolution had to be removed from his see. Skirmishing broke out at a variety of points; freedom of the press was the one most hotly attacked and counter-attacked. There was an episcopal right of censorship for the protection of faith and morals; it was capable of very wide extension, and newspapers of late had smarted severely under it. Under pressure from them the Ministry of Justice issued on 19 August a circular order restricting its exercise.[3] Costa y Borrás was up in arms at once. For the Church he insisted on full freedom of speech: this he represented as merely its right and duty to preach against sin,[4] but it was always apter to preach against Liberalism than any of the older sins, better naturalized in Spain.

There were 349 Cortes seats to be filled; they were distributed among the provinces on the basis of population, Barcelona and

---

[1] See foreword to J. Canga Argüelles (y Villalta), *Tribulaciones de la Iglesia de España* (Madrid, 1858); V. de la Fuente, *Historia eclesiástica de España* (2nd ed., Madrid, 1873–5), vol. vi, p. 257.

[2] See J. M. Carulla, *Biografía de Don Pedro de la Hoz* (Madrid, 1866), p. 50.

[3] Text in J. Nido y Segalerva, *Antología de las Cortes desde 1854 á 1858* (Madrid, 1911), pp. 129–31.

[4] J. D. Costa y Borrás, *Observaciones sobre el presente y el porvenir de la Iglesia en España* (2nd ed., Barcelona, 1857), pp. 135–7.

Valencia having 13 each, Madrid and Granada 11, Álava 2. Single-member constituencies, which since 1846 had facilitated official meddling, were being abandoned in favour of the 1837 system of a single list of candidates for each province. The total number of candidates prodigiously exceeded that of seats; under the law of 1837 there was no property qualification for deputies. In various places public meetings went over lists of applicants, and endorsed some of the names. But there were complaints in the press about swarms of nonentities thrusting themselves forward. 'The scramble to be returned to the Cortes is awful', wrote an English cynic, 'and merely because experience has shewn that a vote is the surest road to preferment.'[1] There was some prejudice here; it was none the less a fact that membership of the assembly, though unpaid, had come to be looked on as a gateway to a smiling garden bordered with jobs or promotions in the services, decorations, public-works contracts for the deputy and all his tribe.

To some in the fragmented Moderado party the elections seemed to offer a first opportunity of drawing together. Their old leader Narváez was going away again in ostentatious disgust to France: Duero was at present the strongest contender for the succession, and could speak in particular for a powerful group of army men close to the Vicalvarists. The *Diario Español*, regarded as their organ,[2] gave much publicity to the stirrings of social revolt in the countryside, and criticized the government freely. On 14 September it printed an aggressive article on the sterility of this and of all revolutions, which according to Howden seemed to strike Progresistas all of a heap: 'the terror was almost ludicrous'.[3] Most Moderados recognized, however, that it would be foolish to fight the elections under their own faded colours, even if they could have agreed on a programme. Liberal Union was their watchword. It had originated respectably enough in the alliance against Bravo Murillo and his successors; and freedom with order, public morality, sound administration made safe slogans. Moderados would ride pillion behind the Progresistas, as Hardman commented, until they could push them out of the saddle.[4]

---

[1] Le Saussage to Clarendon, private, 10 Sept. 1854; Clarendon Papers, vol. c. 20.
[2] It printed, it is true, a disclaimer of any special affiliation: 20 Oct. 1854, 1/1.
[3] Howden to Clarendon, no. 221, 17 Sept. 1854, F.O. 72. 846.
[4] *The Times*, 26 Sept. 1854, 8/2.

Representatives of all the Madrid districts met on 10 September to form an 'election committee'. San Miguel took the chair, and all the speakers favoured Liberal Union. A manifesto drafted by the committee was debated at a big and noisy meeting on the 17th in the Teatro Real. Most of it was mere pious generality.[1] It upheld constitutional monarchy and Isabel II, and depicted the revolution as a triumph of nation over *camarilla*, not of party over party. It was signed by seniors of both parties: Duero, Sevillano, Ríos Rosas, Infante, San Miguel. On 1 October the unadventurous list of eleven candidates recommended by the committee came out. Progresistas were content for the most part to march in the loose Liberal Union procession; Espartero's connexion with O'Donnell might well seem to commit them to it, and often in any case they had nothing fresh to say. The candidate at Ciudad Real who devoted most of his election address to his past services and sacrifices[2] was one of many. But some others were coming forward separately from Liberal Union, and acquiring the title of 'Puros': they were the radicals of the party, and shaded away on the left into Democracy.

Democrats had the choice between figuring as the left wing of Progresismo and setting up as a party on their own; between the risk of being swallowed up in an amorphous mass, and that of isolation. Their decision was to stay in. Some keen men like Pi y Margall thought it feeble,[3] and it must have owed something to discouragement after the setback of 28 August; but they might still hope to draw a reviving Liberal movement bodily along with them. The left-wing meeting that made most stir at Madrid was organized under the vague title of 'Liberal Youth', in the Teatro Real on 25 September.[4] Fernández Cuesta, a radical pamphleteer, took the chair, and Becerra, Sixto Cámara, Martos were on the platform. Proceedings culminated in the famous oration in which the young Democrat Emilio Castelar first dazzled an audience with the *ignis fatuus* of his boundless and often pointless eloquence.

---

[1] Text in J. del Nido y Segalerva, *Historia política y parlamentaria de S.A. D. Baldomero Fernández Espartero* (Madrid, 1916), pp. 629–34.

[2] Gómez de la Mata; text in *Clamor Público*, 15 Sept. 1854, 1/5–2/1.

[3] *La reacción y la revolución*, pp. 49–50, 53.

[4] Press reports next day were brief, and the many later descriptions of the meeting are very divergent. See Morayta, *Castelar*, pp. 49–55; D. Hannay, *Don Emilio Castelar* (London, 1896), p. 63; M. González-Araco, *Castelar. Su vida y su muerte* (Madrid, 1900), pp. 23–26; J. Milego, *Emilio Castelar: su vida y su obra* (Valencia, 1906), pp. 49 ff.

Universal suffrage and religious freedom were his most tangible proposals; and the programme-statement adopted by the meeting contained nothing of a 'social' character beyond free compulsory education, and abolition of excise taxes and conscription. Two grand topics stood out amid the welter of speeches and editorials: the prospective new Constitution, and the economic state of the nation. Ever since 1810 a new Constitution had formed the standard prescription of Spanish politics, and there were still some ready to believe that the one about to be designed would so perfectly reconcile all needs and interests that Spaniards would regard one another no longer as natural enemies.[1] But Spain in 1854 was nearing the end of this illusion; and the smouldering agitation among the disinherited classes was helping to spread the idea that the way to end the country's dissensions was to make it more prosperous. No doubt economic expansion had been trumpeted for several years already. Both Bravo Murillo and San Luis posed as sound practical men and improvers; but the lesson of experience was that *camarilla* rule made economic advance impossible. Much that was being said now showed how the search for a universal panacea, or north-west passage to Utopia, was being transferred from political to economic science. Many were disposed to echo the diagnosis of a French observer that the proper remedy for Spain was 'an economic *coup d'état*'.[2] A country could not subsist on Platonic abstractions, wrote a mining engineer, Nature gave it physical needs as well.[3] In a dithyramb on what the public expected from its chosen representatives the *Nación* set the physical and moral, railways and rights, side by side.[4] National self-respect was another potent stimulus, as it has been in most revolutions in the modern world, for Spaniards who read and travelled were aware of how miserably Spain was lagging behind the advanced nations. A 'rage for new and marvellous inventions' was in the air, *The Times* had commented earlier this year when an electric telegraph line to the

---

[1] *Asamblea Constituyente de 1854!*, p. 9. For a more sceptical view see L. Corsini, *Cuatro palabras sobre las nulidades de las constituciones modernas* (Madrid, 1854), pp. 7–8; cf. L. Rodríguez Camaleño, *Juicio crítico de la revolución española* (Madrid, 1860), p. 11.

[2] Girardin, vol. viii, p. 869 (14 Aug. 1854); cf. pp. 869–87; also 'Juan de Toda Tierra', *Nuestros malos y sus remedios* (Madrid, 1854), p. 9, and V. Bertrán de Lis, *Exposición dirigida al Excmo. Sr. Duque de la Victoria . . . sobre bienes materiales* (Madrid, 1854).

[3] J. Pellón y Rodríguez, *Proyecto de Ley de Minería, presentado a las Cortes Constituyentes* (Madrid, 1855), p. 5.   [4] 8 Nov. 1854, 1/1–2; cf. 12 Sept., 1/1–3.

frontier was begun—it linked Madrid with Paris before the end of
October; the public aspired to 'equality with the most civilized
nations of Europe'.[1]

Provincial governors had been warned on 19 August to leave
the electorate's choice perfectly untrammelled,[2] and for once this
was not mere humbug. Intimidation by local bullies was frequently alleged, but often there was a certain lethargy in the
proceedings, to which the epidemic raging in various regions
contributed. On 24 September and 1 October, two Sundays,
municipal elections were held where they had not taken place
already, or to fill vacancies where the councils of 1843 had been
recalled. Voting was on a broad franchise, and those who thought
it perilous to have too many voters found confirmation in some
disturbances that were reported. Seville was particularly fractious.
Polling in the general election took place on 4 October and the
two following days. Voters began by assembling in each district to
elect by ballot a chairman and two secretaries. Each of them then
chose from the list of candidates as many names as the number of
deputies the province was entitled to. For this, too, ballot papers
were used; they were counted publicly, and destroyed, and the
district figures were added up at the provincial capital and
announced on 16 October. Any candidate receiving more than
half as many votes as the number of citizens actually voting in the
province was declared elected. If fewer than the provincial quota
of deputies were successful a second ballot had to be held among
the runners-up. On paper the procedure might look proof against
any sort of trickery; yet complaints and accusations were legion.

Nearly everywhere the elections that took place went off peacefully, but at points as far apart as Barcelona and Seville they had
to be postponed because of cholera or other impediments. In
many others there had to be second voting: only four for instance
of Saragossa's nine seats were filled at the first round. Altogether
the results that could be declared on 16 October only came to 174,
or half the total. There was thus no dramatic wind-up to the campaign. Abstentions from the poll had been numerous. In the
capital only 4,468 voted out of more than eight thousand on the
rolls. Ten out of the election committee's eleven nominees, and
they alone, were elected at the first ballot: a proof of the stolid

[1] *The Times*, 17 May 1854, 10/3.
[2] R.O. of 19 Aug. 1854; C.L., vol. lxii, pp. 279–80.

political temper of Madrid's middle classes. San Miguel stood first with 9,210 votes, Sevillano second with 8,641. Rodríguez, late of the Junta del Sur and of working-class background, was the most radical of those who got in. Most of the preposterous herd of over three hundred candidates got scarcely any votes. In the end roughly 70 per cent. of the entire electorate voted.[1] Malaga province, with a population of about 450,000, had 17,685 electors (4,569 of them in the city), of whom 13,663 cast their votes. Nine candidates secured the necessary 6,832 or more votes; among them, possibly with some aid from Enrique O'Donnell's influence as governor, his brother, Ríos Rosas, and Cánovas del Castillo. Three places remained, and the second ballot produced an unusually rank crop of charges of irregularity.[2] At Barcelona polling was delayed until late in October. There were then heavy abstentions, and most of the successful candidates were fairly radical Progresistas like Franco, Degollado, and Ribot y Fontseré. But Dulce, who had failed in other constituencies, headed the list, and Duero came eighth. In the second round two other generals joined them: Prim, whose comparative inactivity during the Bienio did little to foreshadow his role as strong man of the revolution of 1868, and Messina.[3]

Hardly any who stood as Moderados got in. Nocedal at Pontevedra in Galicia was one of the very few. Some discreeter conservatives found their way into the assembly under the umbrella of Liberal Union. O'Donnell was elected in two places, and opted for Valencia; he would have a compact group of Vicalvarists round him. Espartero, elected in six provinces, chose Saragossa. Various old associates came in with him: González from Badajoz, Allende Salazar from Vizcaya, Venancio Gurrea from Logroño, his brother Ignacio from Madrid. Among other senior Progresistas were all three who joined the Córdova ministry in July, and their colleague Ríos Rosas was to be one of the assembly's chief ornaments. Among the 'Puros' Olózaga, elected at Logroño, was

[1] Figures in *Novedades*, 9 Feb. 1856.
[2] See Du Bouzet's reports, no. 32 of 9 Oct. 1854, no. 33 of 17 Oct., no. 40 of 5 Jan. 1855, in *Espagne*, Consular, vol. 56.
[3] Election details in Carrera Pujal, vol. iv, pp. 257–8. Prim's election manifesto is printed in F. Giménez y Guited, *Historia militar y política del general D. Juan Prim* (Madrid, 1860), vol. i, pp. 462–70, and F. J. Orellana, *Historia del general Prim* (Barcelona, 1871–2), vol. ii, pp. 53–60. On his activities during the Bienio see R. Olivar Bertrand, *El caballero Prim* (Barcelona, 1952), vol. i, pp. 153 ff. and chap. 13.

the shining light; Madoz, representing the Catalan province of Lérida, and Corradi for Burgos, also stood out, and so before long did a younger man, Calvo Asensio, a newcomer to the Cortes from his native Valladolid: his paper *La Iberia* served as the main Puro organ.

About a score of seats went to Democrats, more probably than they could have got by standing as a separate party. It was in this assembly that Democracy naturalized itself as a force in Spanish politics. A newspaper complimented it on having no leaders, only principles;[1] but its chief spokesman from the first was Orense. Ruiz Pons, Hore's comrade in the February rising at Saragossa, was in; and there were three besides Orense who had sat in the Cortes before: Rivero, Ordax Avecilla, and the Catalan lawyer Figueras, one of the party's readiest debaters if not its strongest character, whose portrait today hangs oddly in a room of the Cortes side by side with Nocedal's. It is noteworthy that only two of the group were elected from the still relatively torpid south; on the other hand only three represented strictly Castilian voters. All the rest owed their seats to regions of Spain's periphery, where the federal idea associated from the outset with Spanish republicanism made its appeal. Four represented provinces of Portuguese-speaking Galicia, three Aragon, four each Valencia and Catalonia, one Extremadura. These successes would naturally reinforce the federalist element in Democrat philosophy.

On the other hand the party's newer, 'socialistic' leaven found little or no place. Younger men, not yet well known, had less chance of election, though ages and opinions did not always coincide: Castelar who failed at Madrid did not share the views of Pi y Margall, defeated at Barcelona.[2] Both of these devoted the coming two years to left-wing journalism. Garrido was outside the parliamentary fraction; so more conspicuously was Sixto Cámara, now busy founding his paper *La Soberanía Nacional*. This was to be, if not specifically 'socialist', ultra-democratic; it cultivated a crisp, popular style in contrast with the measured stride of most of its contemporaries, and made no bones about attacking Espartero's government.

---

[1] *Clamor Público*, 17 Jan. 1855, 2/5.

[2] Pi y Margall failed again, though not too badly, in a by-election at Barcelona next year. He was already a federalist as well as 'socialist', as his *La reacción y la revolución* shows.

Some quidnuncs had been predicting an assembly of 1793 temper. As election results came in estimates of party strength were discrepant,[1] because there were so many independents and unknown quantities. Placemen were less numerous than usual; and a high proportion of the deputies were newcomers. Comparison of membership lists shows that of 380 men who entered the constituent assembly now and at by-elections only 31 had sat in the last Cortes, that of 1853, and only 23 were to survive into the next, elected in 1857 with the Moderados back in power.[2] A sprinkling of them had previously sat in the Senate, and 48 had belonged to the Cortes of April–May 1843. There was plenty of new blood at any rate in the House. In terms of its social composition there was less alteration. A newspaper survey of 281 deputies showed among them 104 proprietors, far too many to augur well for agrarian reform; 73 lawyers, 35 officers, 30 civil servants, 15 doctors, 13 writers, 7 merchants, 4 financiers.[3] From this point of view there was not much to distinguish the Democrats from the rest. There were two noblemen among them, four or five lawyers, four university teachers, three or four writers, and the rest were men of property.[4]

This assembly was to turn out by general consent the foremost in Spanish history for brilliance and learning. Its debates could be summed up as a quintessence of the intellectual life of the country.[5] Quite a number of deputies had a fund of practical knowledge also to contribute; among them, surprisingly, Espartero, who had been setting his neighbours an example of improved farming. Unluckily he seems to have left turnips and everything rustic behind him when he left Logroño, as unsuited to the dignity of a *pater patriae*. There was a general and strong faith in private enterprise, free competition, wealth open to talent.

---

[1] So were subsequent reckonings; see Escalera and González Llana, vol. iv, pp. 134–5; Gebhardt, vol. vi, pp. 1,080–1; Garrido, *Historia*, vol. iii, p. 243; Pi, *Historia*, vol. iv, p. 104.

[2] Not more than 36 of the 380 were successful candidates in any one of the four general elections of 1850, 1851, 1853, 1857. Only 17 were successful candidates in two of these; only 12 in three; only 4 in all four. For lists of deputies see B. Moratilla (ed.), *Estadística del personal y vicisitudes de las Córtes y de los ministerios de España* (Madrid, 1858).

[3] *Clamor Público*, 12 Jan. 1855, 3/4. This is basically the same analysis as the one given by Nido y Segalerva in *Antología*, p. 124, and *Espartero*, pp. 622–3.

[4] Garrido, *L'Espagne contemporaine*, p. 111.

[5] F. de P. Canalejas, 'Las Constituyentes españolas en 1854', in *La Razón*, 1860, vol. i, pp. 190–1.

Though practising businessmen in the Cortes might be few, its spirit was strongly capitalistic. The attempt to modernize the economy without reform of the social structure could have only a restricted reach, but the Bienio was to give it a real if limited stimulus. All the enduring work of the assembly had to do with material advances; its laborious Constitution was destined to flit into the limbo of laws born dead.

VIII

REFORM DEMANDS AND EVASIONS

The Meeting of the Constituent Assembly November–December 1854

MANY, 'I may say an infinite number of persons', wrote Howden a fortnight after Cristina's escape, still believed that Espartero would not refuse the presidency of a republic.[1] Others believed, what is more likely, that a second regency was his secret wish. At bottom perhaps his desire was to be seen on all hands as the grand disposer, to have his indispensability acknowledged—after all these years of waiting—unreservedly and over and over again. To make sure of this he would resign or threaten to resign at every end and turn, as though to relish the sensation of being begged to come back.

Meanwhile his silences about Isabel seemed ominous, and her going or being sent away from Madrid to the near-by royal lodge of the Pardo was enough to fan many rumours. They provoked another outburst on 17 October from the *Diario Español*, which warned all dreamers of republics or regencies that their dreams could lead only to civil war.[2] The *Nación* made haste to repudiate any such ambitions on Espartero's part;[3] but there was at once another uproar over Allende Salazar's election address to his Basque constituents, recommending them (though probably the intention was anti-Carlist) not to trouble their heads about what sovereign reigned at Madrid so long as their own charter of rights was respected. Odds were being laid against Isabel's chances as 8 November, the date for the opening of the Cortes, drew near.[4] It was late in October before she reappeared in Madrid; an elaborate comedy was planned by San Miguel for the 28th. As inspector-general of militia he would present all the militia officers

---

[1] Howden to Clarendon, no. 211, 13 Sept. 1854, F.O. 72. 846.
[2] 17 Oct. 1854, 1/1–2; a reply to an article in *El Siglo XIX*, critical of conscription and the army.
[3] 18 Oct. 1854, 1/1–3; also 12 Nov., 1/2–2.
[4] *The Times*, 13 Nov. 1854 (Madrid, 6 Nov.), 8/4.

of the capital to the Queen, and the affair would be given the look
of a demonstration of loyalty. It was a dismal failure. The officers,
suspicious and on their guard, looked 'as sulky as bears',[1] and
went off as soon as it was over to pay ostentatious respects to
Espartero.

The chief manœuvre was being executed behind the scenes, and
with better success. It consisted in getting the Cabinet to agree
that the Cortes should be opened on 8 November by the Queen.
Many thought that her being allowed to cut a figure on this
occasion would be decisive for her survival on the throne; Howden was one of them, and used all his blandishments in her favour.[2]
On the fateful 8th the House met at 1.15. Esteban Pastor, veteran
of the War of Independence, occupied the chair, as the oldest
member, with the *banco azul* or ministerial bench covered in blue
velvet on his left and the secretaries' table in front. Isabel drove
through heavily guarded and unwelcoming streets, and made her
nervous entry about two o'clock in the same 'sepulchral silence'.[3]
It was an ordeal to tax a more accomplished actress. Her short
speech had been written by Pacheco; she got through the reading not too badly, and withdrew, tremulously, in a less frigid
atmosphere.[4]

The Cortes was inaugurated, but not yet 'constituted', and
there were wearisome preliminaries to be got through. Twelve
unedifying days were consumed in sifting alleged irregularities at
the polls; and then a new *reglamento* or set of standing orders had
to be drafted and discussed.[5] It conformed for the most part with
established practice. Fifty deputies made a quorum, except that a
law could not be passed unless more than half the total number of
349 were present. In divisions the commonest method was for the
Ayes to stand; any seven members could insist on a *votación
nominal*, when every deputy had to declare his vote as his name
was called. Members usually spoke from their own places, but
sometimes chose to speak from the tribune: the acoustics of the

---

[1] Howden to Clarendon, private, 1 Nov. 1854; Clarendon Papers, vol. c. 20.
[2] Howden to Clarendon, no. 263, 19 Oct. 1854, and no. 271, 24 Oct., F.O.
72. 846.
[3] Straten-Ponthoz to Brouckère, no. 187, 8 Nov. 1854; *Espagne*, vol. 8 (1).
[4] See D.S., pp. 1–2. Text of speech in Nido y Segalerva, *Antología*, pp. 145–6.
The *Soberanía Nacional* reported the scene with restraint, but objected to the Queen's
presence (9 Nov. 1854, 1/4–2/1, and 10 Nov., 1/2–4).
[5] Text as finally adopted in App. to D.S., no. 24, 1 Dec. 1854. It was revived in
1869–72.

horseshoe chamber, with its rising tiers of seats facing in towards the presidential chair, were notoriously bad. They addressed the House, not the president, and he was free to intervene in debates himself. Sessions could be held on any day, though Sundays were usually omitted. They were fairly short, four afternoon hours being customary, and left plenty of time for the business of the seven 'sections' into which the House divided itself by lot every month. These nominated members to the half-dozen standing committees, most important among them the budget committee with five members from each section. All bills went first to the sections, and could not proceed further unless approved by at least one of them. If the House then agreed to 'take into consideration' a particular bill it went back to the sections, which appointed one member each to a select committee of seven whose duty was to sift it and submit a *dictamen* or recommendation on it.

Isabel's backers did their utmost to exploit their advantage. On 19 November there was a grand function at the palace, with a drove of deputies among the guests. Howden found an opportunity this evening to give Isabel a private lecture on the duties of a constitutional monarch. She asked his advice in case of a Cabinet split; he told her to hold on to Espartero to the last possible moment, and after that send for San Miguel, under whom he had made a point of ascertaining that O'Donnell would be prepared to serve.[1] For the time being Howden, much more than Turgot, was in a position to exert an influence on events. Unluckily the loose-tongued Queen promptly repeated their colloquy to all and sundry, Espartero took deep offence, and the *Nación* administered a sharp reprimand to Howden for overstepping his duties.[2]

On the 20th the long-awaited crisis blew up. Espartero abruptly notified the Cabinet, and in the evening the Queen, that he intended shortly to resign. Next day as soon as the House met he made a statement lasting about two minutes, the average length of his rare parliamentary performances.[3] Every kind of speculation was let loose immediately. That he should resign when the constituent assembly was ready to begin work was not unexpected, and the natural assumption was that he wanted a free hand to

[1] Howden to Clarendon, no. 306, and no. 307 (cypher), 20 Nov. 1854, F.O. 72. 847.
[2] 24 Nov. 1854, 1/2–3.   [3] D.S., p. 115.

reconstruct his government on more exclusively Progresista lines; in particular, without O'Donnell, perhaps also without Isabel. Madrid was in a ferment that night, troops were in the streets, and the army chiefs, if 'positive information' picked up by Hardman can be relied on, met in secret conclave. Dulce and others argued for marching the garrison out and making a pronunciamiento there and then. More cautious views prevailed.[1] A rising of the Madrid garrison had been tried four months ago and was not likely to fare better now. O'Donnell understood this; his game was to try and keep the coalition going. He said next day, 'and said, I believe, truly', wrote Howden, that in a royalist reaction as much as in a republic 'his head would be the first on the scaffold'.[2] It was a dramatic gage of his fidelity to the revolution, which he was often to make play with.

If it really was in Espartero's mind to treat the coalition ministry as a temporary thing now finished with, he was foolish to leave the Cortes and his own following unprepared. He lacked also political courage to recognize how heavily the odds were on his side, and allowed the trial of strength to slide almost at once into an inconclusive wrangle, not directly about the Cabinet but about the *mesa*, the offices of the Cortes. For the presidency he let his own name be put forward, as a snub to San Miguel who had beaten a friend of his for the provisional presidency. His election was a foregone conclusion, and the real struggle was waged round the choice of the four vice-presidents. It provided the first test of party strength, but in a groping, blindfold fashion prophetic of much to come, because neither friend nor foe could make out what Espartero was really driving at. Puros and Democrats agreed, with difficulty, on a joint list of names. When at last at 1.30 on 28 November the Cortes was formally constituted, election of officers was its first business. Espartero gained the facile triumph he had looked forward to; but of greater political significance was the fact that O'Donnell came first among the vice-presidents, while of the other three only one, the far from radical Marqués de Perales, was on the list of the Left bloc.[3] It would not be easy to drop O'Donnell from the Cabinet now.

---

[1] *The Times*, 30 Nov. 1854, 7/4.
[2] Howden to Clarendon, no. 314, 23 Nov. 1854, F.O. 72. 847.
[3] On the rival lists see *Clamor Público*, 29 Nov. 1854, 2/3; *Nación*, 29 Nov., 1/1. Vega de Armijo and Calvo Asensio were among the four secretaries elected.

Espartero was escorted home by a cheering crowd and a band playing patriotic airs; the Cabinet now resigned, and he was commissioned by Isabel to form another. Having frittered away in advance the occasion for breaking with Liberal Union, he could only reshuffle, not reconstruct. Besides, Collado the Finance Minister wanted to retire, and his gloomy prognostications of bankruptcy made Espartero quail at the thought of being left to cope with an empty treasury by himself. Being indispensable Collado could as Howden pointed out make his own terms, and 'became to a great degree the maker of the Ministry'.[1] Alonso's portfolio of Justice was taken over by the law-lecturer Aguirre, a change that made little difference. Pacheco had given umbrage by some excessively right-wing appointments in the diplomatic service. His removal would make room for Olózaga, who had come on leave from his Paris post to engage in parliamentary activity. To give Olózaga a seat on the front bench would strengthen the government and might be the best means of deterring him from making trouble for it, and also for the palace. The majority in this Cabinet was sure to come down on Isabel's side; and Olózaga was the man who of all Progresistas might rally the assembly against her. Her sworn enemy ever since 1843,[2] at Paris he had just been seeking by private approaches to both the French and the British governments to compass her downfall,[3] and on his return to Madrid all her opponents looked to him for a lead.

Instead Olózaga took up the ambiguous attitude that he was to keep to all through the Bienio. He was not a republican; and his old friend Howden was having 'various conversations' with him.[4] On the other hand he had no mind to be fobbed off with what would amount to merely the third or fourth place in the Cabinet. Another Englishman may have been right in surmising that his real ambition was to be both Foreign Minister and premier, 'keeping D.n Baldomero bolstered up in the Presidential chair of the Cortes';[5] and there seem to have been Progresistas who favoured a solution on these lines, which was very likely the

[1] Howden to Clarendon, no. 328, 30 Nov. 1854, F.O. 72. 847.
[2] On this affair of 1843 see Conde de Romanones, *Un drama político. Isabel II y Olózaga* (Madrid, 1941). Cf. Hughes, *Revelations*, vol. i, pp. 45 ff., and E. Quinet, *Mes vacances en Espagne* (Paris, 1846), in *Œuvres complètes*, vol. ix, pp. 49 ff.
[3] See *The Letters of Queen Victoria*, vol. iii, p. 51.
[4] Howden to Clarendon, no. 319, 26 Nov. 1854, F.O. 72. 847.
[5] Le Saussage to Clarendon, Madrid, 25 Nov. 1854; Clarendon Papers, vol. c. 20.

best that could have been found. At any rate he scornfully refused the proffered post.[1] Foreign Affairs went to Luzuriaga, a close friend of Collado and another old Progresista slowcoach, who had a good reputation as a jurist but no experience of diplomacy, and for whom a seat in the House had to be found.[2] Bringing back such a veteran was a confession that new talents and ideas were not much wanted. And the man who had plunged the country into all this feverish speculation, and gone about it so incomprehensibly, was sitting quietly down again just where he had been before.

It was the cue of the Right to push things on without giving him time for second thoughts, or the Puro-Democrat bloc time to harden. One of a number of resolutions tabled as soon as the Cortes was constituted on the 28th stood in the names of San Miguel, Duero, Escosura (a Moderado turned Progresista), and four others: it invited the House to make use of its sovereign power by declaring constitutional monarchy with Isabel II one of the 'Bases' or fundamental principles of the new Constitution. Soon after the session of 30 November opened at 2.45, with vice-president Madoz in the chair, this resolution was suddenly brought forward. 'I *knew* it would come (as I told the Queen)', Howden wrote privately to Clarendon next day with cynical relish, 'but it was done with unexpected cleverness, just in the nick of time . . . .'[3]

San Miguel delivered an impassioned plea on behalf of Isabel, without whom, he cried, all Spaniards knew by instinct there could be nothing for the country but bloodshed and anarchy.[4] Espartero was left with no choice, and the two old Liberal paladins and jealous rivals fell into each other's arms in a well-contrived embrace. To their credit the Democrats refused to retreat. Orense urged the House not to hurry over this vital decision, on which the national will was still far from clear; he got in a home thrust at O'Donnell by reminding him that there was nothing about Isabel II in the manifesto of Manzanares. Interruptions broke out, the Vicalvarists were on their feet in virtuous indignation. Corradi and Calvo Asensio salved their radical consciences with phrases about 'a throne surrounded by popular institutions'.

[1] A. Fernández de los Ríos, *Olózaga. Estudio político y biográfico* (Madrid, 1863), pp. 523–4.

[2] On Luzuriaga's earlier career see J. Múgica, *Carlistas, Moderados y Progresistas (Claudio Antón de Luzuriaga)* (San Sebastian, 1950).

[3] Clarendon Papers, vol. c. 20.   [4] For the debate see D.S., pp. 219 ff.

Escosura urged the impossibility of a Spanish republic. Prim came to the defence of the sovereign whom fourteen years later he was to dethrone. Olózaga sat silent. At 9 p.m. the long debate reached its end in a vote taken by roll-call 'amidst a religious hush'.[1] There were 194 for Isabel and 19 against.[2] When Olózaga's name was reached he voted with the majority. He hated his Queen, but he loved ribbons and levees. Three of the Noes, including Madoz's brother Fernando, favoured a change of sovereign, and some of the others would have accepted a Braganza.[3] Many more had promised to vote with them, says García Ruiz, one of the nineteen, though they backed out at the end.[4] Democrats had proved their civic courage; two of them resigned government posts before voting; all were closing the doors of office against themselves. As a party, from this evening they would be more definitely sundered from the parent body of Progresismo.

That night Isabel sent Howden a message of thanks for his counsel and aid.[5] It was no more than he had earned, and he was in a mood of 'inexpressible satisfaction'.[6] All conservatives were drawing a deep breath of relief. The *Soberanía Nacional* made the best of a bad job by saying that the monarchy, once held divine, owed its existence from this date forward to a parliamentary vote.[7] And Isabel's 194 voters were after all not much more than half the total membership of the Cortes.

Democrats were eager to counter-attack, and one question above all gave them the chance to do so effectively: the excise taxes, about which they and their newspapers were making a great deal of noise.[8] Progresistas could not afford to hang back; most of them had declared against the *puertas* and *consumos* during the elections, and a group of radicals had taken the lead in tabling

---

[1] García Ruiz, *Historias*, vol. ii, p. 569.

[2] Two absentees added their names to the minority next day.

[3] Rodríguez-Solís, vol. ii, p. 476; and see Pi, *Historia*, vol. iv, pp. 106–7, for the view that most of the Noes would have actually preferred a Braganza to a republic.

[4] *Historias*, vol. ii, p. 571.

[5] Howden to Clarendon, no. 334, Conf., 1 Dec. 1854, F.O. 72. 848. Isabel had called him to the palace on 27 Nov., and written to him on 29 Nov., to ask his advice.

[6] Howden to Clarendon, no. 333, 1 Dec. 1854, F.O. 72. 848.

[7] 1 Dec. 1854, 1/2–2.

[8] On the controversy at this stage see M. Torrente, *Pensamiento económico-político sobre la hacienda de España* (Madrid, 1854). For a defence of the taxes see Santillán, pp. 182, 184–93.

a bill for their abolition. It was moved on 2 December, when Espartero was not present, by Sánchez Silva, a lively journalist and free-trader from Seville. Collado protested in vain. The House resolved to take it into consideration, San Miguel and Madoz and Olózaga all concurring.[1] Ministers walked out in a body. Espartero was furious at the news, and by about 8 p.m. he was on his way to the palace to resign once more. Again the atmosphere of crisis descended, and far into the night a stream of politicians poured through his house, begging him to change his mind. Next day Howden had a go, and exhausted 'every argument, and every entreaty'. Espartero fumed about the vote as an intolerable affront; 'the check in the Cortes', Howden remarked to Clarendon, 'was exactly the first grey hair seen by a beauty, when the idea just crosses the mind that the hour of omnipotence has passed.'[2] It took five hours of humble expostulation by deputies, and the promise of a vote of confidence—moved, on the 4th, for better effect, by the culprit Sánchez Silva[3]—to mollify the duke's bruised pride.

His presidency of the Chamber, once won, he showed no desire to keep, and on the 5th there was a fresh vote. Madoz, the only serious candidate, was an old parliamentary hand, and made a competent chairman. But O'Donnell was succeeded as first vice-president by Infante, older and less energetic than Madoz and a good deal more conservative. Another change that soon followed was the resignation from the Cabinet of Allende Salazar, who presumably felt uncomfortable after the vote on Isabel. The Navy went to Antonio Santa Cruz, a respectable seaman and Liberal of bygone days who like Luzuriaga had to be found a seat in the Cortes.

A vote of confidence did nothing to remedy the money shortage, which was growing more and more acute. The loan obtained in August from the bankers had produced little, because they paid most of their contributions in overdue government bills instead of in cash. In many regions where collection of the excise duties had been at a standstill since July only vigorous action could get it going again. Collado wanted such action, Espartero demurred: it would be bitterly unpopular. Taxation could be reduced for the

---

[1] D.S., pp. 263 ff.
[2] Howden to Clarendon, no. 336, 4 Dec. 1854, F.O. 72. 848.
[3] D.S., pp. 270 ff.

poorer by more being asked from the richer; or for both, by a pruning of the clumsy State apparatus. The richer did not want to pay more, and there were strong vested interests, especially in the army, to impede the government's good resolutions about economies in all departments.

At last, on 18 December, Collado presented his long-awaited budget, while deputies crowded round the tribune in their anxiety not to miss a syllable. It was 'universally set down as a great failure', and the stocks fell.[1] Reduction of expenditure by about one out of fifteen million pounds was envisaged. But no corresponding reduction of taxes was to be seen; and no redistribution of tax burdens except an 8 per cent. impost on the yield of government securities, and a graduated discount on all civil (not military) salaries and pensions, including those of the clergy. As to the *puertas* and *consumos*, the budget put down a sum of 168 million reals as their 'equivalent', thus saddling the Cortes with the responsibility of retaining them or finding a substitute. Negotiations over the next week led to an uneasy compromise: the government gave up its share in the excise taxes, and the Cortes guaranteed to make good whatever deficiency resulted.[2] The makeshift arrangement left untouched the problem of local government finance, which depended heavily on its own share. This would not be worth much to local authorities when the huge cost of collection fell on them alone. Complete abandonment followed, and to avoid a breakdown a series of expedients were soon having to be resorted to, principally surcharges on national revenues such as the land-tax and industrial tax.

Collado resigned as soon as the compromise was patched up. Democrats were indignant when he was replaced by Sevillano, a worse specimen of the same class, illiberal and understanding nothing of finance except how financiers grow rich. But it could not be said that the Democrats had an alternative plan of finance ready. Often they seemed to be against taxation of any kind, and so gave some colour to the charge of obstructiveness and irresponsibility. They were too much inclined to view any and every reduction of public expenditure as a good thing, failing to see that the modernized Spain everyone was talking of could not be had for nothing. Social services like education would not expand if the

---

[1] *The Times*, 5 Jan. 1855, 8/3; cf. *Clamor Público*, 5 Jan., 1/1–2.
[2] App. 5 to D.S., no. 45, 28 Dec. 1854; D.S., pp. 637–9.

State were penniless; nor would the economy, for it was illusory to think that in a country so inert and retarded industrialization could be accomplished, or farming renovated, by unaided private capital. Orense had so doctrinaire a faith in private enterprise that he objected to even stud farms or agricultural schools being run by the State.[1]

Among the other big reform issues confronting the country there was one, that of the army, where Espartero was for once on his mettle. He could not plead ignorance of military matters; and they touched the rivalry between him and O'Donnell closely. What was at stake was the system of conscription.[2] If there was any grievance that bulked as large in the people's mind as the excise, it was this detested 'blood tax'. Exemption from it cost six thousand reals, or £60, a sum far beyond the means of an ordinary family. All Democrats and many Progresistas had for years been denouncing the system; and on 16 December an abolition bill was moved by Labrador, a radical, and passed its first reading. Conservatives on the other hand, not content with the retention of the Civil Guard[3] in spite of the odium it had incurred during the revolution, were agitating for a fresh levy of conscripts. Those in service had been given two years' remission, and normal wastage even in time of peace was very high; in addition it was believed that under San Luis the army had been allowed to drop well below its nominal strength, in order to provide a fat margin for peculation.[4] Such juggling and mystification the War Department practised habitually. Friends of order strenuously contested the argument that the militia was adequate protection, and took as their text various disturbances in the provinces. Rioters at Seville on 3 October had been joined, instead of suppressed, by a number of *milicianos*, whose corps was disbanded.[5] There was the same story at Malaga on 28 December.

Espartero was planning to replace conscription with voluntary, pensionable service. Howden felt that volunteers would be hard

---

[1] D.S., pp. 6,265–72 (18 Jan. 1856).

[2] On the workings of the system see Mas y Abad, pp. 59 ff., 71 ff., 87 ff.

[3] Infante was made inspector-general, and nursed the force back into strength. See E. de la Iglesia y Carnicero, *Reseña histórica de la Guardia Civil* (Madrid, 1898), pp. 122–30.

[4] For official army figures from 1828 to 1858 see *Anuario estadístico* (1859), pp. 628–9. Those for 1855 show only a small drop, and only for the infantry: the other arms were actually strengthened.

[5] Decree of 6 Oct. 1854; C.L., vol. lxiii, p. 155. Cf. Guichot, vol. v, pp. 46–49.

to find, since the 'abominations' of army life had given Spaniards 'a perfect horror' of it.[1] Money to pay them (as well as to equip the militia) would be still harder to come by, and the only man of his epoch whose prestige might have enabled him to transform the vicious military organization was easily daunted by such an obstacle. As so often, he was before long talked into a compromise. Army strength including 10,000 men for the colonies would be fixed at 70,000, somewhat below its previous nominal level; 25,000 would be raised by a fresh levy of conscripts, and whatever shortage remained would be made up by voluntary recruitment. When this came before the assembly, Orense insisted on forcing a division. O'Donnell argued that to abandon conscription would be to throw open the gates to Carlism, and hinted broadly that this was what the Left, bent on exploiting confusion, desired. Orense was defeated by 167 to 26.[2]

Meanwhile in a series of debates on incidental questions the Democrats, and those Progresistas who stood close to them, were making efforts to give the Cortes, what it was not getting from its front bench, a sense of political direction and purpose. Their efforts were meeting with mediocre success. When Ruiz Pons moved that Cabinets should be chosen by the Cortes instead of by the sovereign, Luzuriaga gave the House a lead in dodging the issue.[3] A committee set up to investigate Cristina's conduct was to take eighteen months to produce a report too inconclusive as well as belated to be of any use. An attempt to assert the principle of ministerial responsibility, so little acclimatized in Spain, took the form of a four-day debate, opened by Calvo Asensio, on Córdova's 'Grapeshot government'.[4] It proved a sprawling, ill-managed affair. Three of the men under attack were old Progresistas, and the embarrassed front bench kept out of the debate; and orators were more anxious to tell Spain every jot and tittle of what each personally had seen and done in the great days of July than to make a reasoned case. The motion was talked out. In the debate on the Queen's speech the ministry's programme statement was prolix and academic.[5] By now Democrats were

[1] Howden to Clarendon, no. 286, 1 Nov. 1854, F.O. 72. 847. In fact voluntary recruitment was assisted by the winter's unemployment and hunger.
[2] D.S., pp. 884–5, 887–93, 931 ff. Text of law in C.L., vol. lxiv, pp. 194–7.
[3] For the debate see D.S., pp. 249–53.
[4] D.S., pp. 311 ff., 323 ff., 367 ff., 382 ff.
[5] D.S., pp. 504–7; cf. strictures in *Soberanía Nacional*, 22 Dec. 1854, 1/1–2.

conscious of the danger of isolation that beset them, and their first speaker, Ordax Avecilla, defined their fundamental tenet as not republicanism but thorough-going democracy, which might or might not be found within either a republican or a monarchical framework.[1] They would have done well to make such a declaration earlier.

After the passage of the army bill radicals were provoked into a hardier attempt to check the drift. In a carefully framed resolution moved by Calvo Asensio they professed unlimited confidence in the Duke of Victory but added that his colleagues, worthy as individuals, were unsuited to their posts. Espartero met this offer to save him from himself by asserting that his Cabinet was completely united, and a tumultuous session ended in the defeat of the motion by 138 to 69.[2] This passage of arms was looked back on later as the break-up of the Liberal Union experiment. It brought no end to the assembly's confusions, however, for it left radicals with the baffling task of opposing a government while supporting its putative chief. It was the measure of Liberalism's frailty that it felt obliged to bank so heavily on the prestige of one man, whose lack of energy and other defects his friends were quite ready to acknowledge in private. The assembly was condemned by this situation to a fluctuating incoherence, and a perpetual strife among the more energetic factions for a primacy that was in the long run to elude them all.

So far parliamentarianism was showing little ability to recover credit with the nation. Reform hopes seemed to be losing themselves in a maze of windings and blind alleys, and the Press was growing critical of the assembly's proceedings, as ragged and sterile. About this there was a remarkable consensus of opinion, all the way from the *Soberanía Nacional* to *Padre Cobos*—a new satirical sheet abounding in squibs and epigrams at the expense of deputies of every Liberal shade. While the Cortes floundered, the throne regained confidence. On the last afternoon of 1854 Isabel was to be seen, quite recovered from her alarms, taking her promenade on foot among her subjects on the crowded Prado.

[1] D.S., pp. 477–84. Orense enlarged on this, and said republicans were eager to work with all other progressives, in the next debate: D.S., pp. 571–7.
[2] Debate in D.S., pp. 976–88.

IX

CHURCH AND STATE

The Religious Controversy, January–February 1855

AFTER the vote of 30 November a brand-new Constitution was
less necessary than ever. The old one of 1837 could be restored,
and revised at leisure. Still, there was the lingering notion of an
ideal code laid up in heaven and waiting to be brought down to
earth; and deputies more anxious for practical reform, or for
their own careers, had to reckon that a constituent assembly could
only remain in being for as long as it was dealing with its osten-
sible chief function. On 11 December a committee of seven was
chosen to prepare a groundwork of 'Bases' or fundamental
principles. Its membership was very mixed, though Democrats
had excluded themselves by their vote on the monarchy. General
Sancho, a right-wing Progresista, was chairman, and Olózaga
secretary as he had been in 1837. Lasala and Valera were advanced
Progresistas; M. Lafuente the historian and Ríos Rosas represented moderate conservatism; Los Heros was an Esparterista.
Drafting took a whole month, yet the twenty-seven Bases read out
on 13 January[1] followed, confessedly, the 1837 model. Above all
no serious reduction of the royal prerogative was being proposed.
Lasala and Valera had a long list of minority recommendations
including a broader franchise and more religious freedom, while
Ríos Rosas had several reservations of an opposite complexion.
Howden thought the draft laudably moderate; his private influence, which may have been appreciable, had been exerted to
keep it so.[2] All progressives were disappointed. To the *Iberia* the
draft seemed pallid and cloudy, a mere deception.[3]

The first Base declared sovereignty to 'reside essentially in the
Nation'. Ríos Rosas fought hard to have the formula diluted; he

---

[1] The *dictamen* and minority reports form App. 2 to D.S., no. 57, 13 Jan. 1855.
The draft Bases are printed also in J. Becker y González, *La reforma constitucional en
España* (Madrid, 1923), pp. 124–6.
[2] Howden to Clarendon, no. 50, 7 Feb. 1855, F.O. 72. 864.
[3] 14 Jan. 1855, 1/1–4; cf. 7 Feb., 1/1.

was beaten by 214 to 18.[1] Next the House took up the sixteenth Base, concerning the veto, on which an early decision was required. The commission's wording, 'The sovereign sanctions and promulgates the laws', was highly oracular, and, astonishing to say, the Left endeavoured in vain to discover whether it implied an absolute or a suspensory veto.[2] Only later on was it allowed to transpire that the former was intended. Many who boggled at dethroning Isabel had clearly wanted and expected to see her pushed well into the political background, and in the end the Base was accepted only by 130 against 107, in spite of front-bench support. Luzuriaga had assured the House earlier that ministers would confine their interventions in constitutional debates to the minimum.[3] This sounded well, but often meant that they would give no lead where a lead was badly wanted; and when they did come out with an opinion it was likelier than not to be on the less liberal side.

If they were in an unheroic mood this January it was a good deal owing to the financial troubles that overshadowed them and the assembly. The winter was a hard one, and the relief afforded to the poorer classes by removal of the excise taxes was cancelled out by high food prices and unemployment. Instead of curing last year's commercial depression the revolution had in some ways worsened it, by frightening capital into hiding; though conditions varied, and Basque iron output was expanding while Catalan textiles flagged.[4] In Old Castile the freezing up of the canal at Palencia helped to paralyse movement of goods. Tumults, mostly on a fairly small scale, were reported from places as far apart as Valencia and Bilbao, Granada and Valladolid. In Madrid itself the town hall was daily besieged by crowds of hungry workmen, for whom little could be done. Money for palliative measures was badly needed to hold in check the discontent normally held in check by force. Sevillano as Finance Minister, and Madoz as president of the assembly, were both putting moral pressure on the budget committee by prophesying anarchy, followed by reaction, if cash were not found.

Sevillano very soon resigned, and was succeeded on 21 January by Madoz, whose own place was—to Olózaga's disgust, it would

---

[1] D.S., pp. 1,133–47.   [2] D.S., pp. 1,279–94.   [3] D.S., p. 1,207.
[4] Bruguera, p. 227. Cf. R. de la Sagra, *Remedio contra los efectos funestos de las crisis políticas* (Madrid, 1855), p. 9.

seem—given to Infante. Old enough to have been an *émigré* of 1823, and thus entitled to the respect only accorded to the old guard of Liberalism, Madoz was young enough to be, at 48, a keen, hard-working politician. All the same, the range of experiments open to him was restricted. His connexions with the Catalan *bourgeoisie* hindered him from breaking away from its creed of protectionism and seeking extra revenue, as free-traders like Corradi and Sánchez Silva advocated, from lower duties on an increased volume of imports. An alternative that he was soon privately sounding Howden about was a British loan.[1] But what foreign lenders wanted was to get their old investment back, not to throw good money after bad. A Progresista ministry could not well offer the necessary sweeteners, especially easier entry for British manufactures, for fear of being charged with unpatriotic Anglomania. Espartero as regent had been accused of letting the English lead him by the nose. Only one adequate remedy really lay to hand: a further big instalment of the policy which in the thirties had closed the monasteries and sold off their vast properties. Several variants of it had been talked of or toyed with in the past few years; now, in a situation where the rich were as always unwilling to pay and the poor for the time being could not be made to pay, it beckoned irresistibly.

On 24 January Madoz delivered his inaugural speech. Disamortization, he declared in ringing tones, was the need of the hour, and would be pushed on forthwith. Applause was loud, and a motion of approval was carried by a big majority.[2] But to keep going for the next few months he needed temporary aid from the capitalists who held the government tight in the noose of the floating debt, and his next care was to put them in a good humour by private reassurances. Having thus got promises of assistance to tide him over, he read out on 5 February a bill announcing three grand aims: to give a powerful impetus to the national economy, to supply the Treasury with funds, and to avoid injury to any existing interests.[3] By the 23rd a strong select committee had worked up his rough sketch into a comprehensive measure, with a long preamble.

---

[1] Howden to Clarendon, no. 47, Conf., 7 Feb. 1855, F.O. 72. 864. Cf. Hardman, 'Spanish Intolerance and Insolvency', in *Blackwood's*, June 1855, pp. 719 ff.
[2] D.S., pp. 1,068–71.
[3] Text: App. to D.S., no. 76, 5 Feb. 1855.

In two important features the scheme departed widely from its precedent, the suppression of the monasteries. In the first place it did not apply only to ecclesiastical properties, though the Church still had a good deal to lose: one of its defenders reckoned the wealth still remaining to it after 1845 at above a thousand million reals, nearly half in land.[1] Four categories of real estate, urban or rural, and of *censos* and *foros* or quit-rents, were affected; they held very different places in the country's life, and would have been far better dealt with separately. They were the properties of the Church and military orders; those of the State itself, with scheduled exceptions such as the rich Almadén quicksilver mines; part of the collectively owned lands of villages and municipalities; and endowments of hospitals, schools, and other foundations.[2] In the second place the measure was not in principle one of confiscation. Possessions locked up in mortmain would be compulsorily brought into the market, but their actual owners were promised full compensation. There was some sleight of hand here. Each property taken over would be valued, and an equivalent sum allotted to the owner in the three per cent. Consolidated Debt. The yield to the owner was supposed to be the same as before; but the value in coming years of the real estate he lost would rise, that of the cash income he received would fall. Lots would be sold at public auction, and any margin between the valuation or reserve price and the sum fetched would represent, after expenses were met, a profit for the State. Proceeds were to be applied first of all to covering the budget deficit; subsequently they were to be divided between public works and extinction of the Debt. The entire transaction, however (except as to sales of items already belonging to the State), might be regarded as a vast forced loan, the effective lenders being those who were to hand over their possessions, while the ready cash which was the government's paramount want was to come from the purchasers.

Liberals might calculate that prospective buyers would represent a fresh body of political support. It had always been too much

[1] J. M. Antequera, *La desamortización eclesiástica* (Madrid, 1885), pp. 235–6.

[2] See *Anuario estadístico* (1859), pp. 551 ff., for detailed tables of all these properties, still unsold in 1857; pp. 574–5 give a statistical digest of disamortization from 1836 to 1856. For an elaborate criticism of the scheme by Bravo Murillo, see his *Opúsculos*, vol. i, pp. 181–372, 'La desamortización'; also vol. v, pp. 77–80. Cf. Anon. [L. García], *Apuntes y documentos parlamentarios sobre las doctrinas . . . de D. Juan Bravo Murillo* (Madrid, 1858), pp. 81 ff., 95 ff.

their propensity to bribe a minority instead of going into partnership with the majority. A day would come when there would be no more wealth to buy Liberal votes with; and when that happened there would be no more Liberalism. But more immediate risks were involved. That the Church would resist tooth and nail went without saying. Its income from land was reckoned, it is true, as part of the *Culto y clero*, or State subsidy due to it, just as its new income from three per cents would be under the bill; but possibilities of concealment, and the social influence of ownership, as well as rising values, made the present situation much the more eligible. Cardinal Antonelli, the papal Secretary of State, lost no time in lodging a formal protest in the name of the Concordat.[1] His challenge might prove serious, for so many interests were affected that the Church had a good chance to appeal to the nation at large against its despoilers; and all the forces of reaction would be ready to look to religion for a vantage-ground.

Relations between Church and State had already deteriorated very far. Aguirre at the Ministry of Justice was as zealous a custodian as his predecessor Alonso of every iota of authority over the Church, and during December there had developed an imbroglio of a kind only imaginable in Spain. On the 8th Pius IX promulgated the bull *Ineffabilis* which at long last made the Immaculate Conception a dogma. For centuries Spain had campaigned with crusading fervour for it: the bull was a national triumph, and as such would redound to the advantage of the Church and its conservative allies at a time when the country lay, in the words of the historian of the *Inmaculada*, under the blight of cholera and of the far blacker pestilence of Liberalism.[2] Wisely or unwisely the government felt obliged to assert itself. It had an old weapon in its armoury in the *Pase regio* or right to license or prohibit any documents from Rome. *Ineffabilis* was refused official entry, and referred to the advisory body on ecclesiastical affairs. While religious guilds, cities, and provinces hastened to imitate the palace and organize spectacular rejoicings, no text of the bull could legally be printed.

To cap all this, the next part of the Constitution due for debate,

[1] *Documentos relativos a las negociaciones seguidas con la Santa Sede* (Madrid, 1855), pp. 38–44; J. Becker y González, *Historia de las relaciones exteriores de España durante el siglo XIX* (Madrid, 1924), vol. ii, pp. 290 ff.
[2] N. Pérez, S.J., *La Inmaculada y España* (Santander, 1954), p. 334.

and far the most contentious of all, was the soon-famous second
Base. No Spanish Constitution could leave out religion, though
many Liberals would much have preferred to do so. Erastian or
even anti-clerical they might be, but the difference from there to a
belief in freedom of worship was, reckoning in Spanish leagues,
enormous. Their lukewarmness on this subject did not prove them
all to be either so timid or so unprogressive as they appeared in
English eyes. At their best they had a real hatred of intolerance,
and toleration of a negative sort they could claim to have given
Spain already in the last two decades; for though no religion
except the Roman could be openly practised or advocated, here-
tics and freethinkers were tacitly left to work out their own dam-
nation, the State having lost the will and the Church the power
to persecute them.[1]

To go beyond this point was to court genuine difficulties and
dangers. Very few voices in any quarter were lifted in favour of
disestablishment,[2] which would outrage the clergy and at the
same time deprive the government of its means of keeping them
under watch and ward. Those in favour of taking away from the
Church its monopoly were still a small minority, and the national
will was unmistakably on the wrong side: particularly, as Luzuriaga pointed out, the female portion of it.[3] To authorize Protes-
tants or Jews to worship and proselytize freely was a totally
different thing from allowing them to exist. And in the country of
the Inquisition there were no surviving religious minorities, as
there were in the France of 1789, on which freedom could be
bestowed. It could be granted only in the abstract, to sects that
could be called into existence only by propaganda from abroad,
especially from England. But this might easily galvanize into
fresh life the bigotry that would die out, Liberals hoped, if left to
die quietly. It was only a few years since the butcheries of the
Carlist war. The right course for an enlightened State as they saw
it was to humour an unenlightened Church by leaving it a hollow
supremacy, and domesticate it by degrees into something as
innocuous as the Church of England.

Unfortunately Liberals were not always, or even often, at their

[1] On the legal position under the Penal Code of 1848 see J. D. Hughey, *Religious Freedom in Spain* (London, 1955), pp. 22–23.
[2] One of the few was 'Toda Tierra' (pp. 20–21).
[3] In a debate on 10 Feb. 1855: see D.S., pp. 1,371–87.

best: baser alloys mingled in their philosophy. A true spirit of tolerance could arise only from true social progress, shared in by all classes. Liberal reform had always been designed for the middle classes, and now it was to be financed by further expropriation of others, including both priest and peasant. Some Progresistas would not grudge a sop to Cerberus in the shape of 'Catholic unity' —the current euphemism for Catholic monopoly. Some were even beginning to surmise, as Moderados had done earlier, that the old clerical ascendancy over the popular mind was not altogether a bad thing. One dictum at least of the Bishop of Barcelona had a persuasive ring: 'Religion is the only guarantee of order.'[1] Or, as an English traveller put it, monks had at least helped to maintain 'a spirit of subordination', and been 'perhaps necessary evils'.[2] All these dubitations help to explain why the Bienio offers so inconsistent a picture, of a régime now fiercely browbeating the clergy, now cowering abjectly before them; and why of all the questions that came before the assembly the second Base was the one where a resolute lead from the government was most needed and least forthcoming.

There were conflicting pressures on the drafting commission before the second Base took shape. Howden was dismayed to learn that Isabel had sent for Sancho, the chairman, and warned him that she would not hear of any liberty of cults.[3] He himself was active on the other side, a fact which she and her associates knew and resented. The resultant wording was an uneasy piece of eclecticism. Like the clause of 1837 it promised 'maintenance and protection to the Catholic religion professed by Spaniards', but it went on to stipulate that no Spaniard or foreigner could be prosecuted under civil law (*civilmente*) for his private opinions. It thus seemed to leave the way open for ecclesiastical prosecution of private opinions, as well as for official prosecution of their public profession. A good many radicals like Corradi, and practically all Democrats, thought the formula dismally weak. Clericalists thought it the thin end of a diabolical wedge, and a fresh breach of the Concordat, Article I of which declared Catholicism the religion of Spain 'to the exclusion of any other'.

Ministers were seriously afraid, Howden discovered, of Isabel abdicating and appealing to the country against them in the name

[1] Costa y Borrás, *Observaciones*, p. 280.   [2] Tomkinson, pp. 155 ff.
[3] Howden to Clarendon, no. 2, 8 Jan. 1855, F.O. 72. 864.

of outraged religion.[1] Disamortization meant more to them than
toleration. It was already a sign of their desire to avoid a breach
with the Church, and to pacify Isabel, when the very moderate
Pacheco after leaving the Cabinet in December was appointed to
the long-vacant place of envoy to Rome. On 8 February, the day
debate on the second Base started, and three days after the tabling
of the disamortization bill, ministers rejected a motion in the
Cortes in favour of a new Concordat.[2] On the 11th Pacheco's
instructions were drawn up by his successor Luzuriaga; one of his
duties would be to obtain papal assent to Madoz's bill.[3] Rome
was being offered a bargain.

The debate which began on 8 February was the first full discussion of Church and State in Spain's history, and was followed
with intense interest.[4] Uproar in the galleries was frequent, sometimes spreading to the floor. One speech by Rafael Degollada, a
veteran anticlerical from Barcelona, was said to have sold 10,000
copies there in an afternoon.[5] Lafuente, accounted a broad-
minded Catholic, was the commission's chief spokesman in defending its formula as a reasonable compromise. Few deputies
stigmatized it as going too far, though it was now that Nocedal,
protagonist of 'neo-Catholicism' in the making, first exhibited
his formidable audacity and sardonic wit. There was a prevailing sense that it was time for Spain to put another mile or two
between herself and the ghosts of Torquemada and Philip II, if
only for the sake of appearances in Europe. To go further than
this required courage. When one division was about to be taken
forty-three deputies slipped out of the Chamber to avoid having
to record their opinion.[6] The *Clamor Público*, which had a good
record on this subject, was probably right in believing that another
hundred would have voted for a larger measure of toleration, if
only ministers had pointed the way.[7] As it was, the Democrats
took easily the leading place. In one way it came easier to them to

[1] Howden to Clarendon, no. 63, 10 Feb. 1855, F.O. 72. 864.

[2] It was moved by Batllés; see D.S., pp. 1,319–21.

[3] The instructions form no. 4 of the *Documentos relativos a las negociaciones* (pp.
13–38).

[4] Many of the speeches were reprinted by 'M' in *La Asamblea española de 1854, y la
cuestión religiosa* (Madrid, 1855).

[5] *A Narrative by Dn. A. H. de M. [A. Herreros de Mora] of his imprisonment by the
'Tribunal of the Faith'* (trans. W. H. Rule, London, 1856), p. 5.

[6] Howden to Clarendon, no. 65, 11 Feb. 1855, F.O. 72. 864.

[7] 19 Apr. 1855.

advocate freedom of worship because they tended to be less anti-religious than the older Liberal generation which remembered the Inquisition. A mild undenominational Christianity was fairly common among men like Castelar. Democracy did not mean agnosticism, Ordax Avecilla wrote in the *Soberanía Nacional*, it believed in God as well as in the perfectibility of human nature.[1]

Battle was waged principally over a series of ten amendments, nine of them in favour of more freedom. In divisions the number of votes cast fluctuated about 200, the Left getting from a third to almost half. Ruiz Pons moved the first, adroitly contrived, amendment, asking for the same degree of freedom in Spain as at Rome, where both Protestant and Jewish worship were permitted. He appealed as many others did to history, flagellating Philip II for losing the Netherlands by his bigotry.[2] The second was the most uncompromising of all, demanding 'freedom of conscience and of worship' pure and simple; it was lost by 139 to 73.[3] Scarcely as many Spaniards outside the Cortes as inside it, commented *Padre Cobos*, could have been found to support it.[4] Combating the fourth amendment, Olózaga met the frequently urged view that religious freedom would attract foreign residents and capital by arguing that what would attract them more would be order and security. He announced two concessions none the less that his committee, Ríos Rosas dissenting, felt obliged to make. *Civilmente* was to be omitted, and *creencias* inserted, with the effect of barring prosecutions under ecclesiastical as well as civil law for private opinions *or beliefs*.[5]

Another proposal that failed was that freedom of cults should be introduced for the time being in the larger towns only.[6] On 24 February the second Base itself, as it now stood, was reached, and progressives found themselves uncomfortably obliged to defend it against reactionary onslaughts. Excitement in the country was mounting, and ministers were anxious to have the debate over and done with. On the 28th the House agreed to go into permanent session. Ríos Rosas attacked the new wording, and Nocedal closed a bitterer philippic by holding up religion as

[1] 30 Nov. 1854, 1/2; cf. F. Garrido, *La república democrática, federal universal* (Madrid, 1855), pp. 24, 34–36, and Ruiz Pons, speech of 15 May 1855 (D.S., p. 3,206).

[2] DS., pp. 1,327–33.   [3] D.S., pp. 1,333–5.
[4] 10 Feb. 1855, p. 3.   [5] D.S., pp. 1,373–87.
[6] This came up in two forms; see D.S., pp. 1,406–15 and 1,550–64.

the antidote to social disorder—'in Catholicism alone lies the remedy for the disease from which Europe is suffering'. Olózaga wound up, and half an hour after midnight the second Base without further change was approved by 200 votes to 52, the clericalists outnumbered four to one. O'Donnell voted for, Espartero abstained.[1]

All *libre-cultistas* in Spain and abroad were deeply disappointed with the outcome, which did no more after all than lend the sanction of law to a state of affairs existing by tacit consent for twenty years. British indignation was vehement, and helped before long to push Howden into an unseemly fracas with the Spanish government, ending in a virtual request for his recall.[2] Clarendon turned this off, but the chilling of relations with England subtracted something from the chances of a Liberal consolidation. On the other side the half-heartedness of the second Base did not save it from an outburst of atavistic fury, which convulsed chiefly the highest and lowest classes. Englishmen cherished too fond a belief that Spanish fanaticism was unreal, mere theatrical machinery worked by priests. Yet it does not seem that the frothing passions now being churned up were nearly so deep or ungovernable as in years gone by. In the bigger towns at any rate freedom of worship, and of argument about religion, might well have been inaugurated with success if Espartero had engaged his boundless authority in the cause. In later years Democrats came to attach greater and greater significance to the moral cowardice of 1855 as one of the reasons for his party's collapse.[3]

A degree of firmness was being shown by the Cortes in rejecting petitions against the second Base and refusing to reopen the issue. Ministers continued to look the other way. The army was not in trim yet; and right-wing supporters had been warning them that an affront to orthodoxy, on top of disamortization, would offer Carlism an opportunity too tempting to forgo.[4] There seemed a prospect this winter of Carlists and Polacos making

---

[1] For the final debate see D.S., pp. 1,646–704. It may have been prophetic of Sagasta's future that he spoke for the Base, as a Catholic, rather against the Left than against the Right.

[2] The affair concerned a Rev. Mr. Frith who had some trouble with the authorities at Seville; papers in F.O. 72. 865 and 866, and *Gran Bretaña: Política, 1854–56* (serial number 2,495).

[3] See, for example, E. García Ruiz, *La revolución española* (Paris, 1867), pp. 145–6.

[4] *Diario Español*, 8 Feb. 1855, 1/1–3.

common cause: ever since the revolution various Moderados especially of Cristina's circle were looking towards Montemolín as the last bulwark of order and property.[1] Carlists at Paris and London were observed to be in high feather, and talking mysteriously of a big success just round the corner.[2] Now, with the cry of the Church in danger resounding from end to end of Spain, their day might well seem to be dawning. Conscious that they must do something dramatic or lose face irretrievably, they still hesitated, partly because they were even more hard up for funds than their enemies at Madrid. Spanish legations were devoting much of their limited energy to picking up *émigré* news or rumours: not too exacting a task, in spite of their complaint of having no secret service funds. Carlist strength lay in memories and myths, not in organization. A shadowy *Comisión Regia* at Paris was supposed to be guiding the movement, and there were committees and agents scattered about Spain. How effective were the links no one knew, the Carlist chiefs as little as anyone.

The *émigrés* hottest for action were those who were most impecunious and famished. They had a champion in Elío, who resided at Naples with Montemolín and who in December made his way from there to Paris, and then to London.[3] In London everything depended on Ramón Cabrera, the other great guerrilla chief and the most sanguinary of them all until his marriage in 1850 with the wealthy Miss Richards. Both his name and his wife's money were indispensable, and Elío stayed with him at his town house—81 Eaton Square—though the two men detested each other cordially. There were conferences also with Don Juan, of 17 Alfred Place, West Brompton. Cabrera was in no hurry. He had come to appreciate the difference between a comfortable house in Kensington and a bivouac in the Catalan hills; and he may have recalled that last time he was risking his skin in those hills Montemolín was eloping with his Miss Horsey to the softer slopes of Windermere.[4] Some kind of accord was patched up; Elío

[1] This was noted in a report by the Sub-prefect at Bayonne to the Interior, 18 Aug. 1854; *Espagne*, vol. 845. Cf. Lord Cowley, ambassador at Paris, to Clarendon, no. 1,028, 18 Aug., F.O. 27 (France) 1,021.

[2] Olózaga to Pacheco, private, 31 Oct. 1854; *Francia*, 1854.

[3] Memorandum with España, chargé d'affaires at Paris, to Luzuriaga, Reservado, 22 Jan. 1855; *Francia*, 1855 (in a bundle of papers docketed 'Carlistas'), and 31 Dec. 1854; *Francia*, 1854.

[4] See H. de Lazeu, *Apuntes histórico-contemporáneos* (Madrid, 1876), pp. 23–31.

returned to Paris, his headquarters for the coming months, and on 21 January the *Comisión Regia* drew up its call to action. It fixed no starting-date, however.[1]

On the same day five Carlist agents and a large store of weapons were seized in Madrid. Police searches for suspects and caches were in full swing, in Howden's opinion with the arbitrariness of Spanish police under all régimes.[2] Yet weeks elapsed, and very little else happened. In Old Castile a band of irreconcilables led by Mariano Hierro took the field near Burgos before the end of February. During March small combat groups made an appearance in the Sierra de Ronda and near Huelva.[3] The militia, still in its early flush of ardour, formed one powerful deterrent; along the Pyrenees the French provided another by closing the frontier at Spain's request.[4] The Allies had no wish to see trouble stirred up there just now, and were suspicious of Carlist links with Russia.

Montemolín was being held back most of all, it seems, by the hope of an understanding, not with Cristina merely, but with her daughter. Talk of a marriage between the Princess of Asturias and a son of Don Juan (Montemolín was childless) was current in political gossip, and a dynastic fusion would please many conservatives. But Montemolín's hope was that the crown would be handed over straight away. It was put into his mind by Isabel herself. She too must have overestimated the power of Carlism, and she would rather give up her throne to her cousin than share it with the many-headed beast. She may have been aware that some Moderados were offering Montemolín help to install him in her place.[5] She was probably influenced at first by her mother, certainly throughout the intrigue by her husband. Spite against his wife and her daughter, and qualms of conscience about the Salic law, furnished Don Francisco with motives. In the background stood the Church, with everything to gain from a closing of the dynastic breach that had worked so powerfully to subvert its influence. Like the army it was honeycombed with old Carlists,

[1] Text in Ferrer, vol. xx, App. 6.
[2] Howden to Clarendon, no. 23, 25 Jan. 1855, F.O. 72. 864.
[3] Guichot, vol. v, p. 53.
[4] Papers in *Francia*, 1855 ('Carlistas').
[5] 'Carlos Constante', *San Cárlos de la Rápita, ó el Conde de Montemolín* (Barcelona, 1884), pp. 52–53. Straten-Ponthoz to Vicomte Vilain XIIII, now Belgian Foreign Minister, no. 122, 31 May 1855; *Espagne*, vol. 8 (2), shows he was aware that Moderado approaches to Montemolín were being made.

most prominent among them the redoubtable 'Fray Cirilo'—Alameda y Brea, erstwhile adviser of Don Carlos, now Archbishop of Burgos.

On 10 February Eugenio de Ochoa, editor of the *Amigo del Pueblo* and man of confidence of the King and of Cristina, sought out Brigadier Arjona, the accredited Carlist representative at Madrid.[1] An interview followed at the palace between Arjona and Don Francisco, which was to become a matter of notoriety in not very much later days as Spanish secrets usually did. Further parleys led to a protocol accepted with slight adjustments by Montemolín. Isabel and her consort would retain their 'honours'; Montemolín would reign as Charles VI; the Princess of Asturias would marry his eldest son if he had one, or his brother Juan's; when this prince was twenty-five Montemolín would retire and the young couple would reign as joint sovereigns. Such a plan could not be palmed off on Spain without a trial of strength against Liberalism, demanding a careful choice of the right moment. Meanwhile Nicholas I's death on 2 March was viewed as a serious set-back for Carlism; the Tsar had been its most powerful patron. On the 10th Don Carlos the Old Pretender followed him to the grave. Turgot noticed the absence of any stir of interest in Spain at the news,[2] but it brought the chiefs of the family and the party together for the funeral, and for consultations. Montemolín found time on his journey to Trieste to have a talk with the pope and Antonelli.[3]

The exchanges with Isabel and her husband continued, and there was a great deal of talk at Madrid about a new *camarilla*, directed by Don Francisco's confidential confessor P. Fulgencio and the miracle-working Sor Patrocinio, or María Quiroga. This nun had achieved fame in youth by exhibiting stigmata which a judicial inquiry held to be produced by lunar caustic, and having first won the King's veneration she was now acquiring that of Isabel.[4] Authority had its eye on her; in mid-March, not for the

[1] See Ferrer, vol. xx, pp. 81, 124 ff. The obscure story of the negotiations between Isabel and Montemolín rests on the narrative in 'Constante', pp. 35–43, which purports to be based on an MS. record by an Ignacio Monfort or Montfort, and which (as Ferrer points out: vol. xx, p. 186, vol. xxi, p. 40) appears confused.

[2] Turgot to Drouyn de Lhuys, no. 184, 13 Mar. 1855; *Espagne*, vol. 846.

[3] Ferrer, vol. xx, pp. 138 ff.; also reports from the Spanish consul at Trieste, and other sources, in *Francia*, 1855 ('Carlistas').

[4] On Sor Patrocinio's connexion with Isabel see C. Llorca, *Isabel II y su tiempo* (Alcoy, 1956), chap. 6.

first time in a tempestuous career, she was ordered to remove instantly from Madrid.[1] Howden, who had no doubt that she was working for the Carlists, rejoiced.[2]

[1] Texts of order of banishment, and royal letter of consolation, in Sor María Isabel de Jesús, *Vida . . . de . . . Sor María de los Dolores Patrocinio* (Guadalajara, 1925), pp. 198–201.
[2] Howden to Clarendon, no. 110, 16 Mar. 1855, F.O. 72. 865. On her Carlist sympathies cf. Ferrer, vol. xx, p. 9, N.2.

X

POLITICAL TENSIONS REVIVING

Pressures on the Government from Left and Right
March–April 1855

DURING March the Constitution got one stage further; the question of a second chamber was taken up, as the most controversial item remaining. Lasala and Valera of the drafting commission recommended a return to the unicameral principle of 1812. San Miguel supported this; ministers stated a very emphatic preference for two chambers, coupled with a warning, such as they threw out all too often, that they might feel unable to stay in office if their opinion was overruled. Lasala and Valera were then defeated, though only by 155 to 101.[1]

Ríos Rosas wanted hereditary senators, but it was pretty generally agreed that a House of Lords like England's was impossible because there was no functioning aristocracy. Nomination for life was recommended by the majority of the commission, as giving sufficient independence to senators who had any desire for it. Olózaga produced a third alternative, a variant of the one he had got adopted in 1837: members of the upper chamber to be elected, subject to a property qualification, for twelve years, by the same voters as the lower. This was the solution that found most acceptance, and he was able to beat off a number of amendments, pressed especially by men like Concha, Dulce, and Serrano, who had come to regard the Senate as their appanage and wanted at least some seats to be reserved for them. Replying to the final debate on 17 March he took occasion to defend his own past, and his middle-of-the-road position.[2] It was part of his triumph that he was scoring off the front bench, which disliked an elective Senate but did not feel robust enough to say so.

Constitution-making halted here for six weeks, while more urgent matters demanded attention. Olózaga did not stay to risk

[1] D.S., pp. 1,832–44; 1,845–67; 1,877–81.
[2] D.S., pp. 1,984–92; 2,047–51.

his laurels by trying to grapple with these; he was off again to his comfortable duties at Paris. Economic dislocation was still the biggest problem. Unemployment continued in some trades at a high level. Madrid province suffered during February from incessant rains and flooding. Worst of all was the steep rise in food prices, due in part to the European war which, with bad harvests abroad, was intensifying the demand in England and France for Spanish foodstuffs.[1] Abnormal food exports went on, in spite of protests, throughout the war, exerting an influence steady and pervasive though hard to measure on Spanish affairs. They injured poorer consumers, including the small cultivator who had to sell his crop at once to pay his dues, and then had to buy food;[2] they benefited the trading and landed interests, including the better-off farmer, and helped as time went on to stimulate pipe-dreams of commercial expansion. They were bad similarly for deficit areas like Catalonia which had to import food, and good for those with food surpluses, especially for more go-ahead provinces like Valencia,[3] alert enough to seize the opportunity.

Transport was so deficient that stocks and prices always varied wildly from region to region, and speculators were taking advantage of every local shortage. Agitation for price controls was swelling; the government, wedded to its *laissez-faire* ideas, remained obdurate. Liberals were still too apt to shut their eyes, or, when distress broke out in fits of angry complaint, to blame lurking trouble-makers. On 22 January there was a row at Saragossa, trivial enough, over the arrest of some woodcutters who were helping themselves illicitly to fuel. 'Here is a grave and alarming symptom', cried Escosura in the Cortes, 'of how the enemies of Spain's liberty are incessantly at work.'[4] This was playing into the hands of the Moderados, whose press trumpeted its catchword of Order and accused the Progresistas of being incapable of governing.

Everywhere the authorities were as hard up as most of their

---

[1] In 1855 Spain's share in Britain's total grain import rose from practically nil to 14 per cent. See V. J. Puryear, *International Economics and Diplomacy in the Near East* (Stanford, 1935), p. 218.

[2] On this point see J. M. Álvarez, *Estudios . . . de la prohibición de importar granos y semillas en España* (Madrid, 1864), p. 10.

[3] See trade report from Valencia for 1858 (*Parliamentary Papers*, 1859, vol. xxx).

[4] D.S., p. 1,057 (24 Jan. 1855).

people. At Valencia the whole city council had to be prevented from resigning. Madoz was forced to confess that the Treasury was desperate for funds even to pay the salaries of Madrid's horde of civil servants;[1] and the bankers went back on their undertaking to renew their short-term loans for a year, and haggled for higher interest. He was intensely indignant, and denounced them in the Cortes as saboteurs trying to bring the government down.[2] Little help could be expected from his unenterprising colleagues, none from his leader. No other minister was so often missing from the House, or displayed when there so complete a lack of parliamentary talent, as Espartero. Democrats and advanced Progresistas or 'Puros' were coming together again in search of a remedy for this state of drift. They were meeting regularly in what was coming to be known as the 'Círculo Progresista', one of a succession of experiments at constructing a parliamentary bloc that might impose a coherent line of policy on the government. On 7 March a deputation of Puros tried to convince Espartero that affairs would soon be alarming unless ideas or men more in tune with the needs of the time were brought forward without delay. They got very little out of him; criticism however tactful always ruffled his vanity.

Unity of the Left was marred by disagreement about O'Donnell, whom Puros unlike Democrats were willing to credit with a genuine change of heart. He had energy at least, and ingratiated himself with the other 'Consul' by bearing the brunt of the work while letting him fancy he was doing everything. In the Cortes he was growing into an effective debater, even if his soldierly diction had an uncouth sound.[3] He wasted no breath on trying to conciliate Democrats; the moderate Left he was making every effort to disarm, or at least confuse. From the day when he signed the manifesto of Manzanares, he declared in the course of the Senate debate, he regarded the Constitution of 1845 as dead. With these words he 'linked himself for ever to the Progresista party', exclaimed the *Iberia* jubilantly,[4] only too eager to welcome him as an acolyte. Borrego discussed in a book he was writing this year

[1] See *Asamblea Constituyente de 1854!*, pp. 305 ff., and App. to D.S., no. 141, 28 Apr. 1855; Madoz was forced to resort to a patriotic but irregular loan from Espartero's banker friend Matheu.

[2] D.S., pp. 2,131–3 (22 Mar. 1855); cf. *Clamor Público*, 13 Mar. 2/4.

[3] Nombela, vol. ii, p. 353.

[4] 16 Mar. 1855, 1/5.

the hypothesis of O'Donnell actually becoming the Progresista leader.[1] Liberal Union as advertised during the elections had evaporated; Moderados were cold-shouldering him. According to a story picked up by Fernández de los Ríos a number of generals approached him about this time and asked for an army coup to save the country from going to rack and ruin.[2] He declined, knowing better than they did how premature such an attempt must be.

If Espartero's followers could not persuade him, a push might be tried from another quarter, the militia. By now upwards of 450,000 *milicianos* were enrolled, Madrid province with 28,000 having the largest corps. Service was in principle compulsory, though it was complained that in many areas, including the capital, the authorities were slack about enforcing this; apart from a shortage of muskets, they were interested in the revenue from the toll chargeable on men who did not serve. Militiamen were a mixed lot. Some joined because they had to; others, a cynic wrote, to have the pleasure of dressing up in ornate uniforms, or in order to grind private axes.[3] In the backwoods they may have represented at times a species of gang rule. Howden, who had strong prejudices against the whole force, accused them of setting up 'a little military despotism in the villages'.[4] In the towns various factions were seeking support among them. Democrats made no secret of hoping to permeate the militia with their doctrines, and were more liable than others to be taxed with perverting a national institution to factious purposes,[5] because the sort of men who took an active part in it were likely to be of more radical temper than the average comfortable bourgeois.

Originally the militia had been a mass force of the urban population, warding off absolutist reaction. But now a new kind of contest was unfolding, and it was becoming a practical question whether or not the militia ought to take a hand in it: whether it ought to have, and express, a corporate opinion on the state of the nation. In the official handbook[6] a militiaman was a pillar of both public liberty and public authority; but these attributes might

---

[1] *La revolución de julio*, pp. 150–1.

[2] Fernández de los Ríos, *Luchas políticas*, vol. ii, p. 428; he learned of it, he says, in 1856.   [3] Nombela, vol. ii, p. 172.

[4] Howden to Clarendon, no. 221, 17 Sept. 1854, F.O. 72. 846.

[5] See, for example, F. de P. Montejo, *De la ley de Milicia Nacional* (Madrid, 1855), p. 30.

[6] *Guía del Miliciano Nacional* (Madrid, 1856), p. 3.

come to seem contradictory. If he was under government orders, how could he protect liberty and progress against backsliding rulers? If he was not, how could authority subsist?

A militia battalion was a little republic, made up of eight companies with a captain and two lieutenants to each, and its political feelings if it had strong ones were reflected in its choice of officers. Otherwise mere personal popularity would secure a commission. A wealthy dilettante from Valencia with a residence in Madrid, the Conde de Parcent, was elected captain of an artillery company by honest artisans who enjoyed his custom.[1] At the top the typical figures were not radicals but men in the public eye, chosen simply out of compliment. Some of these might of course be tempted to play on rank and file discontents as a means of furthering their own political careers. Collectively as men of substance they would be sensitive to grumblings among their men, and inclined at least to provide discontent with a safety-valve.

On the evening of 27 March a meeting of senior officers was held at the town hall, General Ferraz the mayor, *ex officio* head of the city militia, presiding by request. Ostensibly the purpose was to discuss means of safeguarding public order by allaying discontent, but what was in the air was a political move—a call for the resignation of the four superannuated Liberals or *Santones*: Luzuriaga, Aguirre, Luxán, and F. Santa Cruz. Some of those present very likely felt themselves to be exactly the right men to take their places; they were sure in any case to be suspected of such a notion.[2] Discussion soon brought out disagreements; Sagasti, civil governor as well as commandant, argued that the militia had no place in politics. Before long threatening crowds were reported to be gathering outside, and though it was speedily discovered that they were only unarmed militiamen waiting to hear what was decided, the conference came to an end.[3] There was some effervescence in the streets, but no semblance of rioting and no refusal of duty by any militiamen.

---

[1] *Asamblea Constituyente de 1854!*, pp. 271–3.

[2] The *Diario Español* made this charge next day (28 Mar. 1855, 1/3). Other papers took it up against one man in particular, Portilla.

[3] On this evening's events see *Asamblea Constituyente de 1854!*, pp. 273–5; Escalera and González Llana, vol. iv, p. 179; C. Massa y Sanguineti, *Historia política del Excmo. Señor D. Práxedes Mateo Sagasta* (Madrid, 1876), p. 21; also speeches by F. Santa Cruz on 28 Mar. 1855 (D.S., pp. 2,256–7) and by Sagasti, Portilla, and Gurrea on 4 Apr. (D.S., pp. 2,386–92).

Ministerial reactions were disproportionately sharp. Towards the close of the session on the 28th F. Santa Cruz as Minister of the Interior read a bill whose single trenchant article prohibited the militia from corporate discussion of politics. A brief preamble gave the pretext: this loyal corps was being exploited by occult influences, unnamed enemies of freedom. On the other side press and parliamentary reactions were equally stiff. A militia deputation waited on Espartero on the 29th, only to be dismissed with a rebuke; O'Donnell, who had most to gain by any weakening of the militia, was going to be able to shelter, as he often did, behind his partner.

On 4 April Sagasti and O'Donnell, amid interruptions from the gallery, defended the bill. So less expectedly did Sagasta, who drew a horrific picture of liberty transformed into 'the most dreadful of dictatorships . . . a dictatorship of half a million bayonets'. A furious wrangle developed, Democrat deputies among the fiercest. Espartero assured the House and the gallery that no one loved, no one 'adored' the militia as he did. Crowds gathered round the building daily during the debate, and on the 11th when it reached its climax the concourse was sufficiently tumultuous to strike panic into many progressives as well as conservatives: both thought they saw sinister agencies at work. Troops were being held ready, with pickets in the main squares. Inside the Cortes strained nerves were in a state to welcome any decent way out, and at last an amendment by Vega de Armijo provided one: it effectively debarred the militia from political activity but added a face-saving reference to the organic law by which all militia questions were to be decided permanently by the assembly. It was approved by 165 votes to 28;[1] as usually happened when the pinch came, only Democrats and a few auxiliaries refused to retreat.

The militia growled, but gave way. It was still under the spell of its self-induced illusions about the Duke of Victory. Politically the damage done was serious; even if the ban on political debate could not be strictly enforced, it betrayed Liberalism's lack of confidence in its own following. The government had all the more incentive to press on energetically with its only big positive project, disamortization, which had begun being debated just before the militia crisis, and which could be advertised as a progressive

[1] For the debate see D.S., pp. 2,455–81.

measure if only because the Church and the right wing were denouncing it. It also gave the Cabinet something to agree about wholeheartedly; O'Donnell was as keen on it as anybody, as the only way out of bankruptcy, and knew very well that only a Progresista régime could handle it. The result was to stand out as the biggest monument of this Cortes,[1] and even to mark the end of an epoch by completing and exhausting the Liberal achievement in Spain.

All parties, a minister was able to assert, concurred in the general principles of the bill.[2] It would be interesting to know how many deputies intended to buy properties brought on the market themselves. At all events, far too little recognition was shown of the injury likely to be done to others besides the Church, and in particular to the peasantry. Of the two main categories of collectively owned land, still exceptionally widespread in most parts of Spain, the *tierras comunes* or lands in communal use were not touched by the bill. But they were not easily distinguishable from the *propios*, lands rented out or otherwise employed so as to produce an income to the community;[3] and the loss or reduction of this income would itself be a blow. No one knew exactly how many *propios* there were; in 1852 they had been estimated at over 100,000 with a total value of over £7,000,000.[4] There was no doubt much petty graft in their management; they were often 'enveloped in a network of jobbery, let at nominal rents to friends and favoured persons'.[5] Each local council down to the smallest was apt to reproduce in miniature the pettifoggery and *caciquismo* of national politics; but this might have been made an argument for further democratizing and closer inspection of local government, instead of for expropriation.

In Spain as elsewhere the nineteenth century saw a conflict of

[1] See, for example, estimates of it in H. Castille, 'Espartero et O'Donnell', in *Portraits politiques au dix-neuvième siècle*, 1st series, no. 14 (Paris, 1857), p. 36; Escalera and González Llana, vol. iv, pp. 171-2; G. Hubbard, *Histoire contemporaine de l'Espagne* (Paris, 1869-83), vol. v, p. 243; Nido y Segalerva, *Antología*, p. 577.

[2] Aguirre; D.S., pp. 2,227-9.

[3] Income from *propios* had for some time paid a 20 per cent. tax, so one-fifth was to be deducted from the compensation paid for them. On the tangle of legal confusions over *propios* and *tierras comunes* after 1855, see Altamira y Crevea, p. 262; J. Costa Martínez, *Colectivismo agrario en España* (Madrid, 1898), pp. 328, 331-2.

[4] Costa Martínez, ibid. p. 309.

[5] Hardman, in *The Times*, 5 Jan. 1855, 8/3, and *Blackwood's*, June 1855, p. 723. The view that communal properties were mismanaged and useless is endorsed by Colmeiro, and by Fermín Caballero, e.g. p. 121.

ideas between those who found virtue in traditional forms of collective ownership, and modernizers intent on crystallizing all ownership into precise individual right. Among the former the great name had been Flórez Estrada, whose ideas Joaquín Costa was to revive: the latter traced their descent from Jovellanos, and were a large majority among Liberals.[1] To these men of the majority it seemed self-evident that the antique modes ought to be swept away. It was an axiom with them that the economic expansion achieved by mid-century owed very much to disamortization; and between economic activity and social justice they did not discriminate too closely. But the more liberal-minded among them, including many or most Democrats, held that transfer of collective property to active private hands could and ought to be managed so as to bring about an increase of small holdings. Political utility as well as social justice seemed to call for this. Pointing out that disamortization, like the *bourgeois* revolution as a whole, had enriched the 'haves' at the expense of the 'have-nots', Garrido emphasized also that those it enriched usually made haste to desert the Liberal cause. 'Nearly all former buyers of national properties are today enemies of the people, royalists, furious *polacos.*'[2]

Two Democrats were members of the select committee on the bill, and there were two elements in this that could be held up as good for the common man. One was that *censatorios*, owners of farms burdened with the quit-rents or annuities known as *censos*, where these were payable to indissoluble corporations, were being offered a chance to redeem them on easy terms. The other was that properties were to be offered for sale in the smallest lots practicable; so that whereas formerly big men, landlords and speculators, had snapped up most of the spoils, now the small man might get a look-in. Only one-tenth of the purchase price of a lot need be paid at once, and fourteen years were allowed for the rest. Men of goodwill were free to hope for a great multiplication of small owners, modifying the agrarian structure of Spain in the

[1] A. Flórez Estrada brought out the 7th ed. of his *Curso de economía política* in 1852, in old age. The ideas of Jovellanos, F. Caballero, and Costa Martínez are discussed in J. Morán Bayo, *Hacia la revolución agraria española* (Cordoba, 1931).

[2] *La república democrática, federal universal*, pp. 4–5. Garrido was strongly for disamortization, none the less, at any rate of Church property; see *El pueblo y el trono*, pp. 11–12, and cf. M. Gómez Marín, *Explicación del programa Democrático* (Madrid?, 1860?).

direction that France took in 1789. This prognosis was being confidently put forward by the ministerial press.

It was cogently criticized during the debate on the principles of the bill by a Progresista deputy from Extremadura named J. A. Bueno, who drew on a wealth of figures and facts. He was against the bill because of its inclusion of the village lands. Expecting poor men to be able to buy he considered chimerical; rich men would be further fattened at the cost of wretched cultivators degraded to the condition of helots in a new feudalism.[1] Madoz in his big speech was at great pains to parry such criticism. All his life, he declared, he had advocated disamortization as the means of increasing the number of proprietors and diminishing the number of paupers.[2] Experience was to prove him wrong, Bueno right. Seven years later Garrido reckoned that of all the land sold more than half was bought by fairly modest middle-class investors, the rest by the wealthier classes, little or none by the peasantry.[3] For the humblest denizens of the countryside, small tenants and labourers, things were made worse instead of better as shrinkage of the village commons deprived them of part of their scanty resources.

Discussion of the bill article by article spread over a month, but there were many interruptions before the final clause was approved on 27 April,[4] and various useful amendments were brushed aside with too little attention. A speaker who dwelt on the extreme poverty of the masses in many rural areas asked for protection against rack-renting for tenants on lands about to change hands.[5] Rivero and others wanted to link the bill with a scheme for rural banks.[6] Meanwhile criticism outside the assembly was left too much to conservatives, the Basque journalist Ortiz de

[1] D.S., pp. 2,213–21. Bueno's speech is cited with approval by Costa Martínez, *Colectivismo agrario en España*, pp. 318–19, and Morán Bayo, p. 100. On the extreme poverty and backwardness of Extremadura, a region of great estates, cf. Fermín Caballero, pp. 68 ff.

[2] D.S., pp. 2,240–9; Bueno's rejoinder is on pp. 2,249–50.

[3] *L'Espagne contemporaine*, pp. 154–5. Cf. A. Ramos Oliveira, *Politics, Economics and Men of Modern Spain, 1808–1946* (trans. T. Hall, London, 1946), p. 56.

[4] Large extracts from the debates are given in I. Miquel and J. Reus, *Manual completo de desamortización civil y eclesiástica* (Madrid, 1856), part 1, pp. 15–132. Final text of law: App. 1 to D.S., no. 142, 30 Apr. 1855, and C.L., vol. lxv, pp. 5–11.

[5] A. J. Arias; D.S., pp. 2,732–4, 23 Apr. 1855.

[6] D.S., pp. 2,791–801, 26 Apr. 1855. Cf. an article in *Iberia*, 20 Apr. 1/1–2, pointing out that land released from mortmain was seldom in good condition, and small buyers would need credit facilities to get it going.

Zárate for instance.[1] Borrego was a veteran supporter of Flórez Estrada's ideas about fair play for the peasantry, and no Spanish publicist of that age wrote more eloquently on any theme. What would befall the social system now forming, he asked, when the Gracchi of the future told their proletarians how it was built upon spoliation of the people?[2]

Clericalists could try to make Liberal flesh creep by predicting that interference with Church property would subvert respect for all property and lead infallibly towards communism.[3] The patrimony of the Church, besides, had often been called, and really had been to some extent, the patrimony of the poor.[4] But the campaign against disamortization, like the one against religious freedom, resorted far more to fanaticism than to argument. It was a raging, tearing attack in which no weapon was neglected, even it was said pressure in the confessional on wives and mothers of deputies. Buckle, reaching the Spain of 1855 in his history, was to be moved to the reflection: 'It is impossible to benefit such a nation as this.'[5] Meanwhile Pacheco as envoy at Rome was trying hard, if his British colleague was not misinformed, to be placatory. He told Antonelli that Spain was passing through a time of storm and stress, and the government was compelled to go with the tide, but was anxious not to be carried too far.[6] Other Spaniards in Rome were at work to frustrate any compromise, among them San Luis and two other ex-ministers.[7] Howden was convinced that another member of the cabal was Bonel y Orbe, the aged Cardinal Archbishop of Toledo,[8] who also spent some time in Rome and then was with Isabel, in residence at Aranjuez, all through April.

[1] See, for example 'El pueblo y los desamortizadores', 18 Sept. 1856, in R. Ortiz de Zárate, *Escritos* (Bilbao, 1899–1900), vol. ii, pp. 96–102.

[2] *La revolución de julio*, pp. 102–3.

[3] Canga Argüelles (y Villalta), *El gobierno español . . . con la Santa Sede*, p. 130; cf. J. Valero y Soto, *Vindicación del partido moderado español* (Madrid, 1856), p. 43.

[4] See this Christian–socialist view, for example, in J. Polo de Bernabé y Borrás, *Apología de la amortización eclesiástica* (Madrid, 1848). On the effects of disamortization on charitable endowments see F. Hernández Iglesias, *La beneficencia en España* (Madrid, 1879), pp. 66 ff.

[5] H. T. Buckle, *History of Civilization in England* (ed. of 1873), vol. ii, p. 592.

[6] R. B. P. Lyons, Agent at Rome, to Lord Normanby, Minister at Florence, no. 15, 14 Mar. 1855, F.O. 43 (Rome) 60. Pacheco himself in his book on his mission— *Italia, ensayo descriptivo, artístico y político* (Madrid, 1857)—says discreetly little about what line he took.

[7] Lyons to Normanby, no. 22, 18 Apr. 1855, F.O. 43. 60.

[8] Howden to Clarendon, no. 132, 25 Mar. 1855, F.O. 72. 865.

Isabel was under strong right-wing pressure to veto the bill; she was only too eager to do so, and was feverishly consulting all and sundry who might help her to defy the consequences. There is some evidence of her trying to induce O'Donnell to break with them and join forces with her, and of his making the temporizing reply that circumstances were not yet propitious.[1] On 21 April she sent a letter to General Pezuela, who had been removed by the government to Segovia. He represented, short of Carlism, the extremest Right, and strained every nerve to enlist army support.[2] In all the plotting the King was taking a busy hand. There seem to have been sketchy plans for a rising in Madrid on 2 May, the national day; also for the Queen to be carried off to some other centre, Valencia perhaps. Ministers could not afford to give way on disamortization; Turgot watched Espartero reviewing the militia and visiting the barracks, and was convinced that they meant to force Isabel to abdicate if she would not sign. He was alarmed into admonishing her through a private channel that obstinacy was likely to cost her the throne.[3] But there were misgivings among ministers too, despite their bold front. On 28 April the papal pro-nuncio Franchi went to Aranjuez to see Luzuriaga, in attendance on the Court as Foreign Minister, and warn him that if the bill became law Rome would denounce the Concordat. Luzuriaga's official rejoinder was stiff; but according to what Franchi told his friend Turgot, he was in tears: 'que la Reine ne signe pas, s'est-il écrié, c'est la révolution et toutes ses horreurs.'[4] It was not of his own side proving too weak that this nervous old Progresista was afraid, but too strong.

At Madrid that evening the Cabinet decided to make one more attempt by going to Aranjuez in a body next day with all the presiding officers of the Cortes, and then, if Isabel held out, to resign and appeal to Cortes and country. Next morning, Sunday the 29th, the town was quiet, but left-wing deputies who knew what was in the wind met in the Cortes building: accounts that got

---

[1] Straten-Ponthozto Vilain XIIII, no. 103, 1 May 1855; *Espagne*, vol. 8 (2), and Howden to Clarendon, no. 274 Conf., 25 Oct., F.O. 72. 870.

[2] Text of Isabel's message in Marqués de Rozalejo, *Cheste, o todo un siglo (1809–1906)* (Madrid, 1935), p. 184. Ochoa was the messenger.

[3] Turgot to Drouyn de Lhuys, no. 194, 1 May 1855; *Espagne*, 847.

[4] Ibid., and *Documentos relativos a las negociaciones*, pp. 66–69; cf. Becker, *Historia de las relaciones exteriores*, vol. ii, pp. 294 ff.; Fernández de los Ríos, *Luchas políticas*, vol. ii, p. 430.

into the press said they were preparing to declare the throne vacant.[1] Isabel made Turgot come to Aranjuez, against his better judgement; he found her drooping. She had done everything conceivable, she exclaimed, to escape signing this impious bill. 'J'ai appelé des Généraux sur lesquels je comptais, des Colonels, tous ont été lâches (cobardes) et m'ont abandonnée.' Turgot told her she had done her duty as a Catholic and must now do her duty as a queen.[2] About noon the ministers and Cortes representatives arrived; and at 4.30 a telegram brought to Madrid the news that the bill was law. Isabel's surrender may have disappointed some on the Left as well as the Right.

The second of May passed off peacefully, but ten arrests were made next night. No prosecutions were launched. Ministers did not want to incriminate the Queen, and O'Donnell, if he really was playing a complicated double game, may have shielded some fellow officers from awkward investigations. But a score of half-pay men were removed to a safer distance, Pezuela to Santander, and the Bishop of Osma to the Canaries; the Archbishop of Toledo was ordered back to his see. On 6 May a decision was taken to push on with the purge of the royal household whose torpid progress had been causing comment. An abrupt descent to burlesque followed when the baffled Don Francisco talked in his treble tones of the new functionaries entering his apartments over his dead body.[3] The government could now afford a graceful concession; on 9 May the bull *Ineffabilis* was at last officially admitted to Spain.

[1] Two Democrats, Figueras and Alonso, were reported as among the boldest speakers. On the events of this day see Howden to Clarendon, no. 188, 30 Apr. 1855, F.O. 72. 866; accounts reprinted in *Diario Español*, 1 May, 1/4–2/1, and *Clamor Público*, 1 May, 1/2–3, and 2 May, 1/2; Pirala, vol. ii, p. 239; Pi, *Historia*, vol. iv, p. 123.

[2] Turgot to Drouyn de Lhuys, no. 194, 1 May 1855; *Espagne*, 847.

[3] See a circumstantial account by Hardman in *Blackwood's*, June, 1855, pp. 722–3; cf. Pi, *Historia*, vol. iv, p. 125, and Nido y Segalerva, *Antología*, pp. 578–80.

XI

THE ASSEMBLY'S DILEMMAS

Carlist Rebellion and Cabinet Obstruction
May–July 1855

THE energies of the Cortes were flagging. By normal standards the session had gone on for a very long time; but on 9 May members came reluctantly to the conclusion that they must complete the Constitution before giving themselves a holiday.[1] O'Donnell strongly supported this, for the government; suspicious minds on the Left were free to conjecture that the assembly was being invited to speed up its work so that it could be the more speedily dissolved, and a tamer one got in its place. A week later absentees had to be summoned back to their duties.[2]

Some of their enemies were wider awake. Religious hysteria was not being allowed to die down; on 15 May a Christ in the church of St. Francis at Madrid sweated blood, and thousands flocked to witness this manifestation of divine displeasure with Liberalism. Two priests, said to be former Carlist chaplains, were arrested. Isabel was surrounded by Carlists, and appeared to Montpensier, who spent some time at Aranjuez hopefully snuffing the air, to be quite indifferent whether she abdicated or not.[3] In all Isabel's talk of abdication and martyrdom, however, there was a good dash of make-believe; she was incapable of playing even the most dishonest game honestly. Carlist sympathy was chilled by her surrender over disamortization, and *émigrés* impatient to force her hand were disgusted at hearing no clarion call from the party conference at Trieste. Whatever Montemolín's own inclinations, this impatience was passing beyond his control; the long-delayed blow must be launched.

What was contemplated was a short, sharp push to bring Liberalism down like a house of cards. It would be fatal for many

---

[1] See D.S., pp. 3,060–81. [2] D.S., pp. 3,265–6.
[3] Howden to Clarendon, no. 229, Conf., 1 June 1855, F.O. 72. 867. Montpensier confided in him as an old friend of the Orleans family.

reasons, Spanish and European, to be locked in another long conflict. Action, moreover, must start or seem to start spontaneously, inside Spain. An appeal to the villages might stand the best chance; but only if accompanied by pledges that the fall of Liberalism would mean lower rents, or land of his own for the tiller, and any such promises would alienate all landlords. Instead the directors were thinking, like O'Donnell a year before, of an appeal primarily to the army. Their highest hopes, Olózaga heard, were fixed on a number of officers of high rank who had been visiting Paris and meeting Elío.[1] Many army men were old Carlists who under Progresista rule could look for no share of the plums; and the officer corps as a whole was distrustful of Espartero, and detested the militia.

When at length the rising broke out it followed the pattern of last year's army plot with almost ludicrous fidelity, for it started with a cavalry squadron at Saragossa *pronouncing*, on the night of 22/23 May, and riding out of the city.[2] All the rest of the garrison remained loyal, and Ignacio Gurrea, the captain-general, was free to march at once in pursuit. Elsewhere, too, the response both in and out of the army was disappointing. A manifesto to Aragon was derisively printed in full by Liberal papers at Saragossa; it began with outraged religion, invoked the Cid, Pizarro, and Lepanto, and denounced disamortization.[3] Guerrilla bands sprang up here and there, but columns were soon beating the districts affected, and dispersing them with ease. There was some spill-over of such bands, half fanatic and half outlaw, into Old Castile and the Maestrazgo; the two regions that had been the hearth and home of Carlism in the great war, Catalonia and the Basque lands, lay inactive. Basque complaints against disamortization were loud, and exemption from the law was being claimed on the basis of the *fueros* or provincial privileges.[4] The government rejected this claim, but its assurances that it had no design to sweep away the *fueros* seem on the whole to have been accepted.

[1] Olózaga to Luzuriaga, no. 348, Reservado, 16 May 1855; *Francia*, 1855 ('Carlista'). Ferrer, vol. xx, p. 149, says that special hopes were placed on discontented N.C.O.s.
[2] See a detailed account in *Iberia*, 29 May 1855, 1/1–3. On the Carlist rising of 1855 as a whole see Ferrer, vol. xx, chap. 7; on Catalonia, Carrera Pujal, vol. iv, pp. 281–2.
[3] Text in Miraflores, *Continuación*, vol. i, pp. 780–2, and Ferrer, vol. xx, App. 13.
[4] This argument is stated in J. L. Maya, *Navarra y la Ley de Desamortización* (Madrid, 1859).

At the first news of the rising Aragon, Burgos, and Navarre were placed under martial law. Bishops were peremptorily ordered to put a stop to any kind of agitation by their clergy;[1] some of them issued appeals for calm, which were viewed by both sides, Straten-Ponthoz remarked, as mere pretence.[2] The Cabinet was not disinclined to exploit the brief emergency so as to strengthen its own hand. One big reason for fearing a Carlist revolt had always been that it might provoke a counter-stroke from the Left, and this government was already smarting under left-wing criticism. On 24 May the Minister of the Interior read a laconic bill authorizing it in case of need to suspend constitutional liberties and prohibit subversive publications. In both progressive and conservative papers reactions were unfavourable. The Cabinet was putting its supporters in a painful dilemma, wrote the *Iberia*, between loyalty to it and to Liberal principles.[3] In the Cortes, where resistance was led by Salmerón, the select committee on the bill tried to soften it by restricting the special powers to 'the government headed by the Duke of Victory', so that they would lapse if he ceased to be premier.[4] On the 30th the bill became law: Nocedal, Ríos Rosas, and Orense were ill-assorted companions in opposition. Not for the first time Democrats were accused of wanting to unbar the door to Carlism and chaos.

Next, on 2 June, Madoz presented to the Cortes a plan, of which there had been newspaper rumours this month past, for a compulsory collection of taxes in advance.[5] Only wealthier taxpayers were to be liable; otherwise it was the same expedient that had helped to bring San Luis down. If this could be regarded as a piece of radicalism at the expense of the propertied classes, it was balanced two days later by a sweeping decree in six articles on the militia.[6] Compulsory enlistment was suspended; volunteers who wished to join must be payers, or sons of payers, of direct taxation; central control was tightened, and the government assumed power to expel unreliable elements. With a rebellion in progress

---

[1] R.O. of 27 May 1855; C.L., vol. lxv, pp. 134–6.
[2] Straten-Ponthoz to Vilain XIIII, no. 126, 11 June 1855; *Espagne*, vol. 8 (2). Cf. *The Times*, 4 June, 10/4: 'The whole movement is greatly aided and stimulated by the priests . . . .'
[3] 26 May 1855, 1/1–3.
[4] Text of report in App. 4 to D.S., no. 163, 25 May 1855.
[5] App. to D.S., no. 170, 2 June 1855.
[6] Decree dated 3 June 1855; C.L., vol. lxv, pp. 229–32.

it could plausibly be alleged that vigilant supervision was essential; while exclusion of the poorest sort could be defended on the ground that men with their daily bread to earn ought not to be burdened with duties. Under such specious reasoning lurked the feeling that the 'lower orders' were taking too big a part in the militia, especially in Madrid, and might turn it into a dangerous weapon of class struggle. And all friends of the militia saw the decree as inspired by prejudice against the force altogether as a popular institution.

There was a chorus of protest. By the evening of 4 June most of the commandants in the capital were offering their resignations. The town council held an indignation meeting, if only for the matter-of-fact reason that ending compulsory service meant ending the graduated monthly tax of 5 to 50 reals payable by men not serving, which formed part of its scanty income. In the Cortes a group of advanced deputies tabled a motion of censure, accusing the government of acting *ultra vires*.[1] At 9 p.m. the Cabinet met, and its four Jonahs resigned. Madoz went out with them.[2] Deserted by fickle favour as a financier he was preparing to move further towards the Left, where popularity with the militia would be an essential asset. Espartero hastily dropped both decree and colleagues, and before he went to bed next night had a new team ready, as well as a new decree shelving the previous one.[3] This abrupt face-about satisfied critics on neither side. Giving way over the militia was a disgraceful retreat, said a right-wing editor.[4] For ministers to resign under outside pressure instead of facing their accusers in the Cortes was unconstitutional, thought the *Clamor Público*.[5] The censure motion was grudgingly dropped on the 6th, after a threat from O'Donnell that the whole government would resign—'El Duque de la Victoria, O'Donnell y los Ministros todos'.[6] It was a mannerism of his to allude to himself in the third person. But fresh offence was given by the announcement on 8 June of the new names.

Not only were they insignificant: any political shift they represented was in the wrong direction. Fuente Andrés who took over

---

[1] D.S., p. 3,643.

[2] He gave the House a complicated explanation of his withdrawal, saying he had always felt uncomfortable in this Cabinet: D.S., pp. 3,704–7, 9 June 1855.

[3] R.O. of 7 June 1855; C.L., vol. lxv, pp. 274–8.

[4] *Estrella*, 8 June 1855, 1/1.

[5] 7 June 1855, 1/1–2.   [6] D.S., pp. 3,666–8.

Justice, and Huelves at the Interior, were the most colourless. Juan Bruil, banker and proprietor, took his seat in that chair of little ease, Finance. General Zabala was known for his heavy-handed repression at Valencia in 1843, and had no visible qualification for the Foreign Ministry except aristocratic connexions. Most obnoxious of all was M. Alonso Martínez, a stripling for whose sudden elevation to the Development ministry no better cause could be discovered than some busy toadying to O'Donnell. The latter's position had been strengthened by Madoz's exit from the Cabinet, where the two men had carried on a running fight. When Ruiz Pons insisted on more information about how and why the change had taken place, Espartero plunged into the oddest speech ever listened to in this assembly. There was no change of ministry, he asserted; nothing had happened except that five ministers had happened to resign. He could not play the orator, he went on incoherently, the only eloquence he had ever practised was on the battlefield. 'In those days, gentlemen, I imagined myself something more than a man . . . I imagined myself the exterminating angel, fighting against tyranny.' Then he was driven into exile, orders were given for him to be shot out of hand if taken on Spanish soil. And why was liberty lost in 1843? Because its friends were seduced into dissension and strife. Let them keep clear of that in 1855.[1]

Espartero's obsession with 1843 helps to explain his distrust of all critics on the Left. A day or two later he struck at the Right, by having published the secret order of November 1844 for his immediate execution if found in Spain. But it was fortunate for a Liberalism so much at sixes and sevens that its antagonist was proving so little formidable. Carlism was still accomplishing nothing beyond some impudent exploits, for instance when the mail-coach was waylaid near Burgos and burned, and a bag containing dispatches from several legations and the Countess of Montijo's jewels perished in the blaze. The army was standing firm, and the militia's share in suppressing guerrillas and patrolling threatened areas was acknowledged by all. Olózaga believed the French watch on the Pyrenees to be responsible for much of the Carlist failure to

---

[1] D.S., p. 3,669. On 9 June Ruiz Pons reverted to the 'unparliamentary' Cabinet changes, and provoked a long and heated discussion. During it F. Santa Cruz insisted on the sovereign's right to appoint and dismiss ministries (D.S., pp. 3,692–714).

rouse Navarre.[1] What mattered most was Carlism's own dimin-
ished strength; it was showing itself, as Otway wrote, 'infinitely
inferior' to what it had been, despite the efforts which he was
convinced the clergy, 'instigated by secret and pressing orders
from Rome', were making to feed the flames.[2]

The Progresista régime then was surviving, but only to relapse
as soon as pressure slackened into its former disarray. Borrego
observed that the government was always shuffling off responsibility for leading the country on to the Cortes, and the Cortes on
to the government;[3] and this was true especially over finance.
Madoz's latest scheme fell with him. On 22 June his successor
Bruil announced his own proposals for making good the deficit.[4]
Stripped of verbiage they meant an increase in taxation, and partial
revival of the excise duties—something the conservative press had
called persistently for. From progressive newspapers and deputies
there was such an outcry that it looked as if Bruil would have to
go forthwith, and there seemed, Otway remarked, no end to this
'continual consumption of Ministers of Finance'.[5] Espartero broke
through the stalemate by resorting once more to his gambit of
resignation. Isabel had to entreat tearfully, and send for O'Donnell
to beg strenuously, before he could be prevailed on to relent. Few
this time suspected him of manœuvring to increase his personal
power; he was too obviously fagged and used up.

By 5 July a group of deputies headed by the statistician Ramírez Arcas was coming to the rescue with a plan that both the
Treasury and the House found acceptable. Essentially it was
Madoz's idea over again, transformed from a tax anticipation into
a partly forced loan. With much wrangling over details it became
a brief law of four articles.[6] There was to be an emission of bonds
worth 230 million reals, issued at 90 per cent. and bearing 5 per
cent. interest, employable exclusively for purchase of properties
about to come up for sale under the disamortization law. A double
object was to be achieved, the Treasury getting ready money and

---

[1] Olózaga to Zabala, no. 422, Reservado, 16 June 1855; *Francia*, 1855 ('Carlistas').
[2] Otway to Clarendon, no. 16, Conf., 30 June 1855, F.O. 72. 867. During the past
year a flight of curés from their parishes, from fear of cholera, had often been alleged.
If this was true to any significant extent it must have lessened their influence.
[3] *La revolución de julio*, pp. 75, 78–79.
[4] D.S., p. 3,956; text in App. 2 to D.S., no. 185, 22 June 1855.
[5] Otway to Clarendon, no. 4, 22 June 1855, F.O. 72. 867.
[6] Final text: C.L., vol. lxv, p. 447.

sales a good send-off. Bonds not taken up voluntarily would be distributed compulsorily among the wealthiest class, payers of over £5 a year in direct taxation. In this scrambling fashion the Cortes was able at long last to dispose of the 1855 budget.[1]

About the same time it finished the main stage of Constitution-making, which it was struggling with amid all these interruptions much as Robinson Crusoe toiled at the ponderous canoe which in the end he could not drag down to the sea. Notwithstanding Olózaga's absence eleven of the twenty-seven Bases had been polished off in May, another eleven in June. Not many of the alterations made in the original draft were substantial, in spite of much criticism from the Left. The third Base, on freedom of the press, was vigorously attacked as too restrictive, though in the end the original wording was adopted.[2] It prescribed trial by jury for all press offences, and allowed publication without previous censorship of anything 'within legal limits'—a nebulous formula too often resorted to. Orense tried and failed to get something like a rule of habeas corpus laid down, arguing that without such protection the security of the individual would be nugatory.[3] The death penalty was abolished for political offences, and confiscation of property or banishment from Spain for any offence. A daring suggestion came from one member that deputies should be paid, since otherwise it was nonsense to speak of all Spaniards being free to seek election.[4] An innovation borrowed from the Constitution of 1812 provided for a *diputación permanente* or standing committee of the Cortes, similar to that of old Aragon, to watch over its interests and those of the nation between parliamentary sessions.[5] When the last section, on control of finance, was reached Lafuente made the remark that in twenty years of representative government only two budgets had ever been properly voted.[6]

It was open to anyone to propose additions. Democrats again had most to say. Two proposals inspired by García Ruiz, free primary education and public works to eliminate unemployment, failed to

---

[1] Budget law of 25 July 1855: C.L., vol. lxv, pp. 513–23. Summary in Pirala, vol. ii, pp. 350–2.

[2] D.S., pp. 3,017–33.   [3] D.S., pp. 3,054–7.

[4] D.S., p. 3,360.

[5] For debate on this see D.S., pp. 3,412–23 (25 May 1855), 3,440–8 (26 May), 3,544–52 (31 May).

[6] D.S., p. 3,868.

gain a second reading.[1] Orense could get only 20 votes for universal suffrage, after making much of its successful working in the U.S.A., a stock theme with Democrats.[2] Even he seems to have regarded as a forlorn hope his plea for gradual extinction of colonial slavery.[3] On 30 June the House adopted a resolution that the organic laws still to be drawn up, on the press, militia, and so on, would form integral parts of the Constitution. This was not a merely scholastic point: it was designed to make it impossible for the constituent assembly to be dissolved before their completion. And here for three months the business slumbered.

All this time the other grand responsibility the assembly had been charged with by the electorate, modernizing of the economy, was not being lost sight of. The Spain of the propertied classes was tremulous with the thought of coming wealth; and the other Spain made itself heard through Figueras when he called for speedy legislation to liberate the country's energies and thereby provide more jobs.[4] After-effects of the hard winter were still felt, and at Santiago on 13 June there was riotous protest at a sudden jump in the price of bread. Construction of electric telegraphs was quickened by a law completed on 31 March.[5] But the keenest interest was in those new highroads to Eldorado, railways; there were inflated expectations of prosperity and modernity spreading over Spain's wildernesses as fast as wheels could roll. Cities and great landowners strained every nerve to get the main lines brought through their territories.[6] Coal and iron would begin at last to develop seriously, it was urged, when they had modern transport to aid them.[7]

On 9 March a batch of nine railway bills became law:[8] one of these granted a concession to the irrepressible Salamanca. A further three laws, each granting, confirming, or quashing some

---

[1] D.S., pp. 4,095–7.
[2] D.S., pp. 3,923–33 and 3,938–43.
[3] D.S., pp. 4,094–5.   [4] D.S., p. 1,996, 15 Mar. 1855.
[5] App. 1 to D.S., no. 137, 24 Apr. 1855.
[6] Segovia and Ávila were fighting a war of pamphlets over the route of the Northern line; see, for example, Anon., *Segovia y Ávila* (Madrid, 1854). On railway enthusiasm cf. I. Gómez de Salazar, *Consideraciones acerca de la importancia de un ferrocarril por León* (León, 1855), e.g. pp. 5–6; F. Coello y Quesada, *Proyecto de las líneas generales de navegación y de ferro-carriles* (Madrid, 1855), e.g. pp. 455–68.
[7] Gómez de Salazar, pp. 8, 24, &c.
[8] C.L., vol. lxiv, pp. 340–55.

concession, were signed on 22 April, seven more on 13 May.[1] One of them annulled the award of 1845 from which a jungle of conflicting claims to the vital Northern line had sprung up, and engineers were appointed to complete the survey. To crown the work a general Railway Law was completed after exhaustive debate on 3 June.[2] It provided for construction of railways either by the State or through subsidized concessions, put up to public auction. Its salient defect was failure to ensure what the best Spanish technical opinion had always recognized the need for, a network of lines rationally planned for the whole country. Its merit was that it did open the way to a considerable expansion during the epoch now being inaugurated.

Agriculture was as always the Cinderella. In December the assembly had been assured that the Development ministry was hard at work on plans,[3] and much talk was heard of reafforestation,[4] and of a cadastral survey.[5] A rural credit scheme to lighten the load of indebtedness was prepared by an official committee early in 1855, but never got so far as to be submitted to the Cortes.[6] The same fate befell another plan later, a private bill which turned on reconstruction of the decayed old *pósitos* or public granaries.[7] As the July revolution ebbed away the official ear was returning tranquilly to its pillow. Only one definite project reached the statute-book: it was reported on by a select committee in June, and authorized the founding of 'colonies' on unused tracts of land;[8] an experiment of limited scope, and like the disamortization law destined in practice to extend landlordism rather than

[1] C.L., vol. lxiv, pp. 441–4, and vol. lxv, pp. 59–69.

[2] C.L., vol. lxv, pp. 233–42; text also in Cambó y Batlle, vol. i, pp. 28–32. 'The Railway Law of 1855 constituted a very important advance' (Boag, p. 17). The previous law of 20 Feb. 1850 had proved very defective.

[3] D.S., pp. 556–8, 22 Dec. 1854. One definite outcome was a decree of 1 Sept. 1855 setting up a 'Central School of Agriculture' at Aranjuez (C.L., vol. lxvi, pp. 4–8).

[4] See, for example, R. de la Sagra, *El problema de los bosques* (Madrid, 1854); J. M. de Nieva, *Discurso sobre la necesitad de los bosques* (2nd ed., Madrid, 1854).

[5] See A. Ramírez Arcas, *Tratados de estadística general* (Madrid, 1855–6), vol. i, p. 58; M. García Miranda, *Observaciones acerca de las calamidades que más afligen á España* (Madrid, 1853); T. Gómez Rodríguez, *Observaciones á la Ley Hipotecaria* (Madrid, 1861); S. Adame y Muñoz, *Manual de la Ley Hipotecaria* (Madrid, 1862).

[6] See Cabanillas, part 3, p. 121.

[7] See D.S., p. 520, 20 Dec. 1854, and App. 1 to D.S., no. 390, 27 May 1856.

[8] Committee report: App. 1 to D.S., no. 179, 15 June 1855; final law of 21 Nov. 1855 in C.L., vol. lxvi, pp. 379–82. On the results see Fermín Caballero, p. 97; Aller, p. 140, N. 1.

small-holding. Most glaring of all was the neglect of reform, so long overdue, in matters like rents and leases. This was what Spain's *bourgeoisie*, semi-feudal by income and at least demi-semi-feudal by instinct, was worst qualified to undertake. When La Sagra recommended increased death-duties on inheritance by collaterals, with the twofold aim of breaking up vast mismanaged estates in Andalusia and of checking excessive fragmentation in Galicia, he was brought to a stop by interruptions, and a minister, faithfully echoed next day by the press, anathematized the idea as revolutionary and socialistic.[1]

In one quality, his freedom from sordid greed, Espartero did not fall beneath what was required of him. He refused all gifts from the public; and in general the standard he set helped to preserve the régime from scandals gross and palpable like those of recent years. Most of his colleagues were unequal to their duties; hardly any were mere unprincipled moneygrubbers. No doubt there was much to be said against a law granting eleven years' seniority to public servants dismissed in 1843.[2] Pluralism, however, was being prohibited;[3] and early this year a decent self-denying ordinance forbade deputies to accept, without special leave of the House, any official post, payment, or decoration, with the exception of Cabinet office or promotion by seniority.[4]

Altogether the legislative achievement of the session now drawing to a close was represented by 91 measures. This performance was on the whole not unimpressive, even allowing that a good deal was trivial or of purely local interest. Some other useful items can be counted in. For example the government had been instructed to revise and codify the law of civil procedure so as to quicken and cheapen justice; by November the task was fulfilled.[5] On the other side various further sins of omission might be pointed to. Little or nothing had been done or was done subsequently in the long-neglected field of colonial reform, about

---

[1] See D.S., pp. 592–4, and Sagra's *Vindicación . . . de un proyecto de ley* (Madrid, 1855), pp. 3 ff., 6 ff. A Utopian socialist of sorts, he found himself isolated in this assembly, and soon resigned: see M. Núñez de Arena, in *Revue Hispanique*, 1924, pp. 490–3, part of a long study of his career.

[2] Text: App. 8 to D.S., no. 208, 1 Oct. 1855.

[3] C.L., vol. lxv, pp. 402–3.

[4] C.L., vol. lxv, pp. 16–17.

[5] The new code was presented to the Cortes on 3 Nov. 1855. See a commendation of it in R. Riaza and A. García Gallo, *Manual de historia del derecho español* (Madrid, 1934), p. 634.

which there was some press discussion stimulated by U.S. designs on Cuba. Hardly any interest was taken at any time in foreign affairs, except in improvement of relations with Portugal; though as the Bienio went on there was a marked need for supervision of the divagations of foreign policy, especially in Latin America. Time-wasting verbosity was one reproach frequently levelled against the constituent assembly. In reality members soon grew impatient of long-drawn sittings, and a speech of more than an hour became a rarity; all the same, there were those who wanted to talk as much as possible, or to gratify voters with multiplied questions which ministers were not obliged to answer. Disorderliness was another common reproach, and the Democrats were singled out as the worst culprits. A small party is almost compelled to make up for smallness by vehemence, and bear-garden scenes did sometimes result. Also prolific of delays was the predilection for voting by roll-call, which as Madoz pointed out took up 45 minutes every time.[1] Its publicity must often have had the worse effect of scaring less resolute deputies into voting against conscience, or staying away.

Private members enjoyed a facility of initiating legislation that had its virtues, but was carried to excess; and inevitably there was more keenness, as a deputy named Gaminde complained, to be chosen for select committees than to perform the tedious grind they often involved.[2] Hence the interval between appointment of committees and production of reports tended to be vastly too long. In mid-June 179 committees had still to report;[3] and there might be an equally long delay before bills came to be considered by the House. No one was really responsible for keeping business moving. Committee reporters had to do most of the steering required to get their measures through; ministers were oftener absent than present, and there were no parliamentary undersecretaries to act as middlemen. If most Spanish administrations were too apt to tyrannize over the Cortes, this one was going to the opposite extreme.

With this went the continuing failure to evolve any stable majority. As the *Diario Español* remarked, journalists who tried to analyse division lists and classify groups were trying to sort out

---

[1] *Clamor Público*, 14 Jan. 1855, 1/1.   [2] D.S., p. 8,051, 26 Apr. 1856.
[3] A mining bill tabled in Nov. 1854 had still not been reported on at the end of 1855; see L. de Aldana, *Las minas y la industria* (Madrid, 1873), pp. 333–4.

a kaleidoscope.[1] The old Liberalism had failed to revive, the new was only beginning to find itself. An old-fashioned Progresista, wrote Pi y Margall, youthfully censorious, 'is the negation of everything, including himself; he is scepticism incarnate'.[2] Older men retorted with hard words about Democrat irresponsibility. Summer's rising tide of heat, and a threatened return of the cholera, were again reducing attendance; in the session's last weeks the Cortes was little better than a cipher, and government and public were being left to face with what fortitude they could the clouds rolling up over the horizon. Carlism was making a fresh effort; friction with the Church was worsening. Most daunting of all was an unprecedented labour crisis in Catalonia. During the spring an intense agitation had developed round the slogan of 'bread and work', together with demands for higher pay and shorter hours and the perennial demand for the right to organize. From April onward a trial of strength was under way in a series of scattered strikes and lock-outs.

Amid these perils the end of the session on 17 July, with no formal prorogation,[3] went almost unnoticed. So tame a finish was the more remarkable since this was the anniversary of the first day of the revolution. Democrats had been trying to arrange demonstrations; but nothing happened except that newspapers paid flowery tribute to the heroes of 1854, and a grand memorial service in St. Isidro was followed by bands and illuminations.

[1] 17 June 1855, 1/1–3; cf. 22 June, 1/1–4.
[2] *La reacción y la revolución*, p. 59.
[3] Since there was no formal prorogation the whole life of this Cortes formed technically a single 'Legislatura' or session.

XII

THE SUMMER MONTHS

Industrial Strife and the Breach with Rome
July–September 1855

A GLOOMY observer saw the country 'hastening with giant strides towards total subversion'.[1] Allowing for rhetoric, there was enough alarmism as summer came on to cause a spate of newspaper talk about a dictatorship of one kind or another as the only resort.[2] Most of the gossips were thinking of plenary powers for Espartero, or for O'Donnell, or for the two jointly. The Moderado press was calling on O'Donnell to break with his lawless associates; privately Cánovas del Castillo was being employed to see what could be made of him.[3] But it was O'Donnell's biggest asset, Borrego remarked, that nobody could tell beforehand what he would do if he came out on top.[4] Papers of the moderate Left were still trying anxiously to convince their readers, or themselves, that he was too loyal to turn against his Progresista allies. He for his part continued willing to humour such notions. Finance was one excellent reason for Fabian tactics; disamortization had to be given time to produce its harvest. Before the Cortes dispersed he assured it that only calumniators could accuse him of plotting a *coup d'état*. 'No, General O'Donnell will never destroy the liberties of his country—never!'[5] A week or two later he was haranguing the 3rd Line Battalion of militia which elected him its commandant.[6]

Before the end of June a good many Carlists must have been regretting their adventure.[7] It would clearly be liable to fizzle out altogether unless some of the old militants in exile were sent back as a stiffening. Once this was resolved no mountains could be closely enough sealed to keep out the indomitable veterans. On

---

[1] Ruiz de Morales, p. 792.

[2] See, e.g., the *Clamor Público*'s comment on this talk: 24 July 1855, 1/1–2; cf. Ortiz de Zárate, vol. ii, pp. 56–58 (21 Aug.).

[3] See Fabié, pp. 35–36.   [5] *La revolución de julio*, pp. 155–6.

[4] D.S., pp. 4,059–61.

[6] Text of speech in *Clamor Público*, 24 July 1855, 1/3.

[7] Comyn reported to Zabala (no. 130, 29 June 1855; *Londres*, 1855) that both Cabrera and D. Juan disapproved of the rising and blamed Elío's ambition.

2 July Gonfaus, alias Marsal, and Estartus entered Catalonia with about a hundred and fifty men. Borges and Rafael Tristany soon followed, the latter with two of his brothers; they came of a legendary clan that gave its volunteers to the cause in every Carlist rising of the century. Yet even with these noted partisans in the field Catalonia like other provinces showed no eagerness to rally to the old banner, and they were hard put to it to avoid immediate capture.

On the other hand their incursion coincided ominously with an explosion of labour trouble in Catalonia. Liberals could not pretend to have lacked warning of this; one petition from the workers to the Cortes had carried thirty thousand signatures.[1] But problems of capital and labour were things not dreamed of in their philosophy. Concessions made by the regional authorities, wage-fixing and restrictions on the new *selfactinas* or 'self-acting looms' from England that the workers blamed for unemployment, were all quashed by an order from Madrid on 21 May, which insisted on perfect freedom of contract.[2] And while Franquet, the civil governor of Barcelona, was a moderate, alongside or above him as captain-general was a man of sterner stuff, Zapatero, who acquired the nickname of 'General Four-shots' because his recipe for labour agitators was a firing-squad of four soldiers.[3] On 6 June José Barceló, a leader of the 'Unión de Clases' or labour federation, was executed on a charge of complicity in intimidation and murder. In the eyes of the workers he died a martyr.

On 21 June Zapatero ordered the dissolution of all illegal unions. On Monday, 2 July they answered with a general strike, the first in Spanish history. It was an astonishing and epoch-making achievement; fifty thousand workers in the Catalan industrial zone came out simultaneously. There was a murder at Sans of a prominent factory-manager and former Cortes deputy, Sol y Padris, and at other places some rioting. Zapatero had to shut himself up in the fort of Atarazanas inside Barcelona; his troops were shut up with him or in the citadel of Monjuich outside the walls. All patrol duties in the city had to be given over to a militia regarded by friends of order as desperately unreliable, because workmen formed a high proportion of its strength.[4] Though not

[1] Carrera Pujal, vol. iv, p. 285.
[2] R.O. of 21 May 1855; C.L., vol. lxv, pp. 118–9.
[3] J. Álvarez del Vayo, *The Last Optimist* (trans. C. Duff, London, 1950), p. 179.
[4] Consul Baker to Clarendon, no. 17, 3 July 1855, F.O. 72. 875.

to be depended on for action against the strikers it was soon admitted to be carrying out all ordinary duties satisfactorily, and no outbreaks of violence occurred here. Militia commanders stepped into the position of mediators, and held conferences with the authorities; though the municipal councillors wanted to resign, and most of them slipped away from Barcelona. As was usually the case, the provincial council was more conservative and stiff-necked.

That ignorant mechanics could have organized on such a scale all by themselves appeared quite incredible. One point that was made much of was that foreign refugees were conspicuous among the strikers: socialists or Mazzinians made up part of the multitude of Frenchmen and Italians in the mills. But most speculations converged on Carlism, very likely with Russian gold in its pocket. Certainly Carlists were now concentrating their efforts on Catalonia. They may simply have foreseen the industrial crisis and reckoned on having a better chance under cover of it; or it may be that some of them, taking their cue from the Christian-socialist teachings of Balmes, were hoping to win the confidence of the working-class and make an alliance with it against the *bourgeoisie*.[1]

The Times asked what any government could do for these strikers who wanted a minimum wage and a maximum working-day—demands 'quite at variance with the first principles of economical science'.[2] The *Iberia* was sufficiently enlightened to argue against mere coercion. Socialism could not be quelled by force so long as the miserable poverty of the mill-workers was allowed, like that of the farm labourers, to continue; the authorities could at least regulate working conditions.[3] Yet the *Iberia* did not want to see workers granted the right to organize and defend themselves.[4] In the conservative press the cry was all for whips and scorpions. There was, too, at Madrid an impatient feeling that Catalans were always troublesome. Huelves as Minister of the Interior reiterated the official resolve to keep the door closed against collective bargaining.[5] No more can be said for this

---

[1] Propaganda on such lines about this time is described by M. Tomás, *Ramón Cabrera* (Barcelona, 1939), p. 268. Ferrer, vol. xx, pp. 120–1, speaks of the Montemolinist variant of Carlism as 'eminently Balmesian'.

[2] 13 July 1855, 10/3.

[3] 13 July 1855, 1/1–3; 14 Aug., 1/1–4; 17 Aug., 1/1–3.

[4] 12 July 1855, 1/1–3.

[5] D.S., pp. 4,246–7.

government than that it refrained from trying to break the strike
by brute force, though army reinforcements were drafted into
Catalonia at once. Even this restraint seems to have been partly
due to jealousies in the sphere of high politics where the two
'Consuls' pursued their uneasy gyrations. A story picked up by
the embassies said that O'Donnell at first wanted to rush to the
scene at the head of his troops, but some who feared he would
return all-powerful went to Espartero and got him to veto the
plan.[1] Turgot's version was that he himself with some of O'Donnell's intimates persuaded him to stay where he was, instead of
leaving the capital an open field for revolutionism.[2]

Espartero was very much on the horns of a dilemma. He had to
show that he knew how to keep order; but he could not forget
that Barcelona still bore the scars of his unlucky bombardment at
the end of 1842. He fell back on a personal appeal to the strikers,
who were shouting his name in the streets with a hopefulness that
sounded to conservatives highly suspicious. On 6 July he sent
off a Colonel Saravia with a manifesto which in paternal accents
reproached the workers for letting themselves be talked into sedi-
tion. Instead they should hearken to 'a son of the people who
has never deceived the people', and trust his government to do
even-handed justice.[3] The manifesto was read to the militiamen,
whose loyalty it was important to ensure. Saravia interviewed the
strike leaders, and then a proclamation was issued summoning the
men to return to work, at the same wages as before, and promising
the setting up of a *jurado mixto* or arbitration panel drawn from
both sides to settle disputes. This was one of the workers' demands, but it would have much less value if they were not allowed
to choose their own spokesmen collectively.

Delegates they had sent to Madrid after the strike began were
very grudgingly received by Espartero, who would only promise
to see fair play once they returned to work.[4] At Barcelona his
appeal must have had some effect on the men, and probably by
now, though neither their organization nor their spirit was

---

[1] Grimberghe, Belgian chargé, to Vilain XIIII, no. 152, 7 July 1855; *Espagne*,
vol. 8 (2), and Otway to Clarendon, private, 7 July; Clarendon Papers, vol.
c. 28.

[2] Turgot to Walewski, no. 6, Conf., 9 July 1855; *Espagne*, vol. 847.

[3] Text in *Clamor Público*, 13 July 1855, 1/2–3.

[4] Carrera Pujal, vol. iv, p. 293; *España*, 10 July 1855, 3/3–4; *Clamor Público*, 10
July, 1/3.

broken, strike funds were running low. On 12 July normal work was being resumed in most places. Yet all the talk Otway heard was of making a severe example of the agitators.[1] Franquet was relieved of his post, and Zapatero and the local Moderados were preparing to act. Their first target was the militia, despite its correct behaviour during the strike. Two battalions were disarmed for a start, and arbitrary conduct by the authorities was complained of, especially nocturnal searches for arms in workmen's homes.[2]

Whatever their disillusionments the workers showed no disposition to throw their caps in the air for Carlos VI. The old movement fading out and the new one emerging in Catalonia overlapped, but could not coalesce. Carlism was making as little headway as before. Its great men would not draw their swords until there was something like an army for them to take command of ; but no army would start up without them. Still less were the princes ready to take the field, as they had talked of doing. They may have been awaiting the seizure of some strong point to serve for a miniature capital; it would be undignified as well as uncomfortable for Montemolín and Don Juan to go sneaking about like a pair of highwaymen. The revolt was frittering itself away, and reducing a mysterious unknown quantity to what now appeared in the light of day a mere nuisance.

Yet its leaders could not well afford to call it off, for conditions were never likely to be more propitious. Most in their favour of all was the breach between the Spanish government and the papacy. An open rupture had been delayed by French efforts; Turgot prevailed on Monsignor Franchi to postpone his departure, and buttonholed ministers to urge concessions.[3] None were forthcoming, and on 15 July Franchi presented a long schedule of grievances and asked for his passports.[4] Otway could see no sign of public opinion being shaken: 'On this occasion the cause of Rome has excited no sympathies, and only inspires a general

[1] Otway to Clarendon, no. 41, 17 July 1855, F.O. 72. 868.

[2] However, some workers sentenced to transportation overseas were removed only to Andalusia, to the distress of the party of order: E. Lagoanère, acting French consul, to Walewski, no. 185, 27 Aug. 1855; *Espagne*, Consular, vol. 52.

[3] Turgot to Walewski, no. 2, 17 June 1855, and no. 7, 12 July; *Espagne*, vol. 847.

[4] Franchi to Zabala, 15 July 1855: *Documentos relativos a las negociaciones*, no. 21 (p. 97).

indifference.'[1] The government drew up a counterblast to Franchi's statement, for circulation to all Catholic countries.[2] It was a masterly composition, the work of Cánovas del Castillo[3] who had been given a post in the foreign ministry, and whose conservatism included all the old Spanish stiffness against papal pretensions. It dwelt on the fact that there was more religious freedom in several other Catholic countries than in maligned Spain; sought to demolish the alleged contradictions between Concordat and disamortization law; and accused the Holy See of 'converting financial and administrative disputes into religious issues'.

Pius IX launched his own appeal to Catholic opinion in an allocution delivered on 26 July, in which he threatened to prohibit good Spaniards from buying Church lands and to withdraw recognition given to earlier alienations by the Concordat.[4] This might be reckoned his most formidable weapon, but it was also the likeliest to rouse the fighting spirit of Liberalism. A series of very free-spoken articles in the *Clamor Público* set the tone at Madrid. From less circumspect mouths came a volley of abuse of the 'King of Rome', or 'Mastai Ferretti', and anticlerical demonstrators had to be restrained from burning him in effigy on the Plaza Mayor. Had the Cortes been in session, public feeling might have swept the government into much more drastic action, with the tearing up of the Concordat for a start. It confined itself to publishing on 11 August its recent circular, and on the 21st its bulky mass of correspondence with Rome extending over the past year,[5] and on the same day closing the ecclesiastical court of the Rota, an appendage of the papal *nunciatura*.[6] There was glowing approval in the Progresista press, acrimonious dissent in the Moderado; the country seemed mostly on the government's side, or else apathetic, and the deepening quarrel with Rome brought little or no fresh support to Carlism. This was so even in Navarre, where a tourist found the lower clergy forming clandestine resistance groups and, their bishop being too timid for them,

[1] Otway to Clarendon, no. 46, 21 July 1855, F.O. 72. 868.
[2] *Documentos relativos a las negociaciones*, no. 24 (pp. 100–15).
[3] Pons y Umbert, *Cánovas del Castillo*, p. 455; cf. pp. 455–6.
[4] Text: *The Times*, 13 Aug. 1855, 10/3–4.
[5] *Documentos relativos a las negociaciones seguidas con la Santa Sede*; soon reprinted separately (Madrid, 1855).
[6] Decree of 21 Aug. 1855; C.L., vol. lxv, pp. 688–90. On the Rota, see P. Cantero, *La Rota española* (Madrid, 1946).

seeking 'the formidable sanction of the Jesuits'.[1] Grimberghe, the Belgian chargé, felt that Pius and Antonelli had overreached themselves;[2] they must have been coming reluctantly to the same conclusion. Only at the end of the year was a fresh papal rejoinder published, a diatribe portentous in length but throwing down no defiance to a more mortal combat.[3]

Altogether the government might congratulate itself on having staved off the challenge of the extreme Right; a challenge, as compared with that of Barcelona, from the dead or moribund past. On the other hand pressure from the Left was not proving strong or steady enough to have a transforming effect. This was partly due to the intrinsic difficulty of marshalling progressive forces in a country so scattered and variegated; of bringing together the heterogeneous discontents of the poorer middle classes and artisans, the peasantry, the new factory proletariat. But it was also partly due to lack of insight on the Left into the motive forces of the new age. Democrats who failed to foresee the social consequences of disamortization were failing likewise to bring to Liberalism a more realistic view of the problem of capital and labour. When they were accused in a debate later this year of flirting with socialism, Orense elaborately disclaimed any slightest leaning towards it. Talk of 'organization of labour', he said, seemed to him as idle as talk of organizing the winds.[4] Even the newer men of the party, preoccupied with social questions, were not getting beyond the vague idea, divorced from any militant struggle, of 'association'. In a pamphlet this year Garrido spoke of the workers supporting society by their toil, yet excluded from its benefits, and asked for aid for the sick and aged; but he thought little more would be needed once the country had a thrifty republican government that would allow everyone to prosper.[5]

In Barcelona and its neighbourhood things remained tense all through the summer, and closures of mills and depression in the textile trade were responsible for a good deal of unemployment. Elsewhere, too, discontents went on gathering outside the

[1] Anon., *Border Lands of Spain and France*, p. 63.
[2] Grimberghe to Vilain XIIII, no. 175, Conf., 23 Aug. 1855; *Espagne*, vol. 8 (2).
[3] Text in Canga Argüelles (y Villalta), *El gobierno español . . . con la Santa Sede*, pp. 253–374.
[4] D.S., pp. 5,432–5, 3 Dec. 1855.
[5] *La república democrática*, pp. 3, 25–26, 26–27.

recognized boundary of politics. Often it was through the militia
that they found expression, and the authorities were quick to take
any pretext for disarming or purging local units. This happened
for instance at Badajoz when some militiamen were accused of
taking part in a riotous demonstration. On such issues Democrats,
especially their 'extremists', did speak up. Sixto Cámara's newspaper was acquitted by a jury on 8 August for a strenuous article
condemning the militia purge at Barcelona; radicals like Madoz,
another Democrat was to complain, who made such a parade of
their own militia uniforms, turned a blind eye to what was being
done.[1]

The 'harlequin government', neither Progresista nor Moderado,[2] gave some of its disjointed thoughts this summer to the
idea of entering the war and sending an expeditionary force to the
Crimea. Drums and trumpets might help to banish dissension, as
they did a few years later in O'Donnell's Moroccan war; and, an
equal attraction, Allied subsidies might be forthcoming. Zabala
made himself chief proponent of the idea, and parleys were carried
on for several months. They ended in nothing. Spain at large
showed no anxiety to enter the war, while the extreme factions
were vigorously against it, on the Right from sympathy with
the Tsar, on the Left from lack of sympathy with Napoleon.
For their part the Allies were afraid of Spain asking too much
and giving too little, and the fall of Sevastopol on 8 September
lessened their need for help.

As the summer went on there was a certain relaxation. One
sedative was the hot weather, often as Turgot remarked a political
peacemaker.[3] Another was the cholera, still continuing. In Madrid
there were 1,738 fatal cases between May and the end of August.
Among healthier influences was a plentiful harvest, whose profits
must have strengthened both desire and ability to buy the land
that disamortization was making available. Auctions of *bienes
nacionales* were getting under way. Lists of properties figured
regularly in the *Gazette*, and the 230 million reals loan sanctioned
by the Cortes was helping to keep bidding brisk, since subscribers
could use their scrip for purchase-money. The loan itself was
going off unexpectedly well, and in the end only one-tenth had to

[1] Garrido, *Historia*, vol. iii, p. 276.
[2] *Clamor Público*, 18 Aug. 1855, 1/2–4.
[3] Turgot to Walewski, no. 11, 10 Aug. 1855; *Espagne*, vol. 847.

be collected compulsorily. This success was said to be partly the result of speculators buying up from smaller tax-payers their allotment of bonds;[1] and big land-buyers were also favoured as against small ones by high bidding at the sales. Over the coming year actual selling prices came to something like double the valuation figures.[2] Clerical obstruction was alleged to be impeding sales, and in some areas perhaps did so, but by and large the Roman thunder had little or no effect. Money was commencing to flow into the exchequer faster than it flowed out, a phenomenon as remarkable in Spain as water flowing uphill. By the end of the summer the extraordinary fact could be reported that 'the Treasury now religiously fulfils its obligations'.[3] It was even able to talk of paying regularly the salaries whose long arrears did so much to nourish clerical disaffection.[4] Things were positively so busy that office hours were lengthened from six to seven.

Nevertheless as 1 October, the date for the reassembling of the Cortes, drew nearer, it seemed unlikely that this ministry could stumble on much longer after coming under parliamentary fire again. Progresistas drew the moral that it was time to stiffen and reinvigorate it, Moderados that it was time to sweep it away. For the latter the first task was to try once more to put their party, or huddle of factions, together. During September there was much newspaper discussion of this. A joint committee was set up, but sectarian differences quickly arose; according to a story got hold of by opponents, Cristina at Paris was consulted, and wanted the San Luis group included, at which some of the more squeamish jibbed.[5] Efforts to get the party into order were to go on spasmodically to the end of the Bienio and after, and never with real success. Still, its newspapers were starting what was evidently a concerted onslaught on the government, and Progresistas were easily startled into supposing their enemies much more united than they really were: they saw the shadow of Narváez already looming over them. Reform had been neglected, reaction allowed a free hand, wrote the *Clamor Público*: all would be lost unless

---

[1] *Clamor Público*, 30 Aug. 1855, 1/2–3. Cf. Otway to Clarendon, no. 15, 30 June 1855, F.O. 72. 867: 'The capitalists of all parties are anxious to increase their money in the purchase of good estates.'
[2] See tables of figures in *Anuario estadístico* (1859), pp. 551 ff.
[3] Otway to Clarendon, no. 124, 1 Oct. 1855, F.O. 72. 870.
[4] Decree of 5 Oct. 1855; C.L., vol. lxvi, pp. 193–7.
[5] *Clamor Público*, 9 Sept. 1855, 1/3–5.

Espartero made up his mind to act firmly and O'Donnell to cast away all thought of a party of political runagates of his own.[1] Puros and Democrats were seeking afresh to consolidate the Left bloc, the 'Mountain', against the Right bloc apparently taking shape.

In the manœuvrings of the Right the Court was bound to be involved. Incense to throne as well as Church, and to the noble character of the present sovereign, formed a large part of Moderado stock in trade. But Isabel, like Espartero, was unmanageable as well as indispensable. Her daydreams of absolutism, and her flirtations with Carlism, were stumbling-blocks to any Moderado who saw himself—as Borrego urged the whole party to see itself—as conservative in a genuinely English, constitutional sense. All this summer contacts between the Court and Montemolín were kept up,[2] even if their seriousness was dwindling: Isabel could scarcely help realizing that her cousin was much less formidable whether as friend or foe than the *camarilla* had made her think him. A steady sibilation of intrigue was audible from the Escorial. Turgot heard that Don Francisco was plotting an escape and trying to induce Isabel to run away with him;[3] what political Gretna Green he wanted to elope to does not appear.

Government talk of a drastic purge of the royal household, renewed after the disamortization crisis, had accomplished as little as before; now another half-measure of reform was decided on. From early in September a remodelling of the Court on English lines was known to be intended. It took some time and the customary scrimmages and hysterics, with comings and goings of Espartero and O'Donnell between Madrid and the Escorial, before resistance was overborne. Then on 15 September a batch of four decrees made the chief posts about the sovereign political appointments at the discretion of the government of the day.[4] Spain was not England, cried the *España*, indignant at this degradation of monarchy.[5] Then on 25 September a Court secretary named Agustín Perales, who had been dismissed late in August,

---

[1] *Clamor Público*, 2 Oct. 1855, 1/1–2; cf. *Iberia*, 6 Oct. 1/1–3.

[2] 'Constante', p. 43.

[3] Turgot to Walewski, no. 12, 24 Aug. 1855; *Espagne*, vol. 847. Cf. *Iberia*, 14 Sept., 2/1.

[4] Decrees of 15 Sept. 1855; C.L., vol. lxvi, pp. 83–89. A few days later Espartero's friend Los Heros was confirmed in the post of *intendente general*, with increased responsibilities.

[5] 15 Sept. 1855, 3/3–5; 19 Sept., 2/5–3/3; &c.

was arrested. His papers had been searched, and a large number of copies of an unsigned manifesto discovered.[1] This showed reaction dabbling in new tactics: it talked of how Liberalism had neglected to give the people the reforms they fought for in 1854, and how the good Queen with better advisers meant to carry them out. There was great excitement in the press, but officially the affair was hushed up. Another opportunity to put the monarchy firmly in its place was being thrown away. Otway heard, however, that Don Francisco was 'dreadfully frightened', as always when caught at his little games, and was suing humbly for pardon.[2] His wife was in a mood of baffled fury, and suffered a miscarriage; a calamity for which loyal newspapers hastened to throw the blame on the brutality of a ruffianly government.

[1] See *Iberia*, 22 Sept. 1855, 1/4–5; *The Times*, 28 Sept., 8/1, and (with copies of this and other documents) 9 Oct., 8/1–2; Grimberghe to Vilain XIIII, no. 201, 25 Sept., *Espagne*, vol. 8 (2).
[2] Otway to Clarendon, private, 1 Oct. 1855; Clarendon Papers, vol. c. 28.

XIII

OPENING OF THE SECOND SESSION

Legislation and Party Manœuvres
October–December 1855

On the last evening of September, when Isabel returned to Madrid, Otway saw her 'most coldly received by the people'.[1] If her welcome was chilly, so was that of the deputies meeting next day to start their new session. Far more than half were still absent, chiefly from fear of the cholera; this inglorious prudence did much to depreciate the assembly in the eyes of the public, and was sternly rebuked by the press on both sides. A start was made on the business of going through the complete text of the Constitution, but not enough members were available for voting on it. Other matters were taken up while the benches slowly filled; and Puros and Democrats tried out their idea of a united front to break the political stalemate. On 3 October they set up a committee, of which Rivero was a member, to discuss co-operation. Clearly the first aim must be a reconstruction of the Cabinet: the question was how to get Espartero to agree, for a new Cabinet could be headed by no one else. Indolence and distaste for real responsibility made him deaf to advice. Before the end of the first week he was said to have refused a request to form a purely Progresista ministry. He had grown used to having O'Donnell at his elbow, and vanity helped to convince him that his War Minister was a rival no longer but a loyal as well as useful lieutenant.

Among radicals some kindred illusions about O'Donnell still lingered, though they were wearing thin. Democrats had regarded him all along as a wolf in sheep's clothing, and they were impatiently ready to denounce as renegades any Progresistas who baulked at joint action by the Left. Within their own ranks discord between the more cautious and the more headstrong was sharpening. Rivero in the Cortes, where Democrats were few and needed friends, was for moderation; Sixto Cámara outside, where

---

[1] Otway to Clarendon, no. 126, 1 Oct. 1855, F.O. 72. 870.

the movement felt stronger, was for plain speaking and action. Not surprisingly Puro feelings about them were always mixed. The *Iberia* could write as if it considered Moderados and Democrats equally disreputable; it could write also of Democrats as, after all, 'important members of the great Liberal family'.[1]

O'Donnell had ready a bill fixing the army's strength for the coming year at 70,000, the same as its present authorized figure.[2] This total had in reality been heavily exceeded, if Zabala was telling the truth when he told Howden in June that the number of men had been brought up to 90,000.[3] Moreover, the Cortes had passed a law to reorganize the 'provincial militia' or territorial reserve force of 60,000.[4] Orense could argue cogently that a total of 50,000 for the regular army would be quite adequate. O'Donnell made play with the Carlist revolt, and with the possibility of Spain being drawn into the Crimean war. This was by now faint, and the revolt was petering out: it was virtually ended by the capture and execution of two of the guerrilla chiefs dodging about Catalonia, Gonfaus or 'Marsal' and Mas. Carlism was vanishing like a ghost at cockcrow from the province it had haunted so long.

In spite of this O'Donnell's bill was allowed to pass without a division;[5] and when another, on army recruitment, came up, a proposal to abolish conscription met with depressingly little support.[6] A professional army would have been even less amenable to civil control, and the best thing might have been a remodelling of the existing system, with a much shorter term of duty, more room for promotion from the ranks, and humaner conditions. As it was, the bill as finally adopted brought no real change. Service was still to be performed for eight years in the line or the reserve, by men chosen by lot. Exemption could be bought, as before, for 6,000 reals. Propertied families had no mind to let their own sons go through the mill; and while they could evade it, service was certain to remain nasty, brutish, and long. The *Clamor Público* lamented that the national militia was being whittled down at the

---

[1] 14 Nov. 1855, 1/1–4; 20 Nov., 1/3–5. The *Clamor Público*, 22 Nov., 1/1–2, also expressed regret at Democrat divisions.

[2] Text: App. 1 to D.S., no. 210, 3 Oct. 1855.

[3] Howden to Clarendon, no. 260, Conf., 22 June 1855, F.O. 72. 867.

[4] Law of 31 July 1855; C.L., vol. lxv, pp. 564–75.

[5] Debate: D.S., pp. 4,579–89. Final text: law of 21 Nov. 1855; C.L., vol. lxvi, p. 377.

[6] Discussion ended on 27 Nov.; final text: App. 6 to D.S., no. 300, 28 Jan. 1856.

same time as the army was being built up. It repeated a charge often made that militia units were kept short of muskets,[1] and it criticized a fresh purge at Seville.[2]

November brought an abrupt clearing up of the epidemic in this region. Madrid heaved a sigh of relief, attended a Te Deum, and reopened its theatres. On the 7th the Cortes felt sufficiently itself again to push on with the Constitution. But its first act was to allow two sections of a minority draft by Lasala and Valera to be eliminated by a procedural manœuvre.[3] They granted unrestricted rights of association and of peaceful meeting. Deputies were relieved at being able to shuffle them out of sight; Barcelona must have overshadowed many of their minds.

On 18 October Olózaga had returned from Paris. Some thought that his friends had persuaded him to come and head the left-wing bloc; others that his own ambitions were prompting him to another essay at acquiring power. He was taking a conspicuous part in the budget committee's work; but it was characteristic of him that the chief episode in his campaign turned on a constitutional nicety. Article 6 of the Constitution declared all Spaniards eligible for all offices. An embarrassing addition was framed by a Left group including Democrats and Madoz: that titles of nobility should not be a condition for any post under the government or—the real sting—in the palace.[4] Figueras moved it, calling to mind the humble birth of the great Ximénez. O'Donnell called to mind Figueras's republican vote of last November. Olózaga announced that he and the majority of the drafting commission accepted the amendment, in the conviction that no sentiment was more deeply rooted in Spain than that of equality. Every country likes to fancy itself in some kind of way more egalitarian than its neighbours. Zabala was indiscreet enough to tell him in a voice audible to members sitting near them that he had no right as a public servant to go against the government's views. Olózaga tendered his resignation on the spot.[5]

Here a principle of very real importance was at stake. Every Cortes contained many placemen, and ministers had often claimed

---

[1] 15 Nov. 1855, 3/5.   [2] 6 Nov. 1855, 1/4.
[3] See D.S., pp. 4,958–9.
[4] For this amendment and the discussion on it see D.S., pp. 4,988–90.
[5] Howden to Clarendon, no. 305, Conf., 10 Nov. 1855, F.O. 72. 870, with two enclosed notes from Olózaga to Howden. Other accounts in *Iberia*, 9 Nov., 1/5–2/1; *España*, 10 Nov., 3/2.

the disposal of all their votes. San Luis was much abused for dismissing parliamentary opponents from public posts. An energetic stand now might secure a definite condemnation of this practice: Zabala's words might also be made to cost him his Cabinet seat, and there seemed a chance of O'Donnell being pulled down with him. The fight over Article 6 was waged in earnest. Rivero declared, with his party's tendency to over-simplify, that all the history of the past half-century was one of conflict, costing torrents of blood, between palace and people. Democrats nevertheless were clearly anxious not to overstrain the alliance of the Left, and several of them gave an assurance that they loyally accepted the decision to retain the monarchy. Ordax Avecilla added an eloquent appeal for unity among all progressives. Shoulder to shoulder they were irresistible; unhappily a hidden enemy was at work to sow dissension among them.

Next day the hidden enemy rose to his long thin legs and counter-attacked, and it was a long time before the House got back to Article 6 and Olózaga could wind up and win the debate with a brilliant speech.[1] The Left bloc had made some progress; Democrat acceptance of constitutional monarchy and methods of legality was welcomed by the Puro press as erasing a barrier. By the more intransigent Democrats on the other hand the statements of their deputies were hotly repudiated. And the crisis that had been set off was fizzling out, because Olózaga could not make up his mind. 'I can not conceive what he is at', his friend Howden wrote privately to Clarendon.[2] His resignation was declined in flattering terms, and on 25 November he withdrew it. Not only was the ministry left intact, but the principle that it had no right to coerce deputies by threatening them with dismissal had not, after all, been vindicated.

Few members had much appetite left—Ríos Rosas was unquenchable—for prolix discussion of the Constitution, though a good many clauses were sent back to the commission for redrafting. All this must come to an end some time, the *España* reflected philosophically, because nothing in our world lasts for ever.[3] Article 38 gave the lower House more definitely the chief voice in finance

[1] For this debate, from 14 to 21 Nov., see D.S., pp. 5,100 ff., 5,112 ff. 5,158 ff., 5,182 ff.
[2] Howden to Clarendon, private, 23 Nov. 1855; Clarendon Papers, vol. c. 28. Howden exerted himself to reconcile Olózaga and the government.
[3] 28 Nov. 1855, 3/4-5.

bills. No. 46 embodied the rule this assembly had bound itself by that members must seek re-election if they accepted place, pay, or decoration from either government or Court. No. 52 on the royal prerogative was approved in spite of criticism of the large powers it still left to the Crown, including the right 'freely' to appoint and dismiss ministers. At the end of November another portion of the Lasala–Valera draft was reached, providing for various social services and in particular for free primary education and State poor-relief. Valera reminded the House in a long speech that monastic charity, formerly the last refuge of the poor, had been swept away.[1] He had to listen to himself, said the *España* sarcastically, in order to have an audience,[2] and more sedate deputies treated his ideas as laudable but visionary. All the same the proposals secured the not unpromising total of 60 votes against 109.

Some winding-up clauses were designed to make alteration of the precious new Constitution as difficult as possible. The seven organic laws were still wanting, and local elections due now had therefore to be put off again. However, on 14 December at 6.45 p.m. the 92 articles of the Constitution proper, the distilled wisdom of Progresismo, stood complete.[3] It was coming too late to be hailed with any outburst of rejoicing; even now it was not promulgated, and controversy about whether it should be brought into force straightaway, or kept back until the organic laws were ready, was never to be settled. Fear of a dissolution cutting short the assembly's work continued to offer a persuasive reason for delay.

Long before the last i's and t's of the Constitution were dotted and crossed, more mundane questions were breaking in. Finance was as always the most troublesome. Disamortization was going well, but its receipts could come in only slowly. On the first day of the session Bruil had submitted his proposals for the eighteen months beginning next January:[4] they included an increase in the land-tax, and restoration of the *puertas* and *consumos*. Moderados noted with gloomy relish that the total to be spent was bigger than in any of their years in office; they were delighted to welcome the excise taxes back. From the radical press there were angry

---

[1] For the discussion, on 28–30 Nov., see D.S., pp. 5,338, 5,349 ff., 5,369 ff.
[2] 30 Nov. 1855, 3/4.
[3] Text in Muro Martínez, vol. i, pp. 167–80.
[4] They took the form of a budget bill and three appended bills, Apps. 16 to 19 to D.S., no. 208, 1 Oct. 1855.

outcries, and Bruil was accused of letting himself be led by reactionary officials. Many Progresistas must have felt that to restore the
hated taxes would be shameful treatment of the people who had
put them in power; others that whether shameful or not it would
be highly imprudent. Some perhaps were reminded of one of the
brighter witticisms of *Padre Cobos*: 'What is left of the revolution
of July? Its causes.'[1] It was speedily apparent that there was no
chance of getting the budget passed before the end of the year,
and the government had to obtain leave to go on collecting taxes
provisionally, as it had done a year since.

On 9 November Bruil suddenly tabled legislation to dismantle
the State monopolies of salt and tobacco at the end of the next
budgetary period.[2] Deputies rubbed their eyes, said the *Clamor
Público* next day, and wondered whether they were asleep or awake
or listening to a tale from the Arabian Nights.[3] Here at last was
a popular proposal, on which Liberal faith in private enterprise
chimed in with the feelings of the man in the street. Nobody
except the legion of smugglers would object. But it would only
be feasible if the revenue sacrificed could be made good, and the
most attractive source was the expanded income that import duties
would yield if more foreign goods were allowed to enter. On 16
November Bruil read a lengthy tariff bill to an absorbed House.[4]
Olózaga became chairman of the select committee, to which every
vested interest and every region with anything to gain or lose at
once began noisily putting its case. One commodity Howden, as
active a lobbyist as any, hoped to get admitted duty-free was coal;
this was objected to by owners of the Spanish mines at this time
'really beginning to be worked', and was effectively blocked by
the members for Asturias in the Cortes.[5] Small in scale and primitive in equipment,[6] the Asturian mines were certainly in no shape
to face serious competition.

Over *bacalao*, or dried cod, a staple article of diet for the
labouring classes, Howden was foiled by the navy, concerned
for Spanish fisheries as 'a nursery of seamen'.[7] But the most

---

[1] 15 May 1855, p. 3.   [2] Apps. 4 and 5 to D.S., no. 240, 9 Nov. 1855.
[3] 10 Nov. 1855, 1/3–4. It questioned Bruil's sincerity.
[4] App. 19 to D.S., no. 245, 16 Nov. 1855.
[5] Howden to Clarendon, no. 306, 10 Nov. 1855, F.O. 72. 870.
[6] See M. Mayo de la Fuente, *Memoria acerca de . . . la Compañía del Ferro-carril de Langreo* (Madrid, 1856), p. 12.
[7] Howden to Clarendon, no. 318, 23 Nov. 1855, F.O. 72. 871.

controversial items were textiles. Argument ran very high between deputies from Catalonia and from Andalusia; the latter having no manufactures to protect would benefit by cheaper imports and hoped besides for reciprocal benefits to exports of wine. A delegation from the cotton-masters of Barcelona was in Madrid, urging Catalan members to do their duty and save their province from ruin. In a statement by the provincial council of Barcelona much was made of the massive unemployment that would result from the crippling of industry.[1] One of the cotton delegates at Madrid developed this theme further when Howden had him to dinner. Catalonia, he said, was 'in a most precarious state, overrun with the purest and indeed most ferocious doctrines of Socialism and ready for an outbreak of the most dangerous kind'.[2] Such highly flavoured accounts were useful for extorting concessions from a nervous ministry. Even in much quieter times it was almost an axiom that talk of tariff reform at Madrid meant rioting at Barcelona, where employers had only to close their mills and throw the blame on the government.[3] By the end of the year Bruil's tariff bill, like his budget, had been brought to a standstill.

Obstruction by millowners could have been faced more firmly if Liberalism had been doing more in other ways to win the confidence of mill-workers. But social legislation on industry was not destined to make even a weak start in Spain for another ten years.[4] Nothing had come of the promises to the strikers this summer of a fair deal once they went back to work, except a bill got ready by Alonso Martínez whose wordy preamble seemed to attribute all the disputes to 'false and perilous doctrines, specious Utopias'. It agreed that child labour ought to be stopped; and it paid lip service to the right of association, while effectively nullifying it by requiring official licence for any kind of union.[5] A distinguished select committee was chosen to go into the bill, with Madoz chairman.[6] Delegates of the Barcelona workers, whom the

---

[1] Carrera Pujal, vol. iv, p. 314.

[2] Howden to Clarendon, no. 379, 25 Dec. 1855, F.O. 72. 871.

[3] Fear of Espartero giving in to free-trade pressure was considered to have done much to turn Barcelona against him in 1842–3.

[4] Martín-Granizo, part 4, pp. 59–60. He dismisses the bill of Oct. 1855 as mere window-dressing (ibid., p. 38); cf. Escalera and González Llana, vol. iv., pp. 211-13.

[5] App. 1 to D.S., no. 214, 8 Oct. 1855.

[6] A similar committee under Madoz had been set up in January to harmonize the

employers were trying to inveigle into company unions, were given long hearings, and made a marked impression. But their efforts were thrown away: the committee was still ruminating when the Bienio came to an end. Matters of greater interest to investors were being dealt with more expeditiously. An Ebro canalization project started in 1851 and held up like many others by want of funds was authorized to raise fresh capital.[1] Attention was given to new railway plans. For Spaniards whose narrow horizons were bounded by day-wages, the value of such things lay in the jobs they might provide. The Bienio was unlucky in nothing so much as in its weather; this autumn and winter rain cascaded over the country. In Madrid province roads were disappearing, the capital was almost marooned. Before the end of October crowds of labourers were clamouring for work, which had to be promised. At Seville in December the river rose and inundated the town, crammed with farm-hands whom four months of rain had driven there in search of relief.[2]

All this was aggravated by the spectacle of food still flowing out of Spain. Ministers wondered whether to follow the example of France and ban further exports,[3] but decided to do nothing, on the orthodox principle that it was futile to interfere with the free movement of grain. As winter came on there was a recrudescence of the elemental unrest of last winter and spring: it broke out first at Saragossa. There as in other regions food prices were rising rapidly, and on 11 November the sight of boatloads of wheat about to be shipped off down the Ebro for export set a match to the town's inflammable temper.[4] About 5 p.m. noisy groups, swelling into tumultuous crowds, began to gather, and the barges came under attack. When the militia was mobilized some of its

interests of capital and labour (decree of 10 Jan. 1855; C.L., vol. lxiv, pp. 32–36); it did little.

[1] Law of 16 Nov. 1855; C.L., vol. lxvi, pp. 364–5.

[2] Guichot, vol. v, p. 65; and see a description of the Seville floods in A. de Latour, *La baie de Cadix* (Paris, 1858), pp. 28 ff.

[3] Howden to Clarendon, no. 272, 21 Oct. 1855, F.O. 72. 870. Britain was anxious not to be prevented from buying Spanish food. Since 1834 export of grain had been allowed freely, import only when prices rose above a certain level; see Álvarez, p. 10.

[4] On the day's events see the statement by Huelves, Minister of the Interior, on 12 Nov. 1855: D.S., pp. 5,045–6; detail from Saragossa press in *Clamor Público*, 17 Nov., 1/3–5 and 18 Nov., 1/5–2/6; Escalera and González Llana, vol. iv, pp. 206–7; Pirala, vol. ii, p. 252; Pi, *Historia*, vol. iv, p. 133.

units were accused of making common cause with the rioters. Gurrea, the captain-general, had a thousand or so troops available, but rather than risk a head-on collision he preferred to hold them back and wait. For three days Saragossa was in possession of the armed people; yet none of the 'anarchy' so often talked of was to be seen. Militia representatives were chosen to discuss the situation with the town council, and on the 12th drew up a remonstrance to the Cortes, complaining that the promise of the revolution was still unfulfilled.

Gurrea was making careful preparations: his delay exposed him to charges of 'blameable weakness', as Howden considered it,[1] but enabled him to manage without any fighting when at 8 a.m. on the 16th his forces suddenly occupied key points and recovered control of the town. As at Barcelona the militia was treated as the chief offender, and a big proportion of names were struck off the rolls, while heavy reinforcements of troops were drafted in. Conservatives wanted more. Firm repression was the only alternative to 'the completest subversion of all social principles', exclaimed the *España*.[2] Radical editors drew the opposite moral that the outbreak was a warning to the government to return to genuinely progressive courses. In between was the stock reaction of old-fashioned Liberalism, that it was all the doing of a few agitators, or criminals, or Carlists.[3]

As to the Cortes, so eloquent just now on Article 6 and equality, it seemed strangely taciturn about this more tangible question. Deputies from Saragossa found as little to say as those from Barcelona in July. One of them of course was Espartero, whom the others would not wish to embarrass. It was Orense who took the matter up, by way of protest, he said, against the habit growing on the assembly of ignoring what was happening in the country:[4] though he himself was inclined to see the affair too exclusively in political terms, with O'Donnell as root cause of all the dissatisfaction plaguing Spain. This was only part of the truth, for on issues like food policy there was no great difference between O'Donnell and his critics. Orense's interpellation on 1 December had little to do with food or with Saragossa; it was a plain-spoken attack on

---

[1] Howden to Clarendon, no. 317, 21 Nov. 1855, F.O. 72. 870.

[2] 13 Nov. 1855, 3/4–5; 17 Nov., 3/3–4.

[3] Borao's continuation of Cortada, vol. ii, p. 291, puts the riot down to criminal elements.

[4] D.S., p. 5,199, 22 Nov. 1855.

the War Minister, who defended himself with equal vigour.[1] Two right-wing Liberals intervened with a motion of confidence in O'Donnell. Homage to a single minister had an unparliamentary look, and by this time Progresistas who had been clinging to the hope that he was really and truly with them were unable to disguise their uneasiness. Calvo Asensio moved an amendment that the House had confidence in O'Donnell under the conviction that he was firmly attached to Progresismo: a clever attempt to force him out into the open, which he evaded with one more allusion to the manifesto of Manzanares as the proof of his bona fides. Progresistas were left suspicious and uncertain. The motion was carried by 132 to 8; Corradi and Madoz voted for it, but Calvo Asensio abstained, and so did 70 or 80 others.[2]

Their uneasiness was deepened by the resignation on 7 December of Ignacio Gurrea, a portentous event because he was 'generally considered as the alter ego of the Duke de la Victoria'.[3] Whether forced on him, or caused by resentment at the criticism of his Fabian tactics, it drew from the *Clamor Público* the remark that Espartero's best friends were drifting out of politics.[4] O'Donnell's success had cost him something, however; he had been compelled to give further offence to Moderados, to whom any mention of Manzanares was a red rag, and he still had to gather a following of his own. Of late there had been talk of a 'third party', a grouping neither Progresista nor Moderado, with him for its natural chief, and the vote of confidence gave it a fillip. Radicals saw it as an exhumation of Liberal Union; Moderados talked of its lack of any binding principle, and of the new Constitution as a gulf between them and it. But a shift of power one way or the other was looking even more inevitable than at the start of the session. The *Nación* stood almost alone in professing to find the situation thoroughly satisfactory;[5] this paper had grown notoriously more ministerial than the ministry itself.

O'Donnell was taken seriously ill at a palace ball on 20 December, and his life was feared for. At the same time his friend Ros de Olano was in danger of losing his inspectorship of infantry; he had let his tongue wag tactlessly about the 'third party', and given

[1] For the debate see D.S., pp. 5,397–413.
[2] On this debate see D.S., pp. 5,416–48, 3 Dec. 1855.
[3] *The Times*, 18 Dec. 1855, 8/5; cf. Gebhardt, vol. vi, p. 1,090.
[4] 12 Dec. 1855, 1/2.
[5] 2 Jan. 1856, 1/1–3; 5 Jan., 1/1–4.

offence to Espartero.[1] What saved the Vicalvarists was the failure of the Left bloc during these three months to develop sufficient cohesion to be able to take command. A good part of the blame belonged to Olózaga. At the end of the year he was going away again, to the disappointment of all who had depended on him for leadership, though he may have counted on being called back very soon to choose his own place in a new Cabinet. His parting shot—if it was correctly traced to him—was typical of the tactics of skirmish and ambuscade on which too much time was frittered away. He was supposed to have got the department of Justice to concoct some change in the form of special marriage dispensations. Madrid was at once agog with a rumour that civil marriage was being introduced, to the utter ruination of religion and morality.[2] This was awkward for the Cabinet, especially for O'Donnell. He, however, survived both illness and intrigue. Zabala held the fort for him, and Isabel lent a helping hand in defence of holy matrimony. Olózaga was delaying his entry into the Liberal government until there would no longer be one for him to enter. An historian was to date from this point the decline of his career;[3] that of his party ran parallel with it.

[1] *España*, 25 Dec. 1855, 3/2; *Soberanía* (now officially the title of the *Soberanía Nacional*), 10 Jan. 1856, 1/3.

[2] See on the episode *Annuaire des Deux Mondes*, 1855–6, p. 272; C. de Mazade, *Les révolutions de l'Espagne contemporaine (1854–68)* (Paris, 1869), pp. 97–98; Miraflores, *Continuación*, vol. i, pp. 736–7; I. Bermejo, *La estafeta de Palacio* (2nd ed., Madrid, 1872), vol. iii, p. 454; A. Matilla, *Olózaga, el precoz demagogo* (Madrid, 1933), pp. 168–9.

[3] Bermejo, *Estafeta*, vol. iii, p. 449.

XIV

LIBERALISM ON THE EBB

Government Inertia and Public Impatience
January–February 1856

Now as when the previous Cabinet collapsed in June 1855, popular tumult proved more effective than subtle intrigue. It began with a petition to the Cortes signed by two or three thousand Saragossans which complained that the country was being kept waiting for its reforms by an unworkable coalition.[1] Petitions as a means of putting pressure on the government were distasteful to many deputies as well as to all ministers, and on 5 January there was a vote against this one being considered. On the 7th the Democrats made a spirited effort to reverse it. It was undeniable, Figueras argued, that revolution principles had been adulterated. The right of meeting was being interfered with, that of association withheld. Sooner or later at this rate an exasperated people would rush to arms. Liberals would then have to choose between anarchy and reaction, and, he went on dramatically, he and his friends would choose the path of Catiline—they would go beyond Catiline, who by freeing the slaves could have broken the patrician power for ever.

His resolution was defeated by 128 to 38, and the House was grappling with a bill on banking when all of a sudden it was told that shots were being fired outside.[2] Guard duty at the Cortes building was always performed by militiamen, and today's picket was rioting. A mysterious sergeant, Mayor, was ringleader; shouts for Saragossa and a republic, some of them with an alcoholic flavour, were heard; one officer received a bayonet scratch. Deputies who hurried to the entrance were jostled and insulted, and a sense of imminent disaster spread round the

[1] Petition no. 883; see D.S., p. 6,005.
[2] The rest of the session is covered by D.S., pp. 6,042–5. Madrid press accounts over the next few days add little reliable detail. See also on the episode *The Times*, 15 Jan. 1856 (Madrid 8 Jan.), 5/3; Escalera and González Llana, vol. iv, pp. 215–16; Pi, *Historia*, vol. iv, pp. 135–6.

benches. Espartero was at home, O'Donnell away ill. Figueras must have been as startled as anyone to see his thunder followed so instantly by the lightning-flash of revolt. He got up again to denounce the brawlers, and proclaimed his party's readiness to perish with its fellow legislators like Marcus Papirius in the curule chair. All the House applauded this swift change of front. Eighteen years later when Figueras was first minister of the Republic and all Spain in an uproar like the steps of the Cortes now, he would play neither Catiline nor Papirius, but catch a train to France.

Alonso Martínez and Escosura followed with similar bursts of the heroic; the early dusk drew on; confused rumours were running through the town. At last Espartero appeared on the scene, and addressed the tense assembly with a brevity which for once it must have found truly majestic. He would quell this riot or perish—'Whilst I breathe, nobody and nothing shall molest the Cortes.' His name had not lost its glamour for those who worshipped from afar, as it had for all who saw him at close quarters, and the riot collapsed at once. No further disturbances took place, but the Cabinet met at 10 p.m., and the military authorities began rounding up the mutineers.

Democrats of course came under suspicion; one foreign observer dwelt on the growth of their local associations, organized on French models and with extensive membership in Madrid and other big towns.[1] The culprits belonged to the 2nd Company of the 3rd Light Battalion, considered 'very "advanced" if not "red" in its principles'.[2] Lurid intentions were ascribed to them, some of which were to pass into accepted legend. While musket-fire emptied the ministerial benches, writes one historian, those deputies who were in the plot were to have seized power and proclaimed a republic.[3] If any such thing had really been intended, there was nothing to prevent it; and the Democrats inside were quite obviously taken by surprise. Their own interpretations of the affair later on were oddly contradictory.[4] Other suspicions fell

---

[1] Grimberghe to Vilain XIIII, no. 8, 9 Jan. 1856; *Espagne*, vol. 9.

[2] Howden to Clarendon, no. 14, 10 Jan. 1856, F.O. 72. 891.

[3] Pirala, vol. ii, p. 270; cf. 'Constante', pp. 56–57, and Becker, *Reforma*, pp. 121–2.

[4] Pi depicts Mayor as an irresponsible drunkard; E. García Ruiz writes similarly in *Dios y el hombre* (Madrid, 1863), p. 321, but in *Historias*, vol. ii, p. 584, he says Mayor was instigated by reactionaries. Garrido curiously calls the affair a bold and well-planned attempt at 'a popular *coup d'état*': *Historia*, vol. iii, pp. 279–80.

on reactionary agencies, including the Moderado party and even the palace. On the whole it seems most likely that the riot was a clumsy popular demonstration; an outburst of impatience as the *Soberanía* called it, 'un ay! de desesperación'.[1] Public and politicians were drifting fatally apart, Liberal mistrust of the masses was deepening month by month.

Rumours and scares multiplying after the riot further shook the flimsy Cabinet, and so did disagreements about what to do with the men arrested. Some wanted a court martial, others feared to antagonize the militia as a body; in the end proceedings dropped out of sight. On 13 January political Madrid was electrified by news that all ministers except the two 'Consuls' were tendering their resignations. What the *Clamor Público* referred to as 'the sacred college of the régime' was to hold a 'conclave' that evening:[2] the elder statesmen, Infante, Luzuriaga, González, Luxán, Portilla, and, despite his membership of the Córdova ministry of 1854, Gómez de Laserna. Cabinet-making was getting harder. Gómez de Laserna declined two portfolios, from motives of delicacy he explained in a self-complacent speech:[3] but González and Infante also declined foreign affairs,[4] which had to be left in the incompetent hands of Zabala. Bruil and Antonio Santa Cruz survived as well, and only three changes were announced on the 16th. Luxán took over again the portfolio of Development which he held in the first period of the Bienio. Justice went to Arias Uría, a respectable but very obscure old magistrate of whom, wrote Howden, 'literally, nobody appears ever to have heard': three newspapers ironically begged readers to tell them who he was.[5] Huelves gave up the Interior to Escosura, whose chief value to the government would be his uncommon brilliance as a debater; it had been known to wring applause from the leathery lips of Narváez himself.[6] This Moderado of not many years ago was still a Moderado, the *Soberanía* maintained, at heart.[7] Nowadays he sometimes took a radical, especially an

---

[1] 8 Jan. 1856, 1/1–3; an issue of a single sheet, the paper having been seized at 3.30 a.m. It applauded Figueras's first speech.
[2] 15 Jan. 1856, 1/1–2.   [3] D.S., p. 6,217, 16 Jan. 1856.
[4] Howden to Clarendon, no. 22, 17 Jan. 1856, F.O. 72. 891.
[5] Ibid.   [6] Wallis, *Spain*, pp. 151–2.
[7] 17 Jan. 1856, 1/1–2. A sketch of Escosura in E. Tajueco Gallardo, *El libro de los diputados, ó fisonomía del Congreso de 1851* (Madrid, 1851–2), part 1, pp. 200–6, begins: 'What is apostasy?' Cf. Rico y Amat, *Libro*, vol. iv, pp. 115–26; and P. de Luz, *Isabelle II, reine d'Espagne* (Paris, 1934), p. 217.

anti-clerical tone; but his ruling quality was to be everything by fits, and his character inspired as little confidence as the talents of the Santones.

Taken all round the reshuffle could be viewed as a slight shift in the conservative direction. Progresista newspapers were disgusted, even the least hard to please of them, all the more because the changes had been carried out, as in the previous June, behind the assembly's back; and many deputies besides disappointed aspirants felt that there ought to be some protest. Espartero made a statement on the 16th of a bare hundred hazy words; that night a meeting of Puro and Democrat members agreed on the terms of a motion rejecting it as inadequate.[1] Sagasta, chosen as mover, took as his main target the frustrating coalition, necessary when first formed after the revolution but now merely confusing and obstructive. Each party ought to stand on its own and peacefully take its turn in office[2]—words oddly suggestive of the game of Tweedledum and Tweedledee that Sagasta and Cánovas were to play after 1875. O'Donnell, not Espartero, replied; he was followed by Escosura, who spoke of the 'red Mountain' and 'white Mountain' as two extremes equally obnoxious. There were 57 votes for the motion, 152 against. A number of those who had voted against the government were dismissed forthwith from their official employments. When its action was challenged in the House both O'Donnell and Escosura brazenly defended it.[3] Thus the Progresista government was openly practising the tactics of its Moderado predecessor, and against its own radicals. The bad effect of this coercion on the assembly's morale was soon patent.

On 19 January the front bench had to face an interpellation by Rivero, on the general condition of the country. His elaborate speech gave the fullest exposition yet heard of the views of the more moderate Democrat section, vowed to legality and to close links with the Progresista party. Spain, he asserted, was drifting towards chaos: it was drifting because reform was frustrated by the government's dualism, O'Donnell being to all intents a Moderado. But Democracy, 'the conciliator of all interests and classes', must be careful never to condone violence. It was the incendiarism of 1848 that provoked reaction in France. After half

---

[1] *Nación*, 18 Jan. 1856, 1/1.
[2] D.S., pp. 6,229–31; rest of the debate: D.S., pp. 6,231–7.
[3] D.S., pp. 6,274–6, 19 Jan. 1856.

a century of conflict Spain needed an orderly public life; and if the time came when he and his friends could no longer agree with the Duke of Victory, rather than act against him they would retire from politics.[1] Democrats of the other persuasion listened with marked distaste to some of Rivero's arguments; his conclusion was indeed remarkably unhelpful. O'Donnell parried the attack by denying that his 1854 movement was a Moderado one. 'The Moderado party had committed suicide.' Escosura opened one of his pungent debating performances by asking how he could answer such an exercise as Rivero's in philosophy and theory. Espartero got up, under some prompting perhaps, to corroborate O'Donnell's statement that there had been no antagonism between the two of them.

Cabinet-shuffling had an epilogue in February when Bruil resigned at last. He had officiated for eight months, a whole lifetime comparatively. Sánchez Silva had been talked of as a successor, but the post went instead to Francisco Santa Cruz, Minister of the Interior before June 1855. Espartero was surrounded, the *Novedades* commented, by the same men who steered the Progresista party to shipwreck in 1843: younger men were given no chance.[2] This suited O'Donnell very well indeed, and allowed him to keep up a while longer his balancing and trimming. His 'third party' was hanging fire; but he could afford to give Liberalism time to run down. He was already becoming *de facto* head of the Cabinet. 'O'Donnell is the person who really rules and resumes the Government in himself', Howden wrote this month.[3] Espartero was content to enjoy the parades and ceremonies where he could wrap the people's breath round him like a warm cloak. It was on 9 March that he perpetrated a piece of eloquence satirists never let him forget, when he pledged himself to be with his militia regiment of lancers in the hour of danger, and went on, plagiarizing Henri Quatre: 'The white plume of my helmet will be your beacon . . . .'[4] His white plume was jam for *Padre Cobos*, which lampooned all Progresistas and the unlucky duke in particular mercilessly. Not General O'Donnell, it said, but general dissatisfaction, was the enemy Espartero had to fear.[5]

[1] D.S., pp. 6,278–87. Rest of the debate: pp. 6,287–99.
[2] 23 Jan. 1856, 1/1–3; 8 Feb. 1/1–2. Cf. Sanromá, vol. ii, pp. 278–9.
[3] Howden to Clarendon, no. 39, 6 Feb. 1856, F.O. 72. 891.
[4] *Clamor Público*, 11 Mar. 1856, 1/1–2.   [5] 25 Jan. 1856, p. 4.

Democrats abused O'Donnell more and more loudly: the *Soberanía* loudest of all, in spite of his having just won a libel suit which cost the paper a stiff fine and its 'responsible editor' (a whipping-boy always useful to opposition papers) a long sentence. Progresistas alarmed by their party's demoralized state wavered between thoughts of an alliance of the Left against O'Donnell, and of sticking to him as not the worst of evils. The *Clamor Público* felt that he and Espartero had been together so long that it would be hazardous to part them: only their union, with all its disadvantages, held at bay the common enemies of all Liberals.[1] What this amounted to was that so long as Espartero was prime minister, his party would be safe in power, but only on condition of not trying to make any use of it. Corradi had given up control of the paper some months since, and now accepted a diplomatic sinecure and went off to Lisbon with a Golden Fleece for Marshal Saldanha.

Reluctance to break with O'Donnell must have been strengthened by nervousness about what the army might do without him to control it; and there was the question of what the discontented masses might do without the army to control them. An invincible new force, wrote a pamphleteer, was taking the place of Carlism all over the peninsula—hunger. He accused Progresistas, much addicted to styling themselves 'sons of the people', of saying in effect to the famished poor: 'There is nothing we can do for you, absolutely nothing. . . . Just be patient!'[2] Patience was giving way; the Saragossa disturbance was followed by others, some trivial and some more grave. Bad weather was once again the immediate cause. In the first weeks of the year Seville was still encircled by water, and food had to be distributed. Seventeen drowned corpses floated into Aranjuez, a macabre *memento mori* to that royal seat. Only late in February did the weather clear up sufficiently to allay fears of widespread famine.

At Barcelona, where 'socialistic' influences could always be blamed and authority had more of a free hand to display what it called 'energy', a fresh bout of industrial strife was followed by summary executions. O'Donnell justified these in the Cortes; so did Prim, who talked of 'a direct attack on Property', with national ruin not far behind.[3] More civilized counsels prevailed at Malaga

---

[1] 3 Feb. 1856, 1/1–2; 17 Feb., 1/2–4.
[2] Busto, pp. 79–80; cf. p. 64.   [3] D.S., p. 6,297.

when a multitude of peasants, washed out of their homes by the rains, flocked into the city on the night of 8 January demanding a levy of contributions from the rich, and were joined by some of the poorer and unemployed townsfolk. The governor rode about the streets and averted a clash by means of firm warnings combined with promises of bread and rice-soup. Escosura as Minister of the Interior circulated instructions that because of financial stringency relief was to be given only in cases of direst necessity, but local authorities should provide as much employment as they could, at subsistence wages.[1] Unluckily local funds for public works were also scanty. Not until this March did government and assembly find time to complete a bill regulating the surcharges on national taxes which now provided the bulk of local revenue.[2] In Madrid a demonstration outside the town hall led to money being found for a programme of road-building.

Unrest among the urban masses was reflected as before in the mood of the militia. When a riotous protest against a local tax took place at the beginning of the year at Alcoy, a town in Alicante province with some paper manufacture, militiamen who were called out, some themselves workmen, sided with the demonstrators, and the governor had to put in an appearance with troops. Four companies were disbanded, whereupon all the rest disbanded themselves. It was much the same at Tarragona in February after a disorderly election of militia officers. At Malaga the corps was getting a name for chronic insubordination. A disturbance broke out in one suburb on the night of 22 February when the magistrates were trying to arrest two offenders: the company they belonged to mutinied and exchanged shots with the police, and a man was killed.[3] For want of guidance this restiveness was too apt to take irrelevant or unworthy forms. In the countryside Howden accused *milicianos* of misusing their power in order to get properties knocked down to them cheap in the auctions.[4] An energetic government would have known how to keep the

---

[1] R.O. of 19 Jan. 1856; C.L., vol. lxvii, pp. 55–57.

[2] Text: App. 7 to D.S., no. 337, 14 Mar. 1856. On the makeshifts of Bienio local finance cf. Dutard, pp. 16–17.

[3] See Consul W. P. Mark to Howden, no. 4, 23 Feb. 1856, F.O. 185 (Spain: Embassy) 317, with copy of governor's proclamation; *Clamor Público*, with detail reprinted from local press, 1 Mar., 3/1, and 2 Mar., 2/4.

[4] Howden to Clarendon, no. 69, 5 Mar. 1856, F.O. 72. 891; similarly *The Times* Paris correspondent, 16 June, 10/1. Cf. strictures in S. Alonso Valdespino, *Qué es el progresismo?* (Madrid, 1863), pp. 15–16.

militia both healthy and loyal; this one could think only of gag-
ging and purging, and the more it weakened the militia the less of
a counterweight was left to it against the army.

Progresista organs complained with good reason of conservatives trying to discredit the régime by blowing up every little
incident into a terrible affray; they complained too of a reactionary
campaign to spread alarmist rumours. But Liberalism, its faith in
its own creed flawed as in all other countries by the events of 1848,
was too easily infected by the panic its enemies were seeking to
spread. These broils in the provinces were really, compared with
troubles of both earlier and later times, very mild. Espartero's
name still gave the people an indistinct feeling that this government was in some sort their own, if only they could make it comprehend their needs. Discontent could safely have been allowed
a clear legal character, by the people's right to meet and talk and
go on strike being ratified. Instead another directive from Escosura expounded the doctrine that if a Liberal ministry was in office
everyone was automatically free and therefore ought to be satisfied and keep quiet.[1] Not surprisingly there were symptoms of an
official wish for better relations with the Church. Arias Uría began
by allowing the court of the Rota to reopen; and on 6 February a
circular went out to the bishops which recalled that in all
epochs the Church had been 'the first auxiliary and best friend
of the State, the noblest and firmest upholder of the principle of
authority'.[2] Punctual payment of clerical stipends was once again
promised. Incense was soon being offered to 'Catholic unity':
provincial authorities were told to put down the preaching of
alien doctrines about which clericalists were raising an outcry. By
March the *Clamor Público* felt constrained to censure the ministry
for obscurantism.[3]

In this atmosphere, what was sometimes called the 'coalición
puro-democrática' made little headway. Puros won small skir-
mishes, remarked the *Novedades*, but never risked serious engage-
ments, while Democrats were eager for the fray but conscious of
their fewness.[4] As Garrido was to say, the former very often took
the same line as the latter in debates, but usually shrank from

[1] R.O. of 16 Jan. 1856; C.L., vol. lxvii, pp. 50–52.
[2] C.L., vol. lxvii, pp. 193–5. Even Costa y Borrás found a good word to say for
this: *Observaciones*, pp. 320 ff.
[3] 28 Mar. 1856, 1/2–3.
[4] 4 Mar. 1856, 1/1–3.

voting with them.[1] This had the further effect of sharpening differences of opinion among the Democrats themselves, for the more moderate wanted to slow down the pace in order to keep in step with Progresista allies, while the more impatient wanted to speed it up in the hope of dragging them along. Despite the growth of Democrat propaganda and influence the party remained very loose, and its improvising style, which promoted initiative, also hindered agreement on tactics. One paper that ran for five months this year, *La Democracia*, had no editor, but was managed by a group of friends, among them Garrido.[2] Such organs were multiplying, and each was inclined to advertise its own opinions as the true and authentic voice of the party.

Most prone of all to do this was the *Soberanía*, whose owner-editor Sixto Cámara combined a Blanquist temperament with a good deal of political insight. An officer of the radical 3rd Light Battalion, he was trying to put the militia all over the country on its guard against the purges by which its ill-wishers were enfeebling it. Progresista opposition in the Cortes his paper tended to write off as spineless and useless. 'The country, only the country can save itself.'[3] It indulged in a good deal of intemperate language that aided opponents of any alliance with Democracy—'that rash, wild, fanatical faction' as the staid *Nación* called it.[4] Even to a fellow Democrat like García Ruiz, who was to look back on Sixto Cámara's propaganda as having done immense harm, it appeared desperately 'socialistic' as well as terroristic.[5]

It was to counteract the fierceness of the *Soberanía* that García Ruiz and Rivero were planning two fresh newspapers, the *Asociación* and *Discusión*. The latter, Rivero's, was the first to come out, on 3 March. Its prospectus advocated an *entente* with radical Progresistas, and assured all Liberals that Democracy was no gospel of class war and disorder: it meant justice for all, harmony

---

[1] *Historia*, vol. iii, pp. 294–5; cf. García Ruiz, *Historias*, vol. ii, pp. 582–3.

[2] Garrido, *Historia*, vol. iii, p. 291. A. de Albornoz, *El partido republicano* (Madrid, 1918), p. 24, lists nine republican papers that appeared in Madrid during the Bienio. See also on the left-wing press of the period R. M. de Labra, *Estudios biográfico-políticos* (part 1, Madrid, 1887), pp. 25–26; Milego, pp. 62–63.

[3] 17 Jan. 1856, 1/1–2.

[4] 25 Jan. 1856, 1/1–2.

[5] *Historias*, vol. ii, pp. 573, 586. It is not easy to be sure how habitually the *Soberanía* played the terrorist, or how much of a social programme it had, because the Biblioteca Nacional has a file of 1856 only for January, and the Hemeroteca none. Its articles, however, were often quoted or referred to in other papers.

of all interests, and this journal would advocate it on strictly constitutional lines. Orense became a contributor to the new paper, though he also appeared for the defence when the *Soberanía* underwent one of its frequent prosecutions, and he must have been trying to keep the wranglings within bounds. At present he favoured caution. The party's organization was gaining ground, he wrote to a friend, only it was hampered by the impetuosity of young men, who failed to see that even if they were strong enough to make a revolution it would be a blunder to do so when the result was sure to be a French intervention.[1]

The *Discusión*'s aims were more easily announced than achieved. Its moderation failed to save it from friction with authority, for it made no truce with O'Donnell. On the other hand, to uphold strict legality when popular feeling was boiling over and reactionaries were scheming counter-revolution, was scarcely enough; especially since the channels open to legal activity were so constricted. There was no need of any violence, Pi y Margall affirmed in another journal, *La Razón*: progress required no weapon but justice.[2] Justice by itself kills no more dragons than any other word of the same length, as Pi y Margall lived to learn; and the conception of Democracy as a painless remedy, which all classes would be ready for as soon as their eyes were opened to the light of reason, was altogether too facile.

Sixto Cámara lashed out at 'cynical apostates and traffickers in public faith';[3] and his rivals' style of sweet reasonableness, which he had some excuse for regarding as mere flummery, goaded him into bloodcurdling outbursts of 'realism'. On 11 March he outdid himself with an article in the vein of Marat, declaring that it might become necessary to chop off the heads of fifty, a hundred, a thousand traitors. There was a storm over this, and two days later young Castelar made known that he was quitting the staff of the *Soberanía* and would find other means of serving Democracy, that beautiful angel sky-descended.[4] Sixto Cámara went on to compare Isabel with Marie Antoinette, and attacked Rivero as an

---

[1] Translation of part of Orense's letter, dated 28 Mar. 1856, with Vice-consul March, San Sebastian, to Hon. Spenser Ponsonby, at Paris, 15 Apr.; Clarendon Papers, vol. c. 58. March does not say how he came by it.

[2] Reprinted in Pi, *Conmociones*, vol. i, pp. 400–1.

[3] García Ruiz, *Historias*, vol. ii, p. 586.

[4] See his letter in *Clamor Público*, 15 Mar. 1856, 1/5; cf. Morayta, *Castelar*, pp. 64–65; Milego, pp. 62–63.

opportunist and careerist: a duel was only prevented by the police.[1] Something like a rancour of Girondin and Jacobin was developing inside this small movement. And neither group was finding an adequate social programme to mobilize mass discontents round. Some of Sixto Cámara's opinions were 'socialistic' enough, but it is not clear how far they fused with his system of political strategy. The *Discusión* programme did not go further than free education for the poor and more equitable taxation; and Pi y Margall, who wanted a social as well as political transformation of Spain, was still convinced that 'The State exists only to protect life and property'.[2]

---

[1] *The Times*, 24 Mar. 1856, 7/4, and 28 Mar., 7/4. Sixto Cámara wounded one of the staff of *Iberia* in a duel: Garrido, *Historia*, vol. iii, p. 296.

[2] Article in *Soberanía*, 30 Jan. 1856, 1/1–2.

XV

THE POLITICIANS AND THE PEOPLE

The Widening Gulf—Taxation and Conscription March–May 1856

When 1856 began the Cortes still had its half-dozen organic laws to make; and work on them was spread out over another half-year, with, a newspaper remarked, truly Spanish incomprehension of the value of time.[1] A separate drafting committee had been set up for each law. The first draft to make much stir was that of the electoral law, under which the basic test for voters would be payment of 200 reals in direct taxation, as under the law of 1837: a trifling sum, but one that a workman would be lucky to earn in a whole month. It might be lowered in any province where fewer than 400 voters per deputy, or 1 per cent. of the population, qualified. González, as chairman of the committee, admitted that a larger electorate would be less at the mercy of illicit pressures; but many Progresistas must have feared that it would favour their Democrat rivals more than them. Much debate and two re-draftings ended in enfranchisement of all male Spaniards over 25 who paid direct taxation up to a minimum not exceeding 120 reals;[2] there would be, it was estimated, an electorate of about a million.[3] The local government law raised similar issues. The provincial franchise was to be the same as the national; but it was a step backward from 1854 for the committee to propose any property test in municipal elections, though voting here was now to be direct instead of indirect. Again the crucial clause emerged somewhat liberalized. In towns of more than 5,000 householders only the upper two-thirds of the tax-payers would have votes, but in smaller places the proportion would rise progressively.[4]

Even more controversial was the press law. San Miguel

---

[1] *Novedades*, 3 Feb. 1856, 1/1–2.

[2] Final discussion on this point: D.S., pp. 6,617–22. Final text: App. 2 to D.S., no. 408, 18 June 1856.

[3] *Clamor Público*, 30 May 1856, 1/2–4.

[4] Final text: App. 4 to D.S., no. 408, 18 June 1856.

observed that newspapers today were far less virulent and scurri-
lous than thirty years ago, because of the general improvement
in public manners.[1] Fairly sweeping restraints were still thought
necessary, all the same. It was made an offence to publish anything
subversive of order or derogatory to Roman Catholicism, to the
sovereign, or to the Cortes;[2] and the outcome was viewed by the
Press as a grievous blow to its liberties. The same restrictive spirit
was shown when the militia law was reached in June. Service was
made compulsory, but confined to men with one of various
property qualifications, and the force was placed under the
Ministry of the Interior. Sorní the Democrat in vain repeated the
charge that Progresismo was going backward.[3] One concession
was secured: any man in the militia at present would be free to
remain in it.[4]

A private bill accepted by the government had proposed an
additional law on the Civil Service, establishing precise rules of
promotion and forbidding dismissals except for misconduct.[5]
Unluckily this attempt to curb the spoils system got no further.
Even the seven organic laws had still to be turned into complete
texts. Only one section of one of them actually reached the statute-
book, as the municipal government Act of 5 July.[6] A good deal
was being left unfinished in other spheres too; notably an education plan, privately initiated, which provided for an elementary
school in every *pueblo*,[7] though not for free admission, a matter
much in dispute.

On the economic side the assembly's activity increased as its
political vitality ran down; as could be said of the moneyed middle

---

[1] D.S., p. 8,096. For a description of the Press in these years see Vivó, pp. 377 ff.;
Annuaire des Deux Mondes, 1855–6, pp. 327–32.

[2] Final text: App. 6 to D.S., no. 408, 18 June 1856.

[3] D.S., p. 8,743.

[4] Final text: App. 7 to D.S., no. 408, 18 June 1856. The three other organic laws
dealt with relations between the two Chambers; the judiciary; and the Council
of State.

[5] The idea came from Escosura: D.S., pp. 1,151–4, 30 Jan. 1855. The bill was
produced by a committee with him as chairman: App. 3 to D.S., no. 295, 22 Jan.
1856.

[6] C.L., vol. lxix, pp. 39–94. Posada, *Evolución legislativa*, pp. 187–9, characterizes
this as allowing rather more scope for local initiative, but not representing any
thorough overhaul.

[7] Text of bill: App. 2 to D.S., no. 273, 22 Dec. 1855. The census of 1860 showed
2,408,620 men and 715,790 women able to read and write.

class at large, caught up in what was fast becoming a financial boom. One of several new business journals to come out in Madrid dwelt lyrically in its first number on the return of peace in Europe (the Crimean war ended in March) and on the vistas of civilized progress thus opened up.[1] It was a sign of the times that a General Prim should be turning his thoughts towards ten per cent. and acquiring shares in a cotton-mill at Reus.[2] More experienced men indeed were sceptical about cotton, because of over-competition and fear of tariff reductions, but companies were being founded in many other lines; by the end of this year Barcelona had forty-five, with £5,000,000 of paid-up capital.[3] True to its own contrariness, capitalism was sweeping away the old collective property-holding of the peasantry and plunging into that new species of group ownership, the joint stock company; so eagerly that pessimists began to recall the disastrous speculation of 1846 and 1847. Howden believed that two-thirds of the avid buyers of shares were only buying in the hope of being able to unload them quickly at a premium.[4]

Banking reforms were very much to the fore, for credit was seen as the grand Open Sesame to prosperity. The existing central bank, the San Fernando,[5] was reconstituted by a law passed in January as the Banco de España, but, actuated by the prevailing faith in competition, the assembly conferred on it no such monopoly of note issue as the government had envisaged,[6] and it was not long before the statutes of a new Bank of Malaga were receiving official approval. Spanish enterprise, however, had stuck too deep in the old rut of usury, and impetus towards more productive investment could come only from abroad. It came from the Crédit Mobilier, the grandiose experiment launched in France in 1852 by the Pereira brothers, who hit on the plan of setting up a Spanish affiliate. They may have hoped to secure exclusive rights, but others were too quick to scent opportunity. A strong select

[1] *Semanario Económico, Mercantil e Industrial*, Apr. 1856.

[2] Olivar Bertrand, vol. i, pp. 176–7.

[3] Barcelona trade report for 1856: *Parliamentary Papers*, 1857, vol. xxxviii.

[4] Howden to Clarendon, no. 122, 8 Apr. 1856, F.O. 72. 892; cf. *Semanario Económico, Mercantil e Industrial*, no. 8, 26 May, and *Annuaire des Deux Mondes*, 1855–6, p. 323.

[5] See J.-A. Galvarriato, *El Banco de España* (Madrid, 1932), pp. 7–9; cf. P. de Essars, &c., *A History of Banking* (New York, 1896), vol. iii, part 3.

[6] Law of 28 Jan. 1856; C.L., vol. lxvii, pp. 93–96. See on it Tallada Pauli, pp. 193, 216–17.

committee recommended a general law to permit flotation of limited liability companies free to make loans and handle all kinds of undertakings. A bill on these lines was passed on 18 January,[1] and on the same day three applications were approved. The Pereiras were allowed to set up their 'Crédito mobiliario'; another French financier, Prost, was the moving spirit of a second syndicate, and in the third were Sevillano and Collado, acting with Weissweiller, a Madrid capitalist connected with the Rothschilds.[2] Manifestly Spain was going to run a risk of being dominated, as well as stimulated, by foreign capital; another reason why the need should have been recognized for the State to play a bigger part in the economic field.

A mining law was issued provisionally, to save time.[3] 'There is at present a great rage for mining', a consul reported from Seville: iron, lead, copper were all being developed, silver with less success.[4] In the railway field most of all the eagerly welcomed influx of foreign capital and technique was setting the pace. By now the route of the Northern railway had been settled as far as the upper Ebro; Ávila had won its long battle against Segovia. When on 20 February the concession for the middle stretch between Valladolid and Burgos was put up to auction, the hall of the Development ministry was 'filled to overflowing'. It was the Crédit Mobilier that asked the lowest subsidy, and was consequently adjudged the contract.[5] Work began in May. Next in importance was the Madrid-to-Saragossa route, secured by a French railway company headed by the Comte de Morny, in alliance with Salamanca.[6] At a celebration banquet the scholar deputy Borao proposed the toast of STEAM, in ecstatic verses on the marvels of the iron horse.[7]

Meanwhile another large share of the assembly's energy was

[1] Law of 28 Jan. 1856; C.L., vol. lxvii, pp. 96–99.
[2] Laws of 28 Jan. 1856; C.L., vol. lxvii, pp. 99–103. The statutes of the Crédito mobiliario are printed in the R.O., approving them, of 22 Mar. 1856; ibid., pp. 387–403.
[3] Law of 11 July 1856; C.L., vol. lxix, pp. 200–1. Cf. Aldana, p. 342.
[4] Parliamentary Papers, 1857, vol. xxxviii.
[5] The Times, 27 Feb. 1856, 9/4; cf. Anon., Manual histórico y descriptivo de Valladolid (Valladolid, 1861), pp. 334–5. Later this year the same corporation secured the other two sections of the line; see N. Villiaumé, De l'Espagne et de ses chemins de fer (Paris, 1861).
[6] A. Gómez Ranero, España geográfica, estadística y administrativa (Madrid, 1856), p. 36.
[7] G. Borao, Poesías (Saragossa, 1869), pp. 59 ff.

absorbed by the budget. Expenditure was gone through with a fine comb;[1] deputies might well feel they owed this to the nation, because scarcely any budget had ever been properly investigated, but they did not succeed in reducing the total bill. All this time petitions against revival of the *puertas* and *consumos* rained on the Cortes; many came from elected local bodies. Bruil's resignation on 7 February was due to this resistance to his revenue plan, and obstruction of his tariff reform bill. Catalan millowners were now demanding total exclusion of British cloth, on the ground that their own higher costs in fuel and material, their workers' militia duties, and idleness enforced by 'the vast number of Feast Days in the year', made competition impossible.[2]

Bruil's successor, F. Santa Cruz, virtually abandoned tariff reform, and disclaimed any wish to revive the *puertas* and *consumos*; but his own plan for making up the anticipated deficit of 136 millions differed from them only in name. In face of this subterfuge it seemed to many deputies that the time had come to draw the line and halt the retreat. A condemnation of revival in any shape or form was signed by 154 of them. The government made its new proposals a question of confidence, and the implied threat of Espartero's resignation had its invariable effect. The *Clamor Público* condemned the proposals in strong terms; now it solemnly adjured members not to vote against them, because the vital need was to keep a Progresista government in being.[3] The *Nación* thought the revolution of 1854 ought to have been kept on a purely political plane; agitators had mischievously dragged in money questions, too complex for the understanding of the vulgar.[4]

On 5 March the budget committee, on which all eyes were fixed, voted 12 to 12 on the decisive clause, and had to confess deadlock.[5] The resulting sense of crisis inspired a fresh attempt to overcome the amorphous confusion of party groupings, which so many bemoaned. There lay ready to hand the notion of a 'third party' that had been in the air in recent months, even if, as the *Novedades* observed, no one could discover what it was supposed to stand for.[6] With men like Cantero, Ríos Rosas, and

---

[1] For detail of expenditure see App. 1 to D.S., no. 358, 15 Apr. 1856.
[2] Howden to Clarendon, no. 93, 25 Mar. 1856, F.O. 72. 892.
[3] 13 Feb. 1856, 1/1-2; 5 Mar., 1/3, and 7 Mar., 1/1-3.
[4] 13 Mar. 1856, 1/1-3.
[5] App. 1 to D.S., no. 332, 8 Mar. 1856.   [6] 14 Mar. 1856, 1/1-3.

Concha taking the lead, a new bloc began to emerge under the title of 'Centro Parlamentario'. Its motto was steadfast support to the government in the interests of stable administration; which meant willingness to canvass and vote for Santa Cruz's budget. A committee was chosen at its second gathering, on 4 March, and next day waited on Espartero with a pledge of loyalty. The *Nación* hurried forward, along with the *Época*, to serve as mouthpiece to the 'Centro' and extol its unselfish patriotism. Even at this late hour the straggling Progresista party could be roused by such a challenge. Calvo Asensio, Fernández de los Ríos, Madoz, Sánchez Silva, and Allende Salazar, who was returning to political activity, set about forming a rival 'Centro Progresista'. Four hours' discussion on 16 March produced a policy statement and a committee. But all the statement amounted to was that they were loyal to Espartero—even more loyal than the other camp— and to Liberal principles. In the circumstances this was a plain contradiction, and it promised no end to the interminable budget bother. On the 17th when the budget debate opened Espartero treated the House to one of his brief homilies, saying that unless it provided the wherewithal to balance the budget the position would be intolerable, and the whole Cabinet would resign.

Panic gripped the assembly, and next day it took the advice of its presiding officers and adjourned until the 26th, in the hope of finding a solution out of earshot of the public. On the 19th the Puros met again, to the number of 103; Allende Salazar, who took the chair, urged that the great object must be to avert Espartero's resignation, and a panel was chosen to thrash out alternative ways of raising money.[1] A plan drawn up by it was accepted without demur by the Cabinet, and laid before the House on the 27th. It began with a ringing declaration that to revive taxes so lately and almost unanimously condemned by this same assembly would be indecent. It went on to propose minor increases in other revenues, including the colonial tribute, and, as its real kernel, an impost to which the title of *derrama nacional* lent a specious air of novelty, but which was really, like Santa Cruz's scheme, the old *consumos* in a fresh disguise.[2]

This manœuvre meant a sharp set-back for the always delicate alliance of the Left. Democrats were being left in the lurch, in

[1] *Clamor Público*, 20 Mar. 1856, 1/2–3; *The Times*, 25 Mar., 8/6.
[2] App. 1 to D.S., no. 342, 27 Mar. 1856.

some degree as the consequence of their own unreadiness with better ideas for raising money: Orense had merely expounded once more their standard contention that all could be set right by proper economies.[1] They could not be blind to the risk of isolation, and their spokesman Figueras picked his words carefully. This plan, he said, was inspired by men whom he would like to see on the front bench; but their *derrama* was suspiciously like the excise system against which some of them like Sánchez Silva had been so eloquent, and he and his friends felt bound in conscience to oppose it.[2] They were left to do so alone, and on 8 April the budget was at last disposed of.[3] Its thirty-nine articles had been beaten out nearly as flat as those of Canterbury.

Government credit improved, and next month the Treasury was able to carry out a conversion of 200 millions of floating debt into three per cents. Prost and the Crédit Mobilier were among the biggest bidders for stock; bids averaged 40.53 per cent. of face value. In Spain such a result could pass for a national triumph, but not all taxpayers were in a mood to rejoice. Labourers were exempted from the graduated imposts by means of which local authorities were to make up their quotas of the *derrama*. But the land-tax was rising by 50 millions, and it was argued that this and the *derrama* between them would burden the multitude of dwarf farmers and tenants more heavily than the *consumos* had done.[4] In fact the new tax was soon encountering the same resistance in the country that a revival of the old one would have met with.

The Centro Parlamentario faded back into thin air; the Centro Progresista, or Puro, continued to meet and talk. In appearance it had won the contest, but it had won only by doing the other side's work. On 30 March a meeting adopted a manifesto which did little more than rehearse Progresista platitudes and advocate unity. Many who had subscribed to the rival Centro added their signatures to it: they did not want to annoy their constituencies, and in any case found it innocuous. Unity on these terms meant immobility; also a further shutting-out of the Democrats. Rivero wrote a set of articles to express the disappointment of his group.[5] He

---

[1] See his minute of dissent, in App. 3 to D.S., no. 335, 12 Mar. 1856.
[2] D.S., pp. 7,445–8.
[3] Final text: C.L., vol. lxviii, pp. 69–87.
[4] *Annuaire des Deux Mondes*, 1855–6, pp. 320–1.
[5] Partly reprinted from *Discusión* in C. de Castro, *Estudio biográfico del Excmo. Sr. D. Nicolás María Rivero* (Madrid, 1915), pp. 84–85.

found fault with the manifesto for its parade of loyalty to the throne, and with its sponsors for welcoming the signatures of men whose votes had been cast against religious freedom and all sorts of good causes, while they rejected the co-operation of Democrats who shared their own beliefs.

Liberalism was subjected almost immediately to another ordeal. This time trouble started at Valencia, with a tumult on 6 April. The province was noted for its social and political extremes.[1] High rents skimmed off much of the profit of agriculture's wartime boom, and in the city, with a population of about a hundred thousand, industry was helping to engender bitterness. It was mostly at a primitive stage of small workshops, compared with Barcelona; silk manufacture was a speciality.[2] Vice-consul Barrie expressed alarm at the subversive ideas spreading among the artisans and silk weavers, particularly those enrolled in the militia, a force here 'composed almost exclusively of the lowest grades of society' and in the habit of listening to 'very untempered socialistic perorations'.[3]

The immediate irritant was a new call-up for the army voted by the Cortes in February. About 7 o'clock this Sunday morning drawing of lots began; two hours later the premises were invaded by noisy demonstrators, the proceedings brought to a halt, city councillors pelted and chased away. Militiamen on duty refrained from coming to their aid. About 2 p.m. the captain-general, Villalonga, arrived at the near-by Plaza de San Francisco where the three garrison regiments had their barracks. His reputation was that of a disciplinarian, not to say brutalitarian, and there had been criticism by Liberals of his appointment. He shunned a pitched battle, however, from fear either of coming off worst or of not being upheld by the government. Two battalions of militia were spoiling for a fight; Barrie, eye-witness of most of these scenes, saw a private strike his officer. Other *milicianos* inside a large building exchanged sporadic fire for a couple of hours with the troops. An officer and four soldiers were reported killed, twenty wounded. Between 5 and 6 p.m. some militia commandants took

---

[1] Landowners were largely Carlist, other property owners Moderado, artisans very radical, the rest indifferent: Vice-consul Barrie to Howden, 30 Apr. 1856, F.O. 185. 318.

[2] See Hoskins, vol. i, p. 116; M. Boucher de Perthes, *Voyage en Espagne et en Algérie en 1855* (Paris, 1859), chap. 16.

[3] Barrie to Howden, 6 Apr. 1856, and 30 Apr., F.O. 185. 318.

the lead in arranging a truce; a number of arrests were made; by ten o'clock the town was quiet, though uneasy.[1]

The entire town council resigned, with obvious alacrity. Its farewell address dwelt pathetically on the cares of office—it had been all along at its wits' end to find money to meet civic expenses. At the capital the news as it trickled in caused great commotion. All Madrid press accounts were garbled, Barrie commented, and serious though the affair was Valencians were astonished to find it given such 'gigantic proportions'.[2] All who saw anarchy looming over Spain were confirmed in their forebodings; and resistance to conscription was a direct affront to the army. A decree of 9 April suspended Villalonga, and conferred special powers on General Zabala to deal with the situation on the spot. It was incongruous employment for a Foreign Minister, though really more in his line than his office work. Next day a resolution moved in the Cortes by Olózaga's brother José, condemning the outbreak and promising support to the government, was approved by two hundred votes to none.[3] Puros were only too anxious to clear themselves of any taint of sympathy with 'anarchy'. Democrats were on slippery ground, as always in such cases; accusing fingers were sure to be pointed at them. With another recoil from radicalism the *Clamor Público* applauded Zabala's appointment, recommended severity, and treated the riot as proof that to give votes and power to the poorer classes, until they were better educated and better informed as to their own interests, would be calamitous.[4]

With Zabala's advent at Valencia some further arrests were made, and prosecutions threatened, though these were left to the civil courts. On 15 April the drawing of lots for the army was carried out in a public square. Troops were kept in readiness, but out of sight, and there was no disturbance. Zabala's real blow fell on the morning of the 17th, when the streets were placarded with a notice disbanding about half the roster of militia companies. Knots of artisans collected, and seemed inclined to defy the order, but were overawed by the powerfully reinforced garrison, and by evening arms were being sullenly handed in.[5] Far more men were

---

[1] This account is chiefly drawn from Barrie to Howden, 6 and 14 Apr. 1856, F.O. 185. 317; Escosura's report to the Cortes on 8 Apr., D.S., pp. 7,669–70; *The Times*, 17 Apr., 10/4.   [2] Ibid.   [3] D.S., pp. 7,716–20.
[4] 10 Apr. 1856, 1/4; 11 Apr., 1/2–3; 17 Apr., 1/2–3.
[5] Barrie to Howden, 18 Apr. 1856, F.O. 185. 317, with copy of the proclamation.

being cashiered than were in any way involved in the tumult, and nearly all the rest abandoned the service in protest; an outcome anything but unwelcome to local conservatives. It was another long stride towards the disarming of the people. Zabala's proceedings were not stiff enough to satisfy Moderados, whose abuse of the government as feeble and irresponsible 'bordered on the incredible'.[1] Tension was being powerfully worked up, and there were fears of an explosion in Madrid on 20 April when an elaborate review of all militia and military forces of the province was due to take place. It went off peacefully, with 40,000 men under arms and the Queen at a saluting post at the Cibeles fountain. This was hailed by self-comforters as a grand demonstration of harmony between people and throne, militia and army, Espartero and O'Donnell. Howden's soldierly eye noted that O'Donnell had stationed artillery at a strategic point and disposed his troops so as to hem in the more numerous *milicianos*.[2]

On the night of the 22nd a crowded and heated meeting of the 'Círculo Puro' rejected a proposed motion of censure against the ministers (except Espartero) for their handling of Valencia. It was left to Democrats to make a stand. Their motion cautiously combined unexceptionable sentiments about order with repudiation of 'illegal and arbitrary methods' of enforcing it; and it was moved on the 24th by Rivero, who could not be depicted as an anarchist, and who had connexions with Valencia. Spectators crammed the gallery as he warned the 'July government' that it was stumbling towards a catastrophe like that of 1843. He reiterated his faith in peaceful persuasion, and lamented that in Spain as in France infernal efforts were being made to foment class hatreds. But this riot at Valencia was not such a dreadful thing. There was no need to send a Cabinet minister from Madrid, like an assize judge in England. Perhaps the government's design was to destroy the Democrat party there: it was really destroying all Liberal influence. Escosura's reply was uncompromising. A state of siege at Valencia had been imperative—'There is no other way, gentlemen: *á la guerra, la guerra*.'[3] Rivero withdrew his motion, pending the return of Zabala.

[1] *Clamor Público*, 16 Apr. 1856, 1/2–3.
[2] Howden to Clarendon, no. 134, 25 Apr. 1856, F.O. 72. 892.
[3] D.S., pp. 8,008–21. Escosura had refused to discuss the merits of the case, while the 'emergency' continued: D.S., pp. 7,983–4.

Espartero listened and sat still. He was going off this evening on a festive tour of Old Castile and Aragon, on the pretext of inaugurating work on the new railways. Valencia's outbreak, one more case of ungrateful people biting the hand that would have fed them if it conveniently could, made him all the happier to get away. As his real authority ebbed he basked more than ever in pomp and show; he would have made a much better constitutional monarch than Isabel ever could. To flit from city to city uttering banalities and gathering the honey of applause was the department of statesmanship that he understood and relished. On the 26th he was at Valladolid, for the opening ceremony of the middle stretch of the Northern railway; a huge crowd attended in defiance of pouring rain.[1] On the 29th he reached Burgos. Everywhere his welcome, especially from the poorer classes, was ecstatic, but his deportment as the Queen's servant, Howden heard, perfectly correct.[2]

But Espartero's reputation was something ludicrously different from his real self. Conservatives were suspicious. Some believed in spite of everything, as Baradère at Barcelona did, that Espartero and Allende Salazar and the rest were still set on a republic and a Jacobin dictatorship.[3] And even yet there were sons of the people for whom Espartero was one of themselves, only awaiting the moment to hoist his white plume and gallop them into some tremendous day of glory. Demagogues at Barcelona were straining every nerve to get him to come there, according to the anxious Baradère.[4] Men like Allende Salazar were not really preparing a republican coup; they were, however, intensifying their efforts to pull the Progresista party together. Local committees were being formed, propaganda toned up. Early in May a letter signed by the organizers of the Centro Progresista appeared in the provincial press, summoning the party to close its ranks and free itself from alien tendencies, whether Moderado or Democrat. But to try to rally the party by barricading it against the Left as well as the Right was to ensure failure. Liberalism could revive only by moving forward, as an expanding alliance of all radical forces.

[1] The official account is reproduced in Anon., *Manual . . . de Valladolid*, pp. 336–8; cf. pp. 122–3.
[2] Howden to Clarendon, no. 158, 17 May 1856, F.O. 72. 893.
[3] Baradère to Walewski, no. 209, 25 Apr. 1856; *Espagne*, Consular, vol. 52.
[4] Baradère to Walewski, no. 212, 20 May 1856; ibid.

A party mistaking purity for strength was all the less likely to succeed in drawing its leader after it. Espartero's tour could not fail to deepen his comfortable feeling that, however much or little the country cared about Progresismo, it loved its duke. Perhaps the *Nación* was voicing his thoughts when it pronounced that the day of the old parties was done, and that the Liberal Union idea of 1854 had been a sound one.[1] A loose medley of moderates, with himself for presiding genius and O'Donnell for executive officer, may by now have been floating in his mind. At all events when on 2 May he arrived at his own town of Logroño, he was in a mood in which to try to reason with him was futile. He was fretful, Straten-Ponthoz learned, when Ignacio Gurrea pleaded with him to break off his partnership with O'Donnell before it was too late.[2] It was the same on 13 and 14 May at Saragossa, where other leading Progresistas collected in the hope that here if anywhere the ark of their covenant might be rescued from the false priests. A bullfight, a review, a play, a Te Deum, and a banquet drowned their croakings. A shrewd almanac-maker, scanning the Aragonese weather and other omens, predicted a great man's downfall.[3]

He got back to the capital on the 16th; Zabala returned on the same day, and on the 20th the Democrats renewed the debate on Valencia. They were striving once more to win Progresistas round to an alliance, and their censure was directed against Zabala alone. Figueras, who moved it, harped again on the duality of this government, and declared that if Progresistas could not impose their ideals on it they ought to go frankly into opposition, and Democrats would stand beside them. On the actual issue of Valencia, he and his friends showed rather too much concern to avoid any appearance of condoning popular violence, and to explain the tumult away in terms of reactionary provocation, which may of course as in every such case have played a certain part. Sorní, who sat for Valencia, maintained that it was all the doing of outsiders brought into the town to make trouble.[4] Espartero condescended to no reasons, but offhandedly approved Zabala's conduct. Again as so often he was forcing his party to vote against itself. Radicals faced a painful choice. Their

[1] 16 Mar. 1856, 1/2–4.
[2] Straten-Ponthoz to Vilain XIIII, no. 84, 10 May 1856; *Espagne*, vol. 9.
[3] J. Yagüe, *Vaticinio de circunstancias* (Saragossa, Aug. 1856), pp. 7–8.
[4] D.S., pp. 8,446–62.

committee met, a newspaper reported, and after hot dispute con-cluded dolefully that they must give way.[1] The motion was defeated by 178 to 18, the Democrats isolated once more; though a score of angry Puros abstained, Allende Salazar among them. Espartero had added one more to the long tale of successes by which he slowly but surely sawed through the branch he sat on.

[1] *Nación*, 22 May 1856, 1/5.

XVI

THE LIBERALS ISOLATED

Plots and Food Riots, June 1856

PROGRESISTAS were divided by now into two sects, one believing that all difficulties would vanish if they only shut their eyes tight enough, the other that something badly needed to be done if only they could tell what it was; among the second sort distrust of O'Donnell was intense. When the party's steering committee was re-elected on 29 May, Allende Salazar admitted that he saw no clear way out of their difficulties; the great crux was whether the league of the two leaders was still desirable, and if not, how it could be ended when even its critics shrank from ever voting against Espartero.[1] Liberalism shrank in other words from the thought of being left without its hero's prestige for a talisman against both reactionary malevolence and mass impatience. Yet so far as reaction, at any rate, was concerned there was no palpable cause for alarm. Carlism had been met and vanquished; and as to other assailants on the Right, neither singly nor, since they were so little able to unite, collectively was there anything in them to warrant panic.

In the Moderado press a furious outcry was being kept up; a few conservatives understood that something more constructive was required. July 1854 was a time of noble ideals, one pamphleteer wrote tactfully: 1856 needed stable administration, and the conservative party ought to close its ranks and give the country a clear view of what it stood for.[2] Clarion calls for party unity had been heard for a long time already, and the *Clamor Público* took comfort from the polemics always going on between Moderado newspapers, as proof that the various factions of Narváez, Bravo Murillo, Mon, and the rest were irreconcilable.[3] To sulk, sneer, and concoct improbable plots was in reality all they were capable

---

[1] *Novedades*, 30 May 1856, 2/1; 31 May, 2/3–4.
[2] J. Romeo y Padules, *Rápida reseña de los principales sucesos que precedieron á la revolución de 1854* (Saragossa, 1856), pp. 6, 8, 21. Cf. Valero y Soto, pp. 38–39, 46–47.
[3] 14 May 1856, 1/1–2; cf. 27 Feb., 1/2–3.

of. Typical of them was Cristina's old friend Istúriz, who shut himself up all through the Bienio and whose house with its 'perpetual conversazione' of malcontents came to be known as the 'Murmuradero'.[1]

Clericalist agitation was in full cry again notwithstanding the government's overtures to the Church earlier this year. A continuous fusillade was kept up by Catholic journals, led by the *Regeneración*. An answering fire came from the Left, especially from the *Democracia*, a chief receptacle of the 'inflammatory and diabolical productions of the enemies of God', which carried the war to the pope's door by cavilling at the defects of his own government.[2] With all its sound and fury clericalist propaganda was failing again to score a real success even where its chances looked brightest, in the Basque provinces. Here the demand for exemption from the disamortization law persisted; there were conferences of provincial representatives, resignations of whole town councils, talk of more than passive resistance.[3] But ideas had changed a great deal here since the first Carlist war, as an observer at San Sebastian remarked.[4] Echagüe, the captain-general, displayed a mixture of firmness and diplomacy, and although grumblings continued, the Basques seemed no more willing to take up arms for Pius IX than for Carlos VI.

Most perturbing of all to Liberals was the attitude of the army. Even the Vicalvarists, well rewarded as they had been, were disgruntled. Ros de Olano was not altogether romancing when he protested tearfully, after the Bienio was over, that for them it had been a long martyrdom which he would rather die than endure again.[5] Such generals felt that they were being relegated to a back seat by the politicians, whom they were accustomed to look down on as civilians and also as, by and large, less blue-blooded than themselves. To all officers the existence of the militia, and Democrat pinpricks, were constant irritants. Progresistas had thrown

[1] A. Conte, *Recuerdos de un diplomático* (Madrid, 1901–03), vol. i, p. 107. Cf. Marqués de Miraflores, *Biografía del Excmo. Sr. D. Francisco Javier Istúriz y Montero* (Madrid, 1871), p. 36.

[2] See J. Canga Argüelles (y Villalta), *Tribulaciones de la Iglesia*, pp. 14 ff., 28 ff., 49. A mass of press extracts, mostly from *Regeneración*, were collected in this volume.

[3] W. C. Brackenbury, consul at Bilbao, to Howden, no. 12, 6 Apr. 1856, F.O. 185. 317.

[4] Vice-consul L. March to Brackenbury, no. 10, 20 Feb. 1856, F.O. 185. 317.

[5] Speech of 22 May 1857; text in Ibo Alfaro, *La Corona de Laurel*, vol. i, pp. 595–602.

away their chance to cut the army's claws; on the other hand it suffered from its own feuds and factions, and as a whole was too much cut off from the country to be able to take action on its own. A number of generals had talked of a coup early this year, it appears, but felt powerless to move.[1] Liberalism hesitated to appeal to the people against its opponents, because it was increasingly unnerved by their predictions of social anarchy, of red revolution about to break out. There was a recrudescence of the same hysterical fear that prevailed after 1848 and was only temporarily relieved by the safety-valve of 1854. The shift of middle-class interest from politics to finance had an effect the more unwholesome because of the febrile mood of get-rich-quick speculation that was bound to accompany any boom in such a country. Liberalism's return to power in 1854 had engendered the optimism necessary for expansion; now, as the investor saw the dragon of anarchy coming between him and his golden harvest, the boom was working against Liberalism. Another of its accompaniments was political pressure from France. As French investments in Spain multiplied the French government could feel, or profess, a duty to shelter them against 'socialism'; and reports he was getting from Spain were of a character to put an edge on Napoleon's genuine fears of a red republic on his doorstep. The controlled press at Paris was impatient to see a turn towards the Right. This meant in particular the elimination of Espartero. It may seem bizarre that anyone should think Espartero, after all he had not done, a firebrand; but his being in office could be reckoned by alarmists a standing incitement to insubordination. Baradère's plaint was one frequently heard: 'Le nom seul du duc de la Victoire est un bouclier dont se couvrent les révolutionnaires.'[2] Espartero might well have lamented like Falstaff that his name was so terrible to the enemy.

From March onward Spanish newspapers were canvassing the chances of an actual French intervention. As usual anxiety was overdone. Britain, for one thing, was looking on, and though sympathy for a Liberal régime was damped by failure to extract concessions to British interests from it, any open meddling by

---

[1] Fernández de los Ríos, *Luchas políticas*, vol. ii, p. 428. Cf. Córdova's account of how, as soon as he returned to Spain at the end of 1855, Dulce and Ros de Olano tried to draw him into plans for a *coup* (*Mis memorias*, vol. iii, p. 413).

[2] Baradère to Walewski, no. 202, 22 Feb. 1856; *Espagne*, Consular, vol. 53. Cf. *Annuaire des Deux Mondes*, 1855–6, p. 299.

Napoleon would provoke serious indignation. In any case he could make no move except in support of anti-Liberal forces inside Spain; the real danger was that a *bourgeoisie* thirsting for quick profits, and counting on an influx of foreign capital to produce them, would be tempted to acquiesce in a situation more conducive to French investment.

Isabel was an essential factor. All right-wing oracles repeated *ad nauseam* that by humiliating throne and altar Liberalism was undermining the country's social as well as political stability. With the public Isabel's personal credit had been slowly reviving. A new favourite seems to have been installed, the young officer Enrique Puigmoltó, but a decent regard was now paid to the proprieties; a paternal admonition from the pope may have helped.[1] Progresistas who strove to see a true convert in her, as in O'Donnell, rejoiced at her good reception by the Easter crowds when she walked from church to church after performing the *lavatorio*, or washing of beggars' feet cleaned up for the occasion. At the beginning of June there was talk of a mysterious plot against her life. Very likely the tale was fabricated for its publicity value, but she herself may have been startled by it. According to a story likely to be true in substance, she sent secretly about this time for the absolutist General Pezuela and asked whether he would undertake to form a ministry : he convinced her that no one could serve her turn except O'Donnell, whom she then sounded, and who gave a guarded assent.[2]

None of the reactionary interests (except Napoleon) would make O'Donnell their first choice; all of them might agree on him as their second. He still had no personal following outside the army. Liberal Union, Third Party, Centro Parlamentario had each in turn proved a mirage. But this very isolation made him in some ways more attractive; for instance to the Court, which could hope to utilize and then discard him. For him it was a spur to action. Having failed to build a party capable of lifting him to the highest place, he must now think of winning this place by other means and then using it as a vantage-point to build a party from. He could not afford to delay much longer, and he could not make his move

[1] Llorca, pp. 126–7.
[2] González-Araco, pp. 35 ff. He gives no date or authority. San Miguel and Infante he says were among the army men who were sounded and seemed well disposed (pp. 42–43).

alone: he needed Isabel as much as she needed him. He must have been plotting and planning as arduously as in the same months of 1854; he spent less time nowadays at the Cortes, the *Novedades* noticed, and more time inspecting troops. It accused him of sending progressive officers to the colonies to be out of his way.[1]

One thing that made Isabel indispensable was that she provided a link between army and Church. The diverse elements banding together against the régime had few positive aims in common, and scarcely any that would bear publication; hence their propaganda had to be couched a good deal in religious terms. The *Regeneración* made a special point in its prospectus of vindicating the gospel against 'the devilish doctrines of Proudhon'. This June the clericalist agitation was rising to a climax, as though at a given signal. 'The hour has come', the *Regeneración* proclaimed on the 2nd, 'when the alarm must never cease to be given. . . . On the alert! On the alert!' A turbid flood of answering letters poured into its postbag. Feminine piety waxed especially furious, and an effusion by a Miss Lozano of Granada ran to seventeen stanzas. 'True Spaniards' apostrophized one another as 'favourite sons of the Heavenly Queen'. One José Pérez, who must have been regaling himself with lives of early martyrs, testified his readiness despite advanced age 'to undergo the cruellest torments and even death'. A tirade by a Sr. Prieto wound up with a recital of what democracy and infidelity had brought on France and were bringing on Spain: 'Guerra!! Muerte!! Sangre!! Ruinas!! Exterminio!! Desolación!!'[2] It would be a cool or callous citizen who did not quail at this catalogue of horrors.

Radicals shaken by their defeat over Valencia were immediately exposed to a series of further trials, in each of which they were fatally hobbled by their inability to defy Espartero. One concerned the insistent question of how much longer the constituent assembly could decently go on. So little had Liberalism consolidated its positions during the Bienio that there was grave risk, as the *Novedades* warned it, of all the assembly's political work being swept away as soon as it disbanded.[3] Howden gathered that ministers wanted to get the session over as quickly as possible, and then dissolve and rely on new elections to give them a docile

---

[1] 13 Apr. 1856, 1/1–2; 17 May, 1/1–2.
[2] J. Canga Argüelles (y Villalta), *Tribulaciones de la Iglesia*, pp. 28 ff.; 54 ff.; 105 ff.; 142 ff; 339 ff. [3] 7 June 1856, 1/1–2.

majority and cripple the 'absolute Democrats'.[1] Paradoxically, therefore, the Right was pressing for the Constitution to be in-augurated at once (Constitutions could after all be ignored), while most of the Left still wanted this postponed, because it would allow the assembly to be treated as a mere ordinary Cortes and put an end to. This exposed the Left to the taunt of being afraid to face the electorate; and a cynic pointed out that for two years now the country had managed to exist without any Constitution at all, like Monsieur Jourdain talking prose.[2]

At the end of May a group of Puros hit on an ingenious plan to prolong the assembly's life and at the same time refresh its popular appeal: it should take another summer holiday before finishing off its work, but should first promulgate the Constitution and in honour of it grant a year's reduction of service to all conscripts.[3] This was taking a leaf out of O'Donnell's book; he had lately raised the pay and allowances of sergeants,[4] and followed this up by announcing that he would personally review each regiment of the Madrid garrison in turn and inquire into its well-being. The Puro proposal was furiously denounced in the Moderado press; what mattered more was that it met with strong disapproval from Espartero,[5] tutored no doubt by his partner. It was twice con-sidered at big gatherings of the Centro Progresista, and then, failing agreement, withdrawn.[6]

Another skirmish arose from Ros de Olano's notorious passion for conspiring, and reputed links with Narváez, which made him obnoxious to all Progresistas. Espartero was brought to ask for his transfer from the inspectorate-general of infantry to the Philippines. He declined to go, and O'Donnell declined to remove him. A face-saving compromise was the upshot. Serrano would give up his inspectorship of artillery to Ros de Olano, who would give up his post to Isidoro de Hoyos, an oldish and pallid Espar-terista, and Hoyos would hand over his present charge as captain-general of New Castile to Serrano.[7] Progresistas saw this game of

---

[1] Howden to Clarendon, no. 170, 25 May 1856, F.O. 72. 893.

[2] L. García, p. 10.

[3] Fernández de los Ríos, *Luchas políticas*, vol. ii, p. 433; Pi, *Historia*, vol. iv, pp. 145–6.　　　　[4] See App. 1 to D.S., no. 368, 26 Apr. 1856.

[5] *Nación*, 31 May 1856, 1/5.　　　　[6] *Novedades*, 1 June 1856, 2/3–4.

[7] On this affair see *The Times*, 14 June 1856, 12/2; Straten-Ponthoz to Vilain XIIII, no. 101, 3 June; *Espagne*, vol. 9; and Howden to Clarendon, no. 199, 7 June, F.O. 72. 893.

musical chairs as another display of feebleness by Espartero; and
it may in fact have been the falling into their hands of the military
control of the capital that made the Vicalvarists and Isabel feel it
safe to go ahead.[1]

A more ignominious rout followed almost at once for the
Progresistas. Their network of local committees and clubs was
spreading in response to the appeal of early May, but it was being
interfered with in various provinces by the authorities. Liberalism
had failed, or not dared, to establish clearly the legitimacy of open,
peaceful political activity; timidity about working-class and religious freedom fostered timidity about public life, and a tacit
assumption that political as well as religious beliefs ought to be
free to everyone, but only in private. Now all of a sudden the Progresistas' organization in Catalonia, where it was solidest, was
proscribed by Zapatero. Here was an affront too blatant for
them to ignore. They met on 5 June and drew up a resolution demanding an explanation. It was moved next day by Valera.
O'Donnell answered with a brazen denial of the right of political parties—even the party supposedly in power—to work outside the Cortes: Zapatero had acted on orders.[2] Espartero sat
silent, although the motion was signed by Allende Salazar and
other old intimates. He would have liked to slip out without
voting, a reporter thought, but was prodded by O'Donnell and
Luxán into voting against it.[3] Even so it was only rejected by
109 to 96.

Espartero did not conceal his resentment against the friends and
followers who had at last plucked up courage to contradict him,
and was even said to be forbidding them his house. Among radicals anger was equally hot, and there was talk of a campaign of
open opposition; but they had already rejected the league with
Democracy that this would imply. When the Puros met on the
7th Gurrea resigned from the committee, and Allende Salazar had
no better advice to give than that having asserted their independence by their vote they should now think twice before doing
anything more. His words fell on the listeners like cold water,
quenching all their new-found courage.

    [1] González-Araco, pp. 44–45, takes this view.
    [2] D.S., pp. 8,755–60. Figueras had complained on 3 May of arbitrary arrests and
banishments in Catalonia (D.S., pp. 8,163–4).
    [3] *Novedades*, 15 June 1856, 1/1–2.

The Centro Progresista had been buoyed up all along by a lurking belief that Espartero was at heart willing to be rescued from O'Donnell's clutches. Now the illusion was at an end, a continuance of the coalition seemed the best, rather than the worst, that could be looked for. Reactionaries were talking openly of a government of O'Donnell alone. Even Espartero could not help seeing that he had landed himself in a very ambiguous position, and he tried to explain it away in an even more ambiguous statement published on 16 June in the *Gazette*. He had abstained from any personal initiative since 1854, he said, because his function could be only that of enabling the national will to express itself freely, and he could only interpret the national will by the light of majority voting in the assembly. If there was any logical calculation behind this apologia, he was offering himself as head or figurehead of any new administration, further to the Right, that might take shape after the next elections. Already a year ago Turgot had judged him sufficiently out of humour with the Democrats and the whole constituent assembly to lend his name to an army coup if one were made.[1] But what really went on in the minds of the two Consuls was, as Howden said, always hard to divine. 'O'Donnell is the most reserved of human beings and Espartero, in spite of his apparent frankness, is as full of dissimulation, not to say falsehood, as any man I ever met.'[2]

Undaunted, Democrats were preparing to carry on the struggle single-handed. On 18 June an imposing banquet was held at the house of the old republican journalist Olevarría, and extension of party work in the provinces—in plain defiance of the government's ban—was discussed. Orense and a whole phalanx of stalwarts were present, García Ruiz, Garrido, Figueras, Pi y Margall, Miralpeix. Fiery toasts were proposed by Castelar and others, and Espartero roundly condemned as a backslider: Rivero, the man of peace and P's and Q's, drank to the triumph of the July revolution without him.[3] *Discusión* and *Soberanía* were speaking in unwonted unison this month, and the *Clamor Público* wrung its hands over the reckless effrontery of these upstarts.[4] They could hope

---

[1] Turgot to Walewski, no. 5, 5 July 1855; *Espagne*, vol. 847 (this part marked 'Très réservée' and sent in cipher).

[2] Howden to Clarendon, no. 134, 25 Apr. 1856, F.O. 72. 892.

[3] *Novedades*, 20 June 1856, 2/2–3; *Nación*, 20 June, 1/5; Straten-Ponthoz to Vilain XIIII, no. 117, 21 June; *Espagne*, vol. 9. Sixto Cámara, reportedly unwell, was not at the banquet.   [4] 22 June 1856, 1/1–2.

to pick up much support in the country that Progresistas were throwing away; they cannot have failed to guess that attempts might be made to cut short their advance. But the ordeal men prepare for is seldom precisely the one that meets them, as history had taught Figueras at the end of his Catilinarian oration in January. Scarcely were the banquet speeches out of their mouths when news astounded the capital of riots, not in seditious Valencia or Barcelona, but in Spain's peaceable home counties, under the placid skies of Old Castile. There could not have been a less foreseeable start to the ultimate crisis of the Bienio.

Food scarcity and dearness worsened by the stormy winter were plaguing various regions. At Malaga wheat imports had lately had to be allowed; at Valladolid too prices had been rising, and on 21 June the town council printed leaflets with promises of cheaper bread, which it seems were not fulfilled. Early on the 22nd a mob collected, and ran riot. The town hall was menaced; a flour-mill was burned, and some houses, including those of two capitalists of the Liberal persuasion, sacked. Local accounts spoke of a strange slowness to act on the part of the military authorities, as if they were deliberately allowing things to get out of hand.[1] The crowd that was for some hours in possession of the town was composed largely of women, even children. Few militiamen if any joined it, and when troops at last appeared on the scene it melted away as quickly as it had gathered.

Next day there were similar outbreaks further north, at Palencia and Medina del Rioseco; even somnolent Burgos was affected. Rioters were nowhere described as armed, and unlike those at Valencia they were responsible for no deaths. Acts of arson however were a recurrent feature, and the simultaneous breaking out of trouble in a number of separate places seemed to bespeak one of those 'vast conspiracies' that Spaniards were always suspecting one another of. The army had a welcome chance to take command of the situation. Scores of people were arrested, and courts martial began pronouncing sentence of death on individuals branded, on little or no evidence, as ringleaders. It was the first time in the Bienio, except against the Carlists or in Catalonia, that such harsh measures were being resorted to; a sad token of Liberalism's moral decline.

[1] The charge is supported by Escalera and González Llana, vol. iv, pp. 233-4, 237-9.

What above all made the riots look portentous, and kept them alive for years in conservative memories,[1] was their coming where they did, in a sleepy province supposed to be infested with nothing worse than highwaymen and suddenly appearing to be infested with 'socialism'. Prosper Mérimée in a letter to his friend the Countess of Montijo exclaimed that to hear of socialism in Old Castile was like hearing of the emperor of China turning monk. 'L'Espagne me paraît être dans la situation où se trouvait la France en 1792. Gare 93!'[2] What had happened was not quite so freakish as such bystanders imagined. Valladolid had lately been taking on a less sedentary character, thanks to the new canals that linked it with Rioseco and enabled it to collect the produce of a fertile region for shipment to the northern provinces and ports. Even if it mustered barely 40,000 inhabitants it struck an English traveller as a 'large and imposing' town.[3] Growth and activity brought with them as usual social strains; and it was the same in the whole surrounding area, where the canals were working as Ramírez Arcas wrote this year a 'miraculous' change.[4] For the poorer classes this expansion, and involvement with distant markets, might mean more loss than gain.

Valladolid's new enterprises attracted labour from outside as well as capital, workmen from industrial areas as far off as Barcelona and Valencia. These outlanders were pitched on as scapegoats by the town council, which resigned after the fracas: it talked of 'a deplorable crusade against property'.[5] Many in Madrid too, Otway reported, were throwing the blame on 'socialistic ideas stirred up and worked upon by French labourers, and easily adopted by an ignorant and impressionable populace who look upon the rich as their natural enemies'.[6] The advent of workers from Catalonia may well have helped to set a match to resentments against an intruding capitalism. At the same time the contrary allegation was at least equally plausible. This old-world land

---

[1] e.g. references in Hannay, pp. 59–60, and Hume, p. 430, which both show the legend swelling as well as lingering.

[2] *Correspondance générale*, 2nd series, vol. ii, p. 75; 15 July 1856.

[3] Lady L. Tenison, *Castile and Andalucia* (London, 1853), p. 385; other descriptions in E. Bégin, *Voyage pittoresque en Espagne et en Portugal* (Paris, 1850?), p. 78; Hoskins, vol. ii, chap. 13; A. L. A. Fée, *L'Espagne à cinquante ans d'intervalle, 1809–1859* (Paris, 1861), pp. 60 ff.

[4] *Tratados*, vol. ii, pp. 83–84.

[5] See Nido y Segalerva, *Antología*, pp. 680–1; he supports the theory.

[6] Otway to Clarendon, no. 11, 6 July 1856, F.O. 72. 894.

of priest and peasant had existed till now in a supralapsarian state
of innocence so far as socialism was concerned, but it was a region
where the clerical-royalist faction would not find it hard to inflame popular feeling against the two-faced *bourgeoisie* with its
worship of liberty and lucre. At Rioseco a mob, chiefly women
and drunkards, was said to have chanted 'Long live religion',
'Down with the Liberals', and 'Down with the millers'.[1]

Right and Left then could each seek to pin responsibility on the
other, and Liberal newspapers were bewildered. Some scented a
Carlist plot to worsen alarm about food shortages by destroying
grain, and the *Nación* hinted at Jesuit machinations, pointing out
that female rioters at least must be supposed 'uncontaminated by
the democratic plague'.[2] But it too saw the socialist 'hydra' rearing
its many heads.[3] A sober article in the *Semanario Económico*, tracing
unrest to ill-informed fears of famine, closed with a prayer that
Spain might 'soon, very soon, slay the monster of communism'.[4]
Portents of impending doom could be found in many other
quarters, including Barcelona where labour trouble was reviving
in an acute form. A minor disorder on the night of 24 June was
reported from Badajoz, chief town of poverty-stricken Extremadura where a woman calling herself 'Sofía' was distributing a
broadsheet which spoke of Christ as a social rebel who took the
wrong path, denounced Catholicism as a lie, and proclaimed the
hour of revolt.[5] With such wild shapes casting their wilder
shadows, the middle classes could scarcely refuse to believe that
they were seeing the harvest of 'the poisoned seeds of socialism
sown so thickly in these two black years over the soil of Spain';[6]
or that O'Donnell's firing-squads, like Louis Napoleon's of late
in France, were the only salvation. Liberal papers were at one in
applauding the government's display of 'firmness', if in nothing
else.

Ministers gave their backing to the red-ruin theory from the
first moment. Questioned on the 24th about the Old Castile riots
Escosura took his stand on the assertion, for which there had been

---

[1] Escalera and González Llana, vol. iv, pp. 235–6. Garrido thought Polacos were
implicated: *El socialismo y sus adversarios* (3rd ed., London. 1862), p. 80.
[2] 26 June 1856, 1/3.   [3] 26 June 1856, 1/1–3.
[4] No. 13, 30 June 1856, pp. 193–4.
[5] Text in Matilla, pp. 175–6; cf. Bermejo, *Estafeta*, vol. iii, p. 459.
[6] Miraflores, *Continuación*, vol. i, pp. 748–9. Cf. *Época*, 4 July 1856, 1/1–2, on the
danger of anarchy.

no time to gather any proofs, that hunger was not the cause, merely the pretext. Wages were high in that region, jobs more plentiful than hands. 'Energetic repression' must be their answer to the malignant influence at work.[1] Seoane, seconded by Orense, got up to protest against the minister's facile explanation, and dwelt on the remarkable sloth of the authorities at Valladolid, where there had been storm signals for a week beforehand. O'Donnell, at whom this was aimed, rejoined by blaming social-ism for all the fevers afflicting Spain. Today its agents were scattering their leaflets up and down Valencia, Alicante, Catalonia. 'The programme of these vandals—they deserve no other name— can be summed up as "War against anyone who owns any-thing" '.[2] Nobody wanted to be labelled a vandal, and Seoane, Calvo Asensio, Sagasta, and others immediately put down a resolution of support to the government in defending order. All must stand together when society was in peril, said Calvo Asensio.

Democrats were in obvious danger of being put into the dock; opponents clearly meant to use the affair to complete their isola-tion. Even their own new-found unity was in jeopardy, for some of them could hardly help feeling that this sort of trouble was what loose talk like Sixto Cámara's led to. Old Castile was one of the few areas where they had failed to establish centres. Yet they were to be stigmatized for years to come as allies of the incendiaries of Valladolid; and they themselves could never agree as to what really kindled the blaze. García Ruiz was to give the verdict of one section of the party by saying that 'the acts of arson sprang from the barbarism of the poor, who have always looked and will always look with envy on the rich'.[3] Unluckily, nearly all Spaniards were poor. Condemning class struggle, Democrats cut themselves off from the only forces capable of making their struggle against inertia and reaction successful; and they left class rancour to curdle into the blind hatred and anarchism that Rivero especially was so fearful of.

On 25 June there was a longer discussion in the Cortes, starting from a proposal of compensation to those whose prop-erty had suffered:[4] members displayed more interest in this than in the executions going on. A speech by Orense showed him

[1] Statement, and discussion following: D.S., pp. 9,142–8.
[2] Garrido, *El socialismo y sus adversarios*, pp. 79–80.
[3] *Historias*, vol. ii, pp. 588–9.   [4] D.S., pp. 9,156–64.

striving to curb hysteria, but himself nearly as dumbfounded as anyone. Palencia was his own constituency. If he had been in China when he heard the news he would not have believed it, he confessed. When this happened in Old Castile, anything might happen. But the remedy was to educate the poor, and bring them to see the folly of attacks on ownership. 'We of the propertied classes must not give ourselves up for lost, we must not despair of the revolution': to do so, he added all too prophetically, would be to drive a wedge between property and liberty.[1] Escosura read a message from the captain-general of Old Castile, Armero: three incendiaries had been shot at Valladolid, courts martial were continuing their work, a column was on its way to Rioseco, order prevailed. 'Signs of approval' found their way into the Cortes record.

On the same day Escosura set out, by decision of the Cabinet, to inquire into the causes which he had already so confidently pronounced on. With this mild assertion of the civil power the assembly was satisfied. It was under intense pressure from O'Donnell's adherents to dissolve, and leave him free to put the tottering social order in a state of defence; and a summer holiday at least was an inviting escape from disagreeable responsibilities. At 6.30 on Tuesday, 1 July, discussion of a fortnightly steamer service to Cuba was left unfinished, and Infante as president announced the adjournment.[2] Thus drably the 422nd sitting of the constituent assembly petered out; the next time speeches were heard in the Chamber they would be broken in on by the louder voices of cannon.

[1] Orense remarked in this speech that he, having enough land to manage already, had not bought any disamortized property. It would be interesting to know how many other deputies had been buying.

[2] D.S., p. 9,306.

XVII

THE FALL OF ESPARTERO

Red Peril and Army Intervention, July 1856

WHETHER the departing deputies would ever be allowed to come back for another positively last appearance was open to doubt. To go away leaving such a government in charge was risky enough, and to leave so many grave problems unsettled made it worse. Prices were still rising; at Seville troops were being held ready to deal with rioting.[1] More helpfully, at Bilbao export of grain or flour was temporarily prohibited. Then it was announced that in order to restore confidence imports of food into Spain would be licensed for the next six months.[2] But by conservative propaganda the necessity of a change of régime to rescue society was trumpeted more shrilly than ever. Progresistas retorted with threats that if any *coup d'état* were attempted committees of public safety would spring up all over the country to resist it. The nervousness behind this bold front was revealed by the way they still clung to a coalition that had lost all meaning.[3] Any of them, it was bitterly remarked later, could have seen through O'Donnell's intentions very easily, if only they had chosen to.[4] At the Buenavista a regular shadow Cabinet was taking shape: Ríos Rosas, his old ally of 1854, Cantero and Collado the bankers, Pastor Díaz the diplomat. Isabel was chafing at her restraints, and if O'Donnell did not cut through them for her she would turn to someone else. His former Moderado associates were insisting, Straten-Ponthoz knew, on a speedy breach with Espartero.[5] Most impatient of all were the army men; cavalry officers at Alcalá in particular talked insolently of dissolving the Cortes with their sabres.[6]

---

[1] J. B. Williams, consul at Seville, to Otway, no. 3, 11 July 1856, F.O. 185. 319.
[2] Decree of 11 July 1856; C.L., vol. lxix, pp. 203–4.
[3] *Clamor Público*, 11 July 1856, 1/2–3; *Nación*, 11 July, 1/1–5, a whole-page article arguing that no new 1843 was at hand, that the Vicalvarists were not anti-Liberal, &c.
[4] García Ruiz, *Historias*, vol. ii, p. 590.
[5] Straten-Ponthoz to Vilain XIIII, no. 132, 7 July 1856; *Espagne*, vol. 9.
[6] García Ruiz, *Historias*, vol. ii, p. 591. Cf. Villa-Urrutia, p. 110.

Espartero had perhaps come to deem himself indispensable to any Spanish ministry, and O'Donnell may have humoured the illusion. To get the duke to lend his name to a new, anti-radical government, with 'Property in danger' for watchword, would usefully confuse the public, and then after a while he could quietly be dropped. Some radicals must have been growing suspicious about him as well as O'Donnell; among them Fernández de los Ríos, who had no doubt that O'Donnell meant to prevent the constituent assembly from ever meeting again. It was agreed that he and Calvo Asensio should try to warn the leaders. They went that same night to see General Ferraz, the mayor, a worthy of 63, in high office before Espartero fell in 1843, now very much a man of the past. With some difficulty they woke him up, and implored him to take immediate precautions against a *coup*. He gaped, mumbled something about doing something, and dropped off to sleep again. 'General Ferraz was a Progresista *pur sang*', remarks Fernández de los Ríos in his narrative of these days.

Next morning the pair were admitted by a private stair to Espartero's sanctum, and explained their fears afresh. The duke rambled off into reminiscences of life in London, and then read out to them Isabel's letter after the July revolution beseeching him to come to Madrid—as if the scrap of paper were a guarantee of her loyalty. At last Fernández de los Ríos succeeded in breaking in and asking bluntly which side he would be on if a *coup* were attempted. Espartero jumped up and protested heatedly his devotion to the constituent assembly. There was no need of soldiers or militiamen to defend it: he himself, with ten men or five men and God and justice, would be its shield. Nothing his visitors could say made any dent in his impregnable self-complacency.[1]

It was symptomatic of the condition of Liberalism that the man about to become the central figure in the crisis was Escosura, a man of few convictions who, Otway wrote, 'had no sympathies in the Chamber and was most deservedly unpopular'.[2] Opportunist that he was, he had kept up some pose at least of radicalism, been elected a militia commandant, and was a favourite target of clerical denunciation. In any swing towards reaction he would risk being left out in the cold. He had an incentive therefore,

[1] Fernández de los Ríos, *Luchas políticas*, vol. ii, pp. 425-9. The dates he gives, 10 and 11 July, must be too late.
[2] Otway to Clarendon, private, 7 Aug. 1856; Clarendon Papers, vol. c. 58.

when he set off on June 25 on his tour of investigation, to handle things in such a way as to establish himself more firmly with the moderate Left. His more radical—or demagogic—brother Narciso accompanied him.[1]

Arrived at Valladolid he gave a vigorous display of open-mindedness, interviewing the notables and collecting confidential statements. Meanwhile the trickle of executions continued, besides prison sentences. Armero, the captain-general, went to Palencia to speed up the proceedings, and four alleged ringleaders were shot there before the end of June, another five on 4 July. There were signs of public disgust, especially when an old woman and a servant-girl were garrotted, and at Madrid a petition against any more death-sentences was got up. It may have struck Escosura that the military men were not taking much notice of the Minister of the Interior. He had played into their hands by committing himself too hastily in the Cortes to the 'socialistic' theory: now the evidence he gathered satisfied him—genuinely, says Garrido, no admirer—that the train had been laid by reactionary and clerical intrigue.[2] His opinion was promptly taken up in the Liberal and denounced in the Catholic press.

He like most others must have expected that the Cortes would wait to hear his report, which dressed up in his electrifying rhetoric might have made a formidable impact. Finding how things stood when he got back to Madrid on the evening of 9 July, he too warned Espartero and urged him to dismiss O'Donnell and all his army clique before it was too late.[3] Failing in this, he fell back on the device, not a very happy one for Liberalism's last gasp, of a gag on the Moderado press. On 11 July when the Cabinet held its Friday meeting at the premier's house Escosura produced a draft decree: O'Donnell retaliated with a call for big alterations in the militia. Both men began threatening to resign, and the meeting was resumed in the Queen's presence and went on inconclusively for hours.[4]

[1] According to an account of his private circle in Nombela, vol. ii, pp. 173 ff., Narciso's chief occupation was gambling.

[2] *Historia*, vol. iii, pp. 299–300. A Jesuit named Cuevas was particularly supected; he is defended by V. de la Fuente in *Historia de las sociedades secretas* (new ed., Barcelona, 1933), vol. iii, p. 57 n. 1, and *Historia eclesiástica*, vol. vi, pp. 258–9.

[3] Pirala, vol. ii, pp. 286–7.

[4] There are difficulties about the time-table and sequence of events of 11, 12, and 13 July. The *Nación* admitted that no one really knew what was taking place: 13 July 1856, 1/3–4. See an interesting narrative, given as by an eye-witness—

Amid vast speculation in the press about what was happening, the cabinet met next afternoon and Escosura pressed his proposal again; O'Donnell demanded his removal. Several others seem to have backed the War Minister: Zabala, F. Santa Cruz, and Luxán, it was credibly reported. Espartero shuffled and fidgeted. As head of party and government he ought to have told O'Donnell to resign, and then called out the militia to prevent the Vicalvarists from calling out the garrison. To abandon Escosura, even if the latter had put the quarrel on not the best footing, meant surrender. But the Duke of Victory had been for two years putting off any real stand, and every postponement left him less capable of ever making a stand. And although his authority in the country was still incalculable, if he chose to exert it, this would mean now, more definitely than two years or a year ago, an appeal to the masses against the classes.

'Crisis is over', Otway telegraphed to London on the Sunday morning: 'Escosura goes out.'[1] But some of Espartero's followers were striving to make him understand how deeply he was humiliating himself and them. Infante as president and Portilla as a vice-president of the assembly had already been consulted, according to custom in ministerial crises, and Espartero sent them to O'Donnell with a request to go on serving along with Escosura.[2] Even now he was putting his foot down only very softly. Infante told Otway afterwards that the intention was merely for Escosura to be kept in the Cabinet for a few face-saving days until a job could be found for him.[3] O'Donnell peremptorily refused any concession at all; the situation he wanted was developing of its own accord. Ministers met once more, and Espartero seems to have grown exasperated enough to tell Isabel that evening that she must either support him or do without him. She too, the longed-for hour of deliverance at hand, grew agitated, burst into tears, and finally said she would preside over another Cabinet meeting this same night.[4]

presumably a minister, in *The Times*, 26 Sept. (Paris, 24 Sept.), 8/1; García Ruiz, *Historias*, vol. ii, p. 592.
[1] 2nd cipher tel. of 13 July 1856, F.O. 72. 894.
[2] Otway to Clarendon, no. 17, 14 July 1856, F.O. 72. 894; Turgot to Walewski, no. 66, 14 July; *Espagne*, vol. 848.
[3] Otway to Clarendon, no. 30, 23 July 1856, F.O. 72. 895.
[4] As n. 2 (above); see also Mazade, *Révolutions*, pp. 118–19, and Bermejo, *Estafeta*, vol. iii, p. 462.

It was after midnight when ministers gathered for the last time. Isabel, who had doubtless conned her part carefully, gave her verdict that O'Donnell should remain and Escosura go. As the latter prepared to leave, Espartero rose to accompany him. For two hours Isabel pleaded with him not to resign. The conspirators had to do everything to make it possible for him not to feel, or not to tell the country, that he was being dismissed. Injured pride if not honour kept him from consenting; but he threw down no challenge: the resignation he wrote out, or signed, was in conventional terms about bad health and desire for leisure. 'O'Donnell will not desert me!' Isabel is said to have exclaimed then, in her play-acting style. He, to be sure, had no intention of deserting her. At 4 a.m. he was receiving his commission to form a new ministry, and the Duke of Victory was descending the great staircase to leave the palace; not as he had left it on his day of triumph two years ago, with Madrid waiting outside to applaud.

Some Puro chiefs were meeting as the crisis came to a head, Straten-Ponthoz heard, and there was talk of summoning the people to attack the palace, and carrying the Queen off.[1] It was talk only, for Espartero was giving no signal. A story became current of his saying to friends who clustered round: 'If you start any resistance, I'll blow my brains out.'[2] He may have clung to a notion that Isabel would soon discover her error, and send him another pathetic letter. But in the sudden tumbling down of his imaginary world he cannot have been capable of much coherent thought. He went to ground in the Gurrea family's house. The one Progresista ready to do something on the spur of the moment was the erratic Escosura. About 4 a.m. a group of Democrats who were on the prowl all that night, Garrido and Becerra and others, encountered him in the Puerta del Sol, on his way to the Principal. He told them with very mistaken confidence that the army was sure to pronounce against O'Donnell;[3] and he sent out from his old office, where he had no right now to be, telegraphic orders for resistance. Most of them went unheeded.

O'Donnell's prospective colleagues seem to have spent the night waiting at the house of Ríos Rosas in the Calle Mayor. They were sworn in at dawn, and very early this Monday morning

---

[1] Straten-Ponthoz to Vilain XIIII, no. 139, 14 July 1856; *Espagne*, vol. 9.
[2] J. Valero de Tornos, *Crónicas retrospectivas* (Madrid, 1901), p. 26.
[3] Garrido, *Historia*, vol. iii, pp. 302–3.

a *Gazette* gave news of the changes. O'Donnell of course kept the War ministry. Ríos Rosas took the Interior; Cantero, another from Córdova's team, Finance, Collado Development, Pastor Díaz Foreign Affairs. None of these men could be considered beyond the Liberal pale. Collado had served in the government of the Bienio, like Luzuriaga who was away from Madrid but was to be offered Justice. If however this Cabinet could not be called at first blush a reactionary one, and all its members except the leader were civilians, the same could have been said with equal truth about Córdova's, of which it was in many ways a reincarnation.

O'Donnell was losing no time in alerting the garrison troops and calling in reinforcements from near-by points.[1] The army was accustomed to look to him, and he had his own men in the positions that counted most. Garrido heard of loyal messages to Espartero from the colonels of the garrison forces.[2] But officers willing to support the duke as premier against a *coup* from the Right would be far less so to back him as a party leader heading a *coup* from the Left; least of all to make one for him while he sat with arms folded. Various senior men were arriving at the palace with offers of their services, while San Miguel at the head of the royal halberdiers vowed to stand by his sovereign to the last drop of his Liberal blood.[3] Nor were the common soldiers likely to give O'Donnell much anxiety. They had too little to thank Liberalism for, either as conscripts or as the peasants that most of them were; as peasants also they can hardly have been untouched by the clerical propaganda against it. They felt, besides, some of their superiors' prejudices against the militia; too often when conscript and *miliciano* performed guard duties together the one had to stand at attention while the other lounged, chatted, or shared a glass with his cronies.

Had Espartero been prepared to say plainly that he considered himself dismissed, every Spaniard to whom his name was faith and hope would have taken up arms to reinstate him. To very many the mere fact of his being no longer premier seemed proof enough of foul play. O'Donnell's apologists would vehemently

[1] Anon., *Relación de los sucesos de Madrid en los días 14, 15 y 16 de julio de 1856* (Madrid, 1856), p. 2. This pamphlet is an army account, almost identical with the one in *Asamblea del Ejército*, no. 3, Aug. 1856, pp. 232–55.

[2] *Historia*, vol. iii, pp. 302–3.

[3] *The Times*, 24 July 1856, 9/5–6. Cf. a graphic scene at the palace in Nombela, vol. ii, pp. 352 ff.

deny that anything else than a normal change of ministry had taken place. Whether or not Isabel was entitled to make a change certain to be repudiated by the Cortes, might be a nice question. The Constitution, which restored her prerogatives, was not yet promulgated, and she might be said to exercise them only on sufferance. But O'Donnell in 1854 had disputed by conspiracy and rebellion her right to appoint ministers without public or parliamentary approval. Whoever else in Spain might properly claim legitimacy, it could scarcely be the new prime minister.

Town council and provincial council met, but seemed inclined to do no more. If there was to be any Progresista initiative, it must come from the Cortes. As in July 1855 there had been no formal prorogation, so that the session could be resumed at any moment. A good many members were soon collecting at the Cortes building, and by about 10 a.m. the unenthusiastic Infante was being urged to give the word for a sitting. O'Donnell, who knew his man, sent for him and seems to have offered some vague assurances. But while Infante conferred with whatever vice-presidents and secretaries were available, the commoners of Madrid were beginning to take action of their own. As on the morning of Cristina's escape, they jumped to the conclusion that their hero was being tricked or coerced and that it was for them to save him. Very soon patriots could be seen scurrying from house to house with lists of names, knocking up fellow militia-men who turned out promptly at the call.[1]

In whole units the Democrat creed had been firmly embraced,[2] especially among the *ligeros* or light battalions, the Third for example whose leading spirits were Sixto Cámara and Becerra. To see men of this temper taking up arms on their own account would alarm staid Liberals as well as their enemies, and when Ferraz, about noon, ordered regular mobilization, his idea was not to prepare for resistance but to bring hotheads under control and to balance the more advanced units with the more conser-vative. So at any rate he was said to have told Serrano when summoned to army headquarters in the Buenavista. Democrats were not far wrong in surmising that General Ferraz's heart was more with the palace than with the people.[3] But solid masses of

[1] G. Hugelmann, *L'Espagne et ses derniers évènements* (Paris, 1856), p. 101.
[2] N. Fernández Cuesta, *Vindicación de la democracia española*, p. 78.
[3] Garrido, *Historia*, vol. iii, p. 304; Pi, *Historia*, vol. iv, p. 150.

armed men were collecting now, 16,000 foot with a few horse and sixteen guns;[1] buildings were being occupied, barricades rising.

On their side the sole act of the new ministers was to lend a sanction to anything Isabel and O'Donnell might do, by signing a decree of martial law. By the time this came out, in a special *Gazette* in the afternoon, it could be contended that the state of Madrid warranted it, but it covered the whole country, and its elaborate wording, which dwelt luridly on the perils of social dissolution, gave it an air of having been got ready beforehand to strangle any opposition, peaceful or not. To make it good O'Donnell had 6,808 infantry and 40 guns, besides cavalry. As in July 1854 the troops were in two divisions, straddling central Madrid; Serrano commanded on the eastern line of the Prado and Concha in the neighbourhood of the palace, where O'Donnell himself was now ensconced.

About 2 p.m. Vega de Armijo, one of the Cortes secretaries, was overborne and a session was announced for four o'clock. Among the waiting deputies antagonism to O'Donnell was sharpened considerably by the declaration of a state of siege, but how to counter this was a question easier asked than answered. Even now if Espartero were to stand forward frankly his authority might avert conflict, by compelling the Court to come to terms; or if battle were joined he could make the people's triumph almost certain. Many *milicianos* must have believed that he was coming to put himself at their head. Oftener than anyone could remember at parades and reviews he had vowed if ever liberty were in peril to draw the sword of Luchana from its sheath. Today he was invisible, or hurrying aimlessly from place to place, the fluttering shadow of a hero. At one time, Otway learned, he was at the town hall, where he 'murmered [*sic*] a few unintelligible phrases' to the councillors; there were glimpses of him in the streets, passing barricades and evasively telling men who shouted to him to join them that he was wanted at the Cortes;[2] then he disappeared again.

Now that Espartero was missing, white plume and all, the politicians who had lived so cheaply on his prestige were faced with the penalty. All round them the capital was splitting into two armed camps, and they must have wondered uneasily whose the ultimate gain would be if the militia overthrew the army. If on

---

[1] For detail of the battalions and their positions see *Relación de los sucesos*, pp. 4–5.
[2] Otway to Clarendon, no. 22, 18 July 1856, F.O. 72. 894.

the other hand the army won a contest in the streets, O'Donnell's success would be complete: he would have proved that the anarchism he had talked of was real and that he knew how to save society from it. Ordeal by battle might be the very chance he wanted. If so, the sensible course would be to keep to parliamentary resistance. But the decreeing of a state of siege seemed to serve notice that nothing of the kind would be permitted. Thanks to its many sins of omission Liberalism was in a predicament where it must fight or surrender, and it shrank from both alternatives. No one wished to tell the militia to open fire, no one wished to tell it to disband and go home.

About 4.30 p.m. the last sitting of the constituent assembly began. Ninety-one members answered the roll;[1] more than the quorum of 50 which sufficed for any business but the passing of laws. Among them were two from the late Cabinet, Escosura and F. Santa Cruz, and two earlier ministers of the Bienio, Madoz and Fuente Andrés. There were eight Democrats, including García Ruiz who was to write the story of these last hours; Orense had left Madrid. Espartero's friend Matheu and secretary V. Gurrea were present. Madoz was the man who was ready with a formula, inspired by the blend of radicalism and respectability that he cultivated: he spoke briefly to a motion of no confidence in the new government.[2] He was in militia uniform, and commended the action of the civic authorities in calling out the militia to protect order and tranquillity. When Tabuérniga argued that any censure of the government would provoke a conflagration, Madoz replied that his motion was simply a statement to the country of the assembly's opinion. In a division 82 votes including Infante's were cast in favour of it, only Tabuérniga's against. But it was followed up only by leisurely procedural rites. Deputies were content to mark time in the hope of an acceptable offer from the palace; cancellation of the state of siege would in all likelihood have satisfied their self-respect. They went through the routine of electing a committee to draft an expostulation to the Queen, and Infante wrote to ask when she would be pleased to receive it. Twelve delegates chosen by lot were given leave to retire and put on formal dress.

But whereas the troops could stand to their arms for any length

---

[1] For the names of those present see D.S., p. 9,307.
[2] For Madoz's speech and the discussion on it see D.S., pp. 9,307–10.

of time, the militia could not. And unluckily for the Progresista game of bluff O'Donnell possessed better nerves, and an intimate knowledge of what phrases from them meant. For hours he ignored Infante's message, and then he refused to recognize the Cortes vote, on the pretext that too few deputies were present.[1] It was to be made a reproach to him later that he could have averted bloodshed by simply condescending to parley; but having burned his parliamentary boats he was compelled to depend on the Court, and one of the first things Isabel required was a good riddance to the assembly which had met twenty months since to sit in judgement on her. About 7 o'clock Turgot had to reopen a dispatch in which he prophesied that there would be no fighting, in order to add a postscript saying that fighting had just broken out.[2]

[1] Text of his letter in *Nación*, 18 July 1856, 1/3–4.
[2] Turgot to Walewski, no. 66, 14 July 1856; *Espagne*, vol. 848.

XVIII

COUNTER-REVOLUTION

O'Donnell in Power, July 1856

THE first shots were fired either by or at the 3rd Light Battalion, posted at the Santo Domingo square. It accused soldiers of attacking it; an army account said that an accidental clash was at once followed by heavy fire from the *milicianos*.[1] Some on both sides must have been ready to precipitate, or at least to welcome, an engagement. There was too little daylight left for a general engagement, but Turgot in his embassy not far from the palace heard bursts of musketry almost throughout the night.[2] The parliament-men had been anxious to avert this clash; once it had started their posture of meticulous legalism could do no good, or could only ensure them personally against future reprisals. There was little meaning in the mere presence of a rump of deputies on these eloquent benches, muffled now by night and doubt. A few of the boldest might be hoping to see history carried forward on the people's bayonets; some others might, in an unkind critic's words, sound the charge when the battle was won.[3] No one had any further move to suggest, except an offer to Espartero of a special mandate to protect the precincts of the Cortes.[4] Even this was too much for Infante, who refused to put the motion because it meant a departure from constitutional correctness. Discouraging news came in from the town hall about 2.30 a.m. of powder and shot already running low. It seems that neither Ferraz nor Escosura had taken care to keep the battalions well supplied; possibly they had taken care not to.

---

[1] *Relación de los sucesos*, pp. 6–7; the most reliable outline of the fighting. Most newspapers failed to appear for several days. There is a synopsis of happenings in the *Nación*, 18 July, 1/4–5, and a compilation of other press reports in the *Clamor Público*, 18 July, 1/1–3. See also O'Donnell's speech of 18 May 1857: Navarro y Rodrigo, p. 121.

[2] Turgot to Walewski, no. 67, 15 July 1856; *Espagne*, vol. 848.

[3] Hugelmann, p. 106. This republican renegade turned Bonapartist was editing a French sheet at Madrid.

[4] D.S., p. 9,313.

Meanwhile Espartero, lying perdu close by in the Calle de Santa Catalina, was being begged and beseeched to do something. He was very reluctant, but still wanted to delay and keep the door open. About six on Tuesday morning he shook off his paralysis so far as to show himself at the Cortes. Its aspect of a forlorn hope can hardly have infused much optimism into him, or he into it. There was some colloquy, and then about 7 a.m. Infante and other prudent men drew him off to the president's room and warned him to think of the extremes—republicanism or worse—that he might let loose by joining the excited populace.[1] He affected to have been merely paying the assembly a courtesy call, and slipped away as noiselessly as he had come. Later on he made it his plea that he could not bear to be the cause of fratricidal strife;[2] which failed to explain why he did not shorten the bloodshed by saying plainly that he meant to take no part.

Militiamen were still waiting for him in vain. After all these hours under arms they cannot have been at their freshest, and such a mass of men would be hard to supply with food as well as powder, but a fair proportion awaited the assault steadily. Their enemies had not been idle. At the outset O'Donnell may have contemplated having to give up Madrid and remove to some other base,[3] but the inertness of Espartero and the Cortes raised his confidence. A proclamation to overawe the citizenry was ready for posting up, another to animate the soldiery with promises of medals and pensions. Concha had arranged with Serrano to launch attacks on both fronts, while their cavalry blockaded the city and cut off supplies.[4]

When morning came Concha opened a cannonade from the Plaza del Oriente in front of the palace, and further south a battery was hastily mounted to sweep the Calle Mayor, along which troops then started advancing yard by yard against stiff resistance. On the eastern side the militia was summoned to disperse within thirty minutes. There was no response, and a column

[1] Espartero's visit to the Cortes seems sufficiently vouched for, though not mentioned in the D.S. because the session was not in formal progress, but it is very variously described: see Otway to Clarendon, no. 22, 18 July 1856, F.O. 72. 894; Pirala, vol. ii, p. 295; Garrido, *Historia*, vol. iii, pp. 309 ff. García Ruiz's account, in *Historias*, vol. ii, p. 595, is the most circumstantial.
[2] 'Manifiesto del general Espartero á los progresistas barceloneses', Apr. 1857: extracts in Orellana, vol. ii, pp. 71 ff.
[3] Pirala, vol. ii, pp. 294–5.
[4] *Relación de los sucesos*, p. 8.

led by Enrique O'Donnell began forcing its way along the Calle de Alcalá, that old millrace of revolution and counter-revolution. A second attack was launched at the junction of the Prado and San Jerónimo, only two or three hundred yards distant from the Cortes. Serrano used his cannon with the same brutality as Gándara on the same ground in 1854, but his attempts to storm the palaces of Medina Celi and Vistahermosa, facing each other at the two corners and held by Madoz's 5th Battalion, were beaten off. The Duke of Medina Celi remonstrated feelingly with the Queen afterwards about his pictures and porcelain.[1]

At 9.30 a.m. Infante reopened the session, to urge that they should seek an honourable end to the fighting; he offered to go in person to treat. There was no demur, and he set off to find Serrano. They agreed on a truce of six hours, to come into effect at 11 a.m.;[2] on Infante's part it was a thinly disguised surrender. His place in the chair had been taken by Portilla. A horrid din shook the walls, and presently a cannon-ball flew in through a window and fell close beside Sagasta, on the third row behind that front bench where he was to repose sedately in years to come. Portilla with Castilian sang-froid put on his hat, and continued in his seat. They all sat on in dogged silence for another hour and twenty-five minutes, with a stoicism entitled to respect, but of no avail to the hard-pressed citizen forces, except to keep floating over their struggle some shadowy banner of legality. At last, at 11.45 a.m., Infante returned, and at his desire the House went into secret session.[3] With this the nine thousand pages of its official record break off; García Ruiz's narrative provides an epilogue. Infante insisted that they were too few to carry on. There proved indeed to be only 43 left: six Democrats, the rest Progresistas. Infante in gloomy accents declared the session closed. It was a whole Liberal epoch that was closing. Individual deputies returned to their posts with the militia, and several, including Rivero, appear to have given a good account of themselves; but the six-hour truce was bound to demoralize the resistance, and early in the afternoon Ferraz sent round word of the Cortes closure and recommended the militia to abandon a hopeless contest.[4] Officers

[1] *The Times*, 15 Aug. 1856, 8/1.
[2] *Relación de los sucesos*, p. 13. Later writers give discrepant times for Infante's movements, and García Ruiz (*Historias*, vol. iii, p. 597) brings him back to the Cortes about 2 p.m., which is much too late.
[3] D.S., p. 9,314.   [4] Pi, *Historia*, vol. iv, p. 159.

found pretexts to slip away, the highest first, then the others in turn.[1] When fighting was resumed later in the afternoon, the position really was hopeless. The stubbornly defended buildings at the entry to the San Jerónimo had been relinquished by the 5th Battalion, which fell back gradually as far as the Plaza de Santa Ana, until it melted away. Its leader, Madoz, was accused of sabotaging the whole defence by this retreat, and Sagasta of weakly withdrawing his engineer unit from the Teatro Real. The 3rd Light Battalion was left exposed, and it too, in spite of the exhortations of Becerra and Sixto Cámara, began to disintegrate.[2] By nightfall a *sauve qui peut* was setting in. Early next morning, Wednesday the 16th, the Plaza Mayor and Puerta del Sol were occupied without a struggle, and soon notices were placarded over the town dissolving Madrid's urban and provincial councils and ordering all *milicianos* to surrender their weapons within six hours. New town councillors were being nominated at once, reliable men like the Duke of Alba who was soon to succeed the Marquis of Perales as mayor.

There was still some resistance on this closing day, chiefly by the working class, vanguard in 1854 and now rearguard of the revolution. It was bitterest in the southern district, especially in the maze of crowded alleys round the Cebada. Pucheta the bull-fighter was again to the fore, and managed to bring off to his stronghold the militia cannon; it may be true that under his handling they instilled more alarm than confidence into his followers.[3] The army approached its remaining foes with circumspection: an elaborate plan for the reduction of the 'South' was first concerted. While Serrano and Dulce pushed down from the centre of the town, Concha and Ros de Olano made a detour round the southern outskirts to take the rebels from the rear by way of the Toledo bridge, and closed in from three sides on the Cebada where the final encounter took place.[4] Pucheta died fighting; or by another report was captured and shot out of hand.[5] He left

---

[1] Hugelmann, pp. 106–7.

[2] Garrido, *Obras escogidas*, vol. i, p. 408, in an admiring obituary article on Sixto Cámara. A tribute to the 3rd Light Battalion is paid by N. Estévanez, who was in the fighting as an army cadet, in *Fragmentos de mis memorias* (Madrid, 1903), pp. 26–29.

[3] Hubbard, vol. v, p. 262.

[4] *Relación de los sucesos*, pp. 16–19. Strong resistance was met with along the Calle de Toledo.   [5] Matilla, p. 180; Cossío, vol. iii, pp. 657–8.

a brother to serve in the revolution of 1868.[1] Chico's ghost, if it haunted this place of death, could feel appeased, and the generals trooped back to the palace ready for their rewards. Enrique O'Donnell got a grand cross; Serrano immediately became a field-marshal, aged 45.

The cost in losses to their men was given as 38 killed, 222 wounded.[2] On the other side it must have been a great deal higher; ten times as high, Turgot thought.[3] Only a minority of militia-men took an active part, and García Ruiz contrasted their showing unfavourably with that of the insurgents of 1854.[4] Marx criticized the militia for letting itself be cooped up in the middle of the town.[5] Elaborate parade-ground training must have lessened mobility and initiative. And too many of the higher officers were of the stamp of Luxán, said to have assured O'Donnell privately that he was trying to induce his 2nd Battalion to lay down its arms.[6] Considering all this, the popular side did not do too badly. Otway spoke of courage worn down only by 'the terrific fire of the artillery', and thought the outcome might have been different had the militiamen not been left in the lurch.[7] Private letters convinced the *Times* man at Paris that the struggle was more stubborn and the bloodshed far heavier than official propaganda gave out; also that the Democrats acquitted themselves best.[8]

O'Donnell granted all conscripts at Madrid six months' reduction of service and promised similar benefits to loyal soldiers in the provinces.[9] He had won the decisive round already by quelling the capital. In 1854 Madrid rose only after other cities gave the signal; in 1856 it was in the forefront. This was evidence of its political growth, but its defeat was a proportionately severe blow, worsened by the moral as well as physical collapse of the leadership. One of the two stone lions outside the Cortes had had its head carried off by a cannon-ball, and presented 'a most ridiculous

---

[1] L. de Taxonera, *Un político español del siglo XIX. González Bravo y su tiempo* (Barcelona, 1941), p. 240.

[2] *Relación de los sucesos*, pp. 20, 23.

[3] Turgot to Walewski, no. 68, 17 July 1856; *Espagne*, vol. 848. Angelón took it for granted that bloodshed in Madrid was much heavier than in 1854 (pp. 460, 463).

[4] *Dios y el hombre*, p. 326.   [5] Marx, p. 150 (18 Aug. 1856).

[6] Hugelmann, p. 119; his account of the incident is, however, confused.

[7] Otway no. 22 (above). Even Hugelmann admitted as much (pp. 121–2).

[8] *The Times*, 23 July 1856 (Paris, 21 July), 10/1.

[9] Decree of 22 July 1856; C.L., vol. lxix, pp. 230–1.

appearance':[1] it made no bad emblem of decapitated Liberalism. The Duke of Victory was hiding his head in an obscure lodging, and his portrait was being burned in streets where a week ago he was worshipped. O'Donnell's main strength lay, as Turgot saw, in the bankruptcy of Progresismo—'une religion dont le Dieu a abdiqué'.[2]

In many areas the new régime met with scarcely a show of recalcitrance. There was none at Valladolid or the other towns so lately depicted as breeding-grounds of anarchism. Outlying regions were more inclined to resist, partly because the fall of Madrid became known to them more slowly. In the north-west Lugo and other towns came out against O'Donnell, and F. de P. Ruiz at Corunna was one of the few captain-generals who did the same. He however was promptly deposed by his second in command, General Vasallo; and after a scuffle and some shooting it was agreed between the militia and the army that they should wait and see how things turned out at Madrid. Then the militia surrendered its arms.[3] In southern and eastern Spain many town councils resigned in a body, or declared against O'Donnell and had to be dissolved. They seldom went beyond passive protest; among Liberals of the sort who became councillors disillusion and apathy were too widespread. Yet behaviour of the militia seems proof that the will to resist was keen enough in the citizen mass, and that only leadership and combination were wanting to make it effective.

In one place after another militiamen banded together of their own accord on hearing of Espartero's fall, but found themselves without plan or guidance, and broke up in discouragement when the tidings of defeat arrived from Madrid. At Jaén the senior army officer at first had to escape into the hills.[4] Troops and milicianos at Granada stood facing each other from the 17th to the 19th, when captain-general and town council agreed to wait for the news.[5] At Cadiz, where serious trouble was feared, the militia sullenly submitted to being disarmed. When the state of

---

[1] Otway to Clarendon, no. 21, 18 July 1856, F.O. 72. 894.

[2] Turgot to Walewski, no. 72, 25 July 1856; Espagne, vol. 848.

[3] E. Santos, vice-consul at Corunna, to Otway, no. 1, 21 July 1856, F.O. 185. 319.

[4] Bouzet, consul at Malaga, to Walewski, no. 81, 16 Aug. 1856; Espagne, Consular, vol. 56.

[5] G. Williams, vice-consul at Granada, to Otway, 20 July 1856, F.O. 185. 319.

siege was proclaimed on the 17th at Seville the city council resigned, but did nothing else; on the 21st and 22nd the militia was disarmed without difficulty; some trivial attempts next day to get up a fight only resulted in the deaths of a few rioters.[1] Here and elsewhere discord between Progresistas and Democrats helped to immobilize both.

Of all the southern cities industrial Malaga stood out longest; its militia, so often taxed with ruffianism, showed both firmness and discipline. News of Espartero's fall came on the morning of 17 July; the men at once took up arms and occupied all strategic points. Their commandants and the city and provincial councils drew up a joint remonstrance to the Queen.[2] Next day the troops gave their adhesion to the popular cause, while Domingo Velo the respected civil governor took charge. Shortly before 6 p.m. Malaga learned of the rout at Madrid. Not surprisingly the soldiers wavered, and on the 21st their officers got them to declare for O'Donnell and shut themselves up in the fortress. Even now the citizen forces were not cowed; they turned out and built barricades, and some were eager for an assault on the citadel. No battle took place, thanks to mediation by the consular body and to Velo's anxiety for a pacific settlement, which he employed much skill in inducing the militia to accept. Then he slipped away on an English ship to Gibraltar.[3] On the 26th O'Donnell's lieutenants made their entry, proclaimed martial law and dissolution of the militia, and ordered the surrender of arms by sunset. Both British and French representatives paid tribute to the militia's conduct during the nine days; there was no anarchy, no subversion of society, not even any looting.

It was the weakness of Spanish centrifugalism that these disaffected areas had nothing to draw them together for a combined stand. When Sixto Cámara escaped from Madrid in a southbound train, after lying low for a week, his hopes of a struggle were dashed, and he made his way abroad.[4] Orense was arrested

[1] Guichot, vol. v, pp. 82–85.
[2] J. A. Mark, acting-consul at Malaga, to Otway, no. 26, 18 July 1856, F.O. 185. 319, and R. Lagoanère, acting-consul, to Walewski, no. 74, 18 July; *Espagne*, Consular, vol. 56. Printed copies of the protest with both.
[3] Much detail on these developments, and copies of correspondence, with W. P. Mark, consul at Malaga, to Otway, no. 29, 25 July 1856, F.O. 185. 319, and Lagoanère to Walewski, no. 77, 26 July; *Espagne*, Consular, vol. 56.
[4] Garrido, *Obras escogidas*, vol. i, pp. 409–11.

on suspicion at Valencia. Here the late government had done O'Donnell's work for him beforehand. Democrats tried to get the civil governor and captain-general, both Esparteristas, to re-arm the militia, and might have succeeded but for some officers of the garrison. On the night of the 17th news of the defeat at Madrid put an end to any such thoughts.[1] It was much the same at near-by Alicante. Barcelona was the only place outside Madrid where a serious clash followed. Little had been done by the fallen régime to endear it to the public there; but national events happened to coincide with a fresh surge of industrial unrest, and produced one of the worst storms in the city's stormy history.

Word arrived only on 17 July of O'Donnell being in power and of Madrid and other cities having risen. Next afternoon demon-strators had to be dispersed, and some of the more determined city councillors and militia chiefs were endeavouring to set up a junta.[2] But here too Liberalism had hamstrung itself in advance by giving up Catalonia, from fear of the workers, to the rule of Zapatero, and he and his Moderado friends were pining for an opportunity like this to settle accounts. He had six thousand in-fantry ready for action, drawn out along the water-front between their main base, the Atarazanas fort at the south-west corner of the town, and the Plaza del Palacio.[3] Early in the evening of the 18th Zapatero promptly poured soldiers into the mutinous areas and opened fire. Soon the insurgents had to fall back into the factory districts, where resistance was continued till midnight, mainly it would seem by the workers there. They were joined by at least one battalion and some other companies of militiamen, many of these probably themselves workmen; and it was alleged that French refugees and prominent Democrats took part.

In the morning things were at first quiet. Zapatero ordered four militia battalions to be disbanded and gave the men one hour to hand in their arms.[4] Only half of them did so, and by noon battle was joined afresh. Armed bands flocked in from neighbouring

---

[1] Vice-consul C. Barrie to Otway, no. 11, 17 July 1856, F.O. 185. 319.

[2] Capt. R. Aguirre, 'Sucesos de Barcelona', in *La Asamblea del Ejército*, no. 4, Sept. 1856, pp. 301–2. Cf. Carrera Pujal, vol. iv, p. 323. No newspapers came out at Barcelona for several days.

[3] 'Sucesos de Barcelona', pp. 303–5; and see Zapatero's report of 26 July 1856, partially reproduced in Chamorro y Baquerizo, part 2, p. 460.

[4] Acting-consul Prat to Clarendon, no. 23, 19 July 1856, F.O. 72. 901, and to Otway, no. 18, 19 July, F.O. 185. 319; Baradère to Walewski, tel. 19 July, 3 p.m.; *Espagne*, Consular, vol. 52.

districts to aid the Barcelona rebels, and according to Zapatero's report practically the whole militia was making common cause with them. Next day, the 20th, he was hard-pressed enough to resort to firing the guns of Monjuich fortress into the streets. Various committees of town councillors and others failed to patch up a compromise, and all that night an obstinate conflict raged. At last on the 21st, soon after midday, Zapatero was in a position to order a decisive onslaught with the bayonet; by 4 p.m. all the principal barricades were taken by assault.[1] He followed up his success by dissolving the town council—he had already arrested four members—and nominating a fresh body, mostly businessmen and millowners. On the 23rd, as though to give his new council an impressive start, three prisoners were shot. Many others were being jailed and condemned to hard labour, and houses were under search for arms.[2] Baradère spoke for all friends of order, now drawing a deep breath of relief, when he gave the captain-general credit for saving society. The violence of the encounter could be cited as corroboration. Army losses were given as 13 officers and 50 men killed, 11 officers and 198 men wounded;[3] the official total of dead was thus appreciably higher than at Madrid. Rebel casualties must have been much heavier. One estimate put them at 403 in killed alone.[4]

As always the troops had been more effectively organized and led. They tried, too, an experiment in mechanized street warfare, with a primitive armoured car, a contraption on wheels sheltering two snipers that could be propelled from inside. Between middle-class radicals and the working class there was too little solidarity; and, as Marx noted, there was division within the working class itself, not all of which joined in the fray.[5] From the rest of Catalonia support was inadequate, though Barcelona's resistance was seconded by Tarragona, Reus, Gerona, and other towns. In Gerona province the movement seemed particularly firm. But General Ruiz was abandoned by his own forces when he threw in his lot with the militia; and the brittle state of Liberalism could be seen in the bestowing—or forcing—of a post on a Cortes

---

[1] On the fighting of 21 July see 'Sucesos de Barcelona', pp. 314–17; Prat to Clarendon, no. 26, 21 July 1856, F.O. 72. 901, and to Otway, no. 21, 22 July, F.O. 185. 319.

[2] Carrera Pujal, vol. iv, p. 324.

[3] 'Sucesos de Barcelona', p. 321. Slightly different figures are given elsewhere.

[4] Ibid.   [5] Marx, p. 151.

deputy, E. de Climent, secretly disillusioned with his Progresista party and longing to see parliamentarianism supplanted by dictatorship.[1]

While Barcelona struck its blow, Saragossa waved its sword. Elsewhere in Spain, and abroad, it was believed that a rival government was taking shape at this city, with a large contingent of Cortes members to lend it a mantle of legality;[2] and for a week or so it really looked as if Saragossa meant to assume the leadership of the country, or conceivably to lead Aragon out of it. There had been talk before 1854 of a revival of the old franchises of the 'eastern realms', Aragon and Valencia and Catalonia, to give them the same autonomy as the Basque provinces; during the Bienio a plan was mooted to restore old links by grouping the three together as in bygone days.[3] In left-wing propaganda the federal idea had been taking a salient place. Besides all this, Saragossa had like all regional centres a population of civil servants whose salaries were in jeopardy the moment the Progresista government fell.

Falcón, the captain-general, and Polo, the civil governor, took the initiative by calling a meeting of public bodies on the evening of the 15th, and a junta was set up with Falcón president and Polo vice-president.[4] Manifestos were drawn up, militiamen drilled and paraded daily: Ruiz Pons was elected commandant of one of the battalions. Troops were being reviewed likewise, and the two forces seemed prepared to stand together; Gurrea while captain-general had conferred posts on officers of Progresista affiliation. But the 'socialistic' character of the militants of Madrid, and especially of Barcelona, was likely to make Liberal dignitaries chary of combining with them, especially after Saragossa's own food riot and militia outbreak of the previous winter. Only one radical and one Democrat found a place in the junta, and the men in control were not really trying to organize a struggle, any more than at Madrid. Their object was to secure the best

---

[1] Carrera Pujal, vol. iv, pp. 324–7.

[2] e.g. The Times, 21 July 1856, 9/4; 22 July, 10/2.

[3] Its chief advocate was the writer V. Balaguer, who founded a journal, La Corona de Aragón, and in 1857, with L. Cutchet, another, published—a new departure—in Catalan. See M. García Venero, Historia del nacionalismo catalán 1793–1936 (Madrid, 1944), pp. 83–84.

[4] Escenas contemporáneas, vol. i, pp. 9–10, in an anonymous article, 'Zaragoza (desde julio de 1856)'.

terms for themselves while providing a safety-valve for public anger, or at most to be ready if by some chance O'Donnell were overthrown.

Madrid and Barcelona were soon beaten down, and Saragossa left isolated. And nowhere else in Spain could the collapse of Espartero make for more doubt and dudgeon than here. Among the military there was a speedy drift towards the government side. Dulce was coming up with a column and a siege-train, and on 24 July a deputation from the junta went out to ask him not to start a bombardment. Diplomacy set to work, warlike spirit evaporated: militia officers quitted their men, units melted away. Last-ditch efforts by Democrats failed to muster support, and Bruil and Borao took a zealous part in arranging a capitulation on terms considered sensible by moderates, an amnesty, and no dismissals of government servants.[1] On the 31st the junta issued its last proclamation, recommending submission. Next day Dulce made his unhindered entry into the city which half a century before it took a French army three months to reduce.

---

[1] *Escenas contemporáneas*, vol. i, p. 20. Bruil was accused of using influence and perhaps money to undermine resistance; Pi, *Historia*, vol. iv, p. 162.

XIX

EPILOGUE

Spain after the Bienio

O'DONNELL was free at last to try out the Liberal Union experiment he had meant to try in 1854. Coming to power from the Right instead of the Left, he had to be all the more careful to look moderate and level-headed. He must seem able to offer constitutional government tempered by discipline, as the man who, a panegyrist declared, had saved monarchy and society by his patient vigil during the Bienio and now meant to go on in the same spirit, 'supporting the throne with one hand, brandishing the sword of law with the other'.[1] The extravagances of the Bienio would be corrected, all its useful work brought to fruition. A keynote circular was drawn up at once by Cantero the Finance Minister: legislation of the Constituent Cortes was to be scrupulously observed, and in particular the disamortization law.[2] To defend this was indeed both a political and a fiscal necessity.

His attitude procured for O'Donnell, what was worth something to him, the approval both of Paris, where his advent was warmly welcomed, and of London, where he was grudgingly accepted. At home he had to depend on stifling criticism until by manipulation and cajolery he could hope to disarm it. The state of siege was maintained; newspapers were censored with a thoroughness that could be called remarkable even in Spain.[3] But it was equally part of his tactics to abstain magnanimously from reprisals. At Madrid there were many arrests, but no executions. Rebels captured on 16 July were 'mainly operatives',[4] and so probably were those deported subsequently from the capital. Most of the bigger fish, Madoz for instance, were left alone. Orense had to leave the country for a while, and some others thought well to do

---

[1] J. M. de Losada, *Ahora ó nunca* (Madrid, July 1856), pp. 5–6, 10. The *Época* said the same more moderately: 17 July, 1/4–2/1.

[2] R.O. of 14 July 1856; C.L., vol. lxix, pp. 219–20.

[3] *The Times*, 22 July 1856, 10/3.

[4] Circular of 26 July 1856; C.L., vol. lix, pp. 268–9.

the same. O'Donnell abstained too from the usual wholesale dismissal of employees; some Progresistas returned unmolested straight from the barricades to their office desks. Their pay would be surety for their docility.

A circular of 26 July, noting 'with pained surprise' how many elected bodies had joined or countenanced the resistance in the provinces, directed them to be replaced with nominated councils chosen without respect to party. For the time being, however, it was to conservatives that O'Donnell had to look for enough public support to keep him from becoming the prisoner of the palace; and in the first flush of the counter-revolution, 'the magnificent drama of 1856' as Miraflores hailed it,[1] all of them were ready to applaud its author. Very soon this gratitude was dwindling. Of the seven Moderado newspapers of Madrid only one followed the *Época* in continuing to extol O'Donnell. Even moderate Moderados like Borrego held against him his demagogic phrases of the past two years;[2] and job-hunters who poured into Madrid by every coach were disgusted to find him reluctant even to accept Progresista resignations. Before long he was having to angle for the support of his late opponents against those who had helped into into power.

Progresistas could scarcely be regarded any longer as a party, Otway remarked, for the more respectable were by this time conservatives in all but name, while the more audacious were turning democratic.[3] If their party survived for another dozen years it was only as a shell, pulverized by the next serious collision with events. Espartero lay low in Madrid until all was quiet, and then requested a farewell audience with the Queen. She received him on 3 August and, the papers said, bantered him on his recent invisibility. Next day when the common diligence rumbled away it carried him with it out of Madrid and out of history. This left the leadership, for what it was worth, open. One candidate was Madoz; another was Olózaga, who gave up his embassy and moved from Paris to Bayonne, where a rump of Progresistas was collecting. They all saw the need for a new chief, the Spanish chargé at Paris heard, but most of them felt that only a military

[1] *Reseña histórico-crítica de la participación de los partidos en los sucesos políticos* (Madrid, 1863), p. 170; cf. L. García, p. 27.
[2] A. Borrego, *Lo que ha sido . . . el Partido Conservador* (Madrid, 1857), pp. 44 ff., 48–49; cf. on the Moderado press Pirala, vol. ii, p. 305.
[3] Otway to Clarendon, no. 44, 6 Aug. 1856, F.O. 72. 895.

man could fill the bill.[1] In the upshot Espartero was left with the nominal position; so that there was really no leader, as well as virtually no party.

Some radicals like Calvo Asensio and Sagasta went abroad for a time. Too many feebler spirits were sunk in the perpetual Hamlet mood of Liberalism, and would rather bear the ills of a reaction than fly to those of a revolution. A week after the fighting Infante confided to Otway that he 'rejoiced at the triumph of the Government', for a victorious militia would have gone to fearful lengths.[2] Of this state of mind the *Nación* was the faithfully quavering voice; it advocated helping to prop O'Donnell against reactionary pressure, for fear of worse befalling. Corradi, whose resignation from Lisbon was declined, put the blame on his own side—Escosura's rashness, Espartero's incompetence—more than on O'Donnell, and was even ready privately to think him the most eligible leader for the Progresista party.[3]

It was to the Democrats that the Liberal inheritance might be expected to fall. 'Democracy, I regret to say, is gaining ground, and making proselytes', wrote Otway.[4] He exaggerated, as many probably were doing, the extent of its influence. The *Discusión* hobbled along under frequent prosecutions, while the *Soberanía* announced on 23 July that as its issues were being confiscated daily it preferred to stop altogether. Garrido and Becerra and others had sought safety abroad; Ordax Avecilla had just died of an illness contracted in his prison days. At such a juncture the lack of a well-knit party organization, one of the things Sixto Cámara advocated, made itself painfully felt. Many Democrats, as his friend Garrido observed, fancied that since history was working for them there was no need to bother about organizing.[5] Linked with this fallacy was their failure to enlist the support of that permanent majority of Spaniards to whom politics meant food, and whose hopes the Bienio had stirred up only to leave them unfulfilled and ready to seek violent expression.

Elemental unrest, not political opposition, was O'Donnell's preoccupation on the Left. He was relying on palliatives as well

[1] Muro to Pastor Díaz, private, 31 Aug. 1856; *Francia*, 1856.
[2] Otway to Clarendon, no. 30, 23 July 1856, F.O. 72. 895.
[3] H. F. Howard, minister at Lisbon, to Clarendon, no. 207, Conf., 6 Sept. 1856; copy in F.O. 185. 310.
[4] Otway to Clarendon, no. 48, 7 Aug. 1856, F.O. 72. 895.
[5] Garrido, *Obras escogidas*, vol. i, p. 413.

as on coercion. At the end of July the new town council of Madrid was paying a daily subsidy of 30,000 reals to the bakers to keep bread prices down. In August the permission to import food-stuffs was extended to next June.[1] A week later import bounties were offered. This further disrespect for Spain's corn laws cannot have been palatable to the landed interest and the speculators, and it failed to cure the shortage. At Barcelona the long-continued trade depression was worsening, while Zapatero and the employers made a fresh effort to destroy the unions. In the countryside the Civil Guard had to be alerted against attempts to burn crops and woods, always endemic, the government commented, in some provinces but deplorably frequent this summer everywhere.[2] Conservatives could exploit against O'Donnell the red scare that he himself had helped to conjure up. Pidal came back from a tour fully convinced that all sorts of subversive ideas were still spread-ing, and told Isabel.[3] There was indeed a measure of truth in this, as the next few years were to show. By comparison the Bienio would come to look, as it really was on the whole, orderly and well behaved.

Liberal Union, essentially a double negative, was in danger from the first of sliding into simple reaction. In a circular of 13 August, a sort of political manifesto, the Cabinet complained that too many local government bodies of San Luis's day were being reinstated, and ordered all councils nominated since July to be replaced by fresh men, chosen impartially; and it pronounced legitimate all opinions compatible with order and constitutional monarchy.[4] A little later captain-generals were cautioned to resort to their exceptional powers only in case of actual breach of the peace.[5] O'Donnell was hankering for the amenities of a constitutional system without its risks and fatigues. And he was not really master even in his own Cabinet, where shades of opinion were quick to develop. Least unprogressive among his colleagues were Cirilo Álvarez, an unknown who was given Justice when Luzuriaga declined it, and Pedro Bayarri, a younger lawyer who

---

[1] Decree of 11 Aug. 1856; C.L., vol. lxix, pp. 355-6. Local authorities had been told not to raise their contributions to the *derrama* by taxing articles of prime neces-sity: R.O. of 4 Aug., ibid., pp. 291-3.

[2] Circular of 26 Aug. 1856; C.L., vol. lxix, pp. 412-3.

[3] Straten-Ponthoz to Vilain XIIII, no. 232, 15 Oct. 1856; *Espagne*, vol. 9.

[4] C.L., vol. lxix, pp. 360-3.

[5] R.O. of 8 Sept. 1856; ibid., pp. 471-2.

took the Navy. Collado and Cantero the bankers were in the middle. Ríos Rosas was credited with the paternity of Liberal Union philosophy. He was credited too with sincerely constitutional views, but this summer he was in a markedly backward-looking mood. He had for ally the new Foreign Minister. Pastor Díaz[1] was a distinguished jurist, whose outlook was deeply tinged with the fatal pessimism that Liberalism was always prone to. In his celebrated Ateneo lectures of 1848 and 1849 he despaired of any economic cure for the social problem, and concluded that religion alone could ward off socialism;[2] now in his dread of socialism he was forgetting something he had written before 1848—that it was a mockery to talk of parliamentary government while deputies could be silenced by cannonades.[3]

Before long the French chargé, Guitaut, thought that O'Donnell's desire to conciliate was being overborne by his more right-wing colleagues, and by influences working through them.[4] The result could be recognized in a series of major decisions. First came in mid-August a laconic decree with a long-winded preamble putting an end to the national militia and asserting that it had become, through middle-class dislike of service, perilously working-class in composition.[5] Having effectively disarmed the militia already, O'Donnell would probably have liked to postpone this measure. Liberal papers were perhaps not sorry to be able to plead the censorship as an excuse for not attacking it.

The constituent assembly, in its state of suspended animation, was an even more ticklish problem. Lengthy Cabinet wranglings only ended on 2 September, when another decree declared it dissolved. Another monstrously long preface, ascribed by knowledgeable readers to Ríos Rosas, argued in Burke's vein that political science and hard experience ought to have cured the country of the fanciful hope of transforming itself overnight; also that the session of 14 July was illegal and seditious.[6] Much as the assembly's prestige had drooped, this *coup de grâce* was an

---

[1] See an obituary account of him in Rico y Amat, *Libro*, vol. iii, pp. 55–68, and a sketch by Juan Valera prefixed to vol. vi of Pastor Díaz's Works (Madrid, 1866–8). His honesty is emphasized by J. del Valle Moré, in *Pastor Díaz. Su vida y su obra* (Habana, 1911), pp. 7–8.

[2] *Los problemas del socialismo*; these lectures fill vol. iv of his Works.

[3] *Á la Corte y á los partidos* (1846), in Works, vol. vi, p. 33.

[4] Guitaut to Walewski, no. 87, 14 Sept. 1856; *Espagne*, vol. 849.

[5] Decree signed 15 Aug. 1856, published 22 Aug; C.L., vol. lxix, pp. 369–77.

[6] C.L., vol. lxix, pp. 432–7.

affront to all who had ever believed in it or still believed in parliamentarianism. Corradi now felt bound to insist on resigning; the *Clamor Público*'s editorial was deleted by the censor. On the other hand intransigent conservatives were still not satisfied: they wanted every act of the obnoxious assembly annulled, beginning with its Constitution. Palace adherents wanted that of 1845 back again; ministers preferred, O'Donnell and Ríos Rosas for once concurring, to revive it with some extenuations. There was a Portuguese model, as for many things of this epoch, in Marshal Saldanha's 'Acto Adicional' of 1852. On 15 September a third decree restored the 1845 Constitution and tacked on to it an 'Acta Adicional', by virtue of which the Senate could not be swamped by excessive nominations; the Cortes must sit four months in every year; mayors would be government nominees only in the few biggest towns.[1] Thus trying to please both sides, O'Donnell pleased neither. Both fastened on the anomaly of a constitutional revision by mere fiat.

By leaguing with rampant clericalism he had helped to raise a spirit he could not lay, and the Church's mood after July was militant and triumphant. Returning to Barcelona at last Costa y Borrás insisted on having a steam-warship to chariot him back to his rebellious diocese.[2] Having got rid of the second Base, churchmen wanted next a stoppage of the sale of their properties. They could count on the *camarilla*, and there was the question of relations with Rome. O'Donnell wanted to restore these, but he wanted even more to go on auctioning all classes of disamortized property. Of the total of sales between the passage of the law in May 1855 and September 1856, more than a third took place under his auspices.[3] They gave the Treasury resources it was hard up for, and also helped to maintain commercial confidence. Railway and banking expansion were going on encouragingly. Cantero as Finance Minister was the firmest against any interruption of sales; Ríos Rosas and Pastor Díaz were diverging more and more from the agreed line.

---

[1] C.L., vol. lxix, pp. 494–502; also in Nido y Segalerva, *Ríos Rosas*, pp. 440–50.

[2] Baradère to Walewski, no. 231, 22 Sept. 1856, no. 232, 4 Oct., and no. 233, 16 Oct.; *Espagne*, Consular, vol. 53.

[3] There were sold in this year and a half 52,164 lots of real estate and 88,207 *censos*, with a total value of 941,407,112 reals, of which 240,195,044 reals were already paid up. See *Anuario estadístico* (1859), pp. 570–1; figures also in Miquel and Reus, part 2, pp. 123–5, and Antequera, pp. 456 ff.

Things came to a head at a Cabinet meeting on 12 September when Isabel demanded an end to disamortization. After a week-long crisis it was O'Donnell's turn to go through the retreat disguised as compromise that he had so often forced on Espartero. Cantero resigned, and on the 23rd an order halted sales of all endowments of the secular clergy. This time ministers had the good taste, Guitaut remarked, to leave out any rigmarole of philo-sophy:[1] there was a bare allusion to 'high reasons of State'. O'Donnell's brief period of indispensability was over. From having been Isabel's saviour he was becoming her factotum, and might soon be not even that. It was a great point to have got one of the men responsible for the disamortization law to make the first breach in it: something more might be extracted from him, and then he could be shown the door.

Narváez had been as much outraged at seeing O'Donnell snap up power under his nose in July 1856 as O'Donnell at seeing Espartero do the same in July 1854. He rushed down from Paris to the frontier to offer Isabel his services; she declined them politely, but he remained a bugbear that could be used to coerce O'Donnell. On 20 September, towards the end of the Cabinet crisis, she wrote to him to come:[2] on 5 October the old dictator stood once more in Madrid, in the frame of mind of a famished dog off the chain at last. Five days later took place the famous Court ball in honour of the Queen's twenty-sixth birthday, and the 'rigadoon of State'. She gave the customary first dance to her prime minister, the second unexpectedly to Narváez.[3] It was a pointed snub to O'Donnell; and before the evening was out she called him aside, put a handkerchief to her practised eye, and in-dulged in a long outpouring of old grievances against him. So at any rate says an oft-repeated narrative, couched somewhat in the style of an historical novel.[4] Next day she was amicable, but made it plain what she was after—the winding up of disamortiza-tion altogether. There was a cabinet, then another audience.[5]

[1] Guitaut to Walewski, no. 91, 25 Sept. 1856; *Espagne*, vol. 849.
[2] Howden to Clarendon, cipher tel. 25 Sept. 1856, F.O. 72. 896—from Paris, where he had been seeing Narváez. Cf. Révesz, p. 222.
[3] Straten-Ponthoz to Vilain XIIII, Separate, Conf., 16 Oct. 1856; *Espagne*, vol. 9, gives what is clearly the correct version of this incident.
[4] Its source is Bermejo, *Estafeta*, vol. iii, pp. 466–7.
[5] See *Discusión*, 14 Oct. 1856, 1/3–2/1; *Clamor Público*, 15 Oct., 1/5–2/1; Otway to Clarendon, no. 137, 16 Oct., F.O. 72. 897.

O'Donnell seems to have been trying even now to temporize, but it was too late. Some time about midnight he was seen leaving the palace in a state of visible chagrin;[1] an hour or two later a missive reached him at the Buenavista requiring his resignation.[2]

Democrats might rejoice at the fall of 'the most hated and hateful man in our annals', as the *Discusión* termed him,[3] but the average Liberal shivered at the spectacle of a Cabinet in which the tyrant of 1848 was the least, not the most, illiberal figure. Pidal and Moyano were decent if bigoted conservatives, but Lersundi had been the forerunner of San Luis; Nocedal at the Interior represented the neo-Catholicism into which Spanish conservatism was decomposing; and Urbistondo, the War Minister, was a former Carlist. It may be a safe guess that Narváez had not been allowed a free choice, and the decrees that were pouring out by 15 October look as though they had been got ready in advance and simply put before him for signing. The Acta Adicional was promptly scrapped, the reorganization of the Household of September 1855 was quashed, and the sequestration of Cristina's possessions cancelled. She had fairly earned her share of the spoils by energetic intriguing against O'Donnell from Paris. Everything since 1851 that could be held to infringe the Concordat was declared invalid; and to crown the whole edifice the disamortization law was suspended altogether.[4]

By this time even reactionaries of the less purblind sort were in 'a veritable panic',[5] and Narváez must have been anxious to call a halt. His idea was to take up again the Moderado tradition of the years after 1843, to be the exponent of sound administration, while like O'Donnell he proposed to build further on the material achievements of the Bienio. As always he was for constitutional government, on the two conditions that it satisfied solid men of property and kept the Duke of Valencia permanently in power. On the 20th he made a reassuring move by issuing a full amnesty to all involved in the July risings; three weeks later he lifted the state of siege. He had indeed little to fear from the bewildered Left.

---

[1] Llorca, pp. 131–2, citing an Italian diplomatic report.
[2] The diplomats' accounts of the change of government broadly tally: Guitaut to Walewski, no. 95, 14 Oct. 1856; *Espagne*, vol. 849; Otway no. 137 (above); Straten-Ponthoz, 16 Oct. (above).
[3] 14 Oct. 1856, 1/3–2/1.
[4] For these decrees see C.L., vol. lxx, pp. 77–80, 82–84, 93–95, 100–1.
[5] Otway to Clarendon, no. 138, Secret & Conf., 17 Oct. 1856, F.O. 72. 897.

An attempt by Sixto Cámara at an insurrection in Malaga on the night of 12 November was easily crushed; he had to escape to Portugal, and his party's more prudent men repudiated any connexion with the adventure.[1] As to O'Donnell's following, most of it shrivelled away the moment he was dislodged from office. Narváez's embarrassments, like his rival's before him, came from the Right. He was speedily discovering that a good deal was still expected from him by the *camarilla*, and that the day had gone by when he could lay down the law. Like the Espartero of 1854 he was too much the shadow of a great name, a hero living on his past. Turgot found him faded, and was not deceived by the jaunty air with which Narváez assured him that 'he felt stronger than all the priests in Spain'.[2]

What the *camarilla* wanted was to drag the country back as far as it could be dragged in the direction of absolute monarchy. As in 1852 a revision of the Constitution to facilitate this was the first objective; Spanish history seemed to have slipped back by three years. Clericalists were dreaming of a further, vaster triumph —recovery of all the wealth lost by the Church since 1833. No less than this, it was rumoured, Isabel called on Narváez to perform. It is easy to believe that at the mere thought of so immense a revolution in landed property the old soldier 'literally stood aghast, and the very hairs of his moustache twisted with affright'.[3] To be able to put a stop to such dreams or schemes he needed the backing of a party; but the Moderado factions that had clamoured for his return, to mortify O'Donnell, now squabbled and straggled as before, and many individuals were trying privately to insure themselves against the drift by coming to terms with Carlism. In the coming year or two a surprising number of them seem to have made at least tentative approaches to Montemolín : Bravo Murillo, Salamanca, Fernández de Córdova, González Bravo.[4] Dynastic fusion, partnership between Isabel and the Pretender, was again loudly advocated; moribund Carlism in spite of its fiasco was being given another lease of life.

[1] Detailed accounts of the attempt in W. P. Mark to Howden, no. 41, 13 Nov. 1856, F.O. 185. 319, and Bouzet to Walewski, nos. 85 to 88, 13 to 25 Nov.; *Espagne*, Consular, vol. 56. Official and other reports in *Clamor Público*, 18 Nov., 1/5–2/2. Cf. García Ruiz, *Historias*, vol. ii, p. 604; Rodríguez Solís, vol. ii, p. 480.
[2] Turgot to Walewski, no. 107, 10 Dec. 1856; *Espagne*, vol. 849.
[3] *The Times*, 25 Oct. 1856 (Paris, 22 Oct.), 10/1–2; cf. Castille, *Espartero et O'Donnell*, p. 58.   [4] 'Constante', pp. 58 ff.; cf. Ferrer, vol. xxi, chap. 2.

It was another hard winter. Travelling from the frontier to Madrid Turgot saw everywhere 'une horrible misère';[1] and the government rubbed in salt by restoring this December the *puertas* and *consumos*, combined henceforth in a single tax. On another question it could not agree so cordially: that of when, if ever, a new Cortes was to be allowed to meet. 'Señor Nocedal desires boldly to rule without a Parliament', wrote Howden, 'and in this desire Queen Isabel participates with all the blind earnestness of our own Stuarts.'[2] Narváez doggedly insisted on an election; and on 16 January 1857 the Cortes was summoned to meet on 1 May. For him it was a means of asserting himself against palace dictation; even the shadow of a parliament would have some symbolic value. It could be little more. A shrunken electorate was firmly handled by Nocedal, Progresistas were divided on whether to boycott the whole affair; only half a dozen of them got in. Nocedal carried through this assembly his new press law, formidable enough to threaten political journalism with extinction.[3] Moyano followed with an education law designed to educate primary-school children into religious and political conformity. And the Constitution was revised, very much as Bravo Murillo had intended, with the special aim of ensuring that opposition should never again find a stronghold in the Senate.[4] In July the brief session ended.

This summer the resentful mood of the people broke out in agrarian disturbances in Seville province. They gave Narváez a welcome chance to work off his own ill humour and play his role of 1848 over again. More than a hundred rioters or suspects were shot. It was easy work, for army strength was rising this year from 92,000 to 122,000, and the peasants found no political leadership. Progressives, as at the time of the Old Castile riots a year since, anxiously disclaimed any sympathy with 'anarchism'.[5] This did not save them; mass arrests were carried out at Madrid, and with calculated brutality. By tampering with the Constitution

---

[1] Turgot to Walewski, no. 107 (above).

[2] Howden to Clarendon, no. 235, Conf., 7 Nov. 1856, F.O. 72. 897.

[3] On this press law and its effects see Garrido, *L'Espagne contemporaine*, chap. 23; Eguizábal, pp. 213–16, 334–6.

[4] Text in Abad de Aparicio and Coronel y Ortiz, vol. iii, pp. 516–17, and Padilla Serra, pp. 99–100; and see Becker, *Reforma*, pp. 152 ff.

[5] See, for example, Garrido, *Obras escogidas*, vol. i, p. 414, and *Historia de las asociaciones obreras*, vol. i, pp. 73–75, where he attributes the social disturbances of both 1856 and 1857 to 'neo-Catholic Machiavellianism'.

and terrorizing the opposition Narváez had performed his allotted task, and could be dispensed with in his turn. He was dropped on 15 October.

Next month Isabel succeeded at last in having a son, the future Alfonso XII, to strengthen her position. Two palace ministries, headed by General Armero and Istúriz, followed Narváez, and it looked as if Spain was on the brink of a complete relapse into autocracy and obscurantism. But before the brink was reached there was a turning away. For this there were various reasons. Financial problems were growing difficult again. The army—even now, viewed from palace windows, deplorably 'Liberal' in spirit[1]—pined for the return of chiefs it could respect. To the bulk of the propertied classes autocracy in itself might not appear very undesirable, but to take refuge from the hazards of the age with an Isabel II and an Istúriz was a different matter; and as long as it clung to fantasies of a return to its golden age the Church was even more irresponsible, because more anachronistic, than the monarchy. Moreover, the Bienio had given Spain's economy a momentum not yet exhausted, which its beneficiaries did not want to lose. They could not help seeing also that intensified reaction, and the economic running down sure to accompany it, must sooner or later drive political radicalism and mass revolt together and produce a worse explosion than 1854.

Fear of such an uprising may, as Garrido thought, have been what decided Isabel in June 1858 to come to terms with O'Donnell.[2] He was taking office this time for the unprecedented spell of four and a half years. His restoration marked no sharp break with reaction; if he ever dreamed in Fernández de los Ríos's garret in 1854 of being independent head of an authentic new movement experience had taught him to be content with a good deal less. It was easier for him now no doubt to recruit a following of his own. Decomposition of the old factions had gone further, providing a sediment that could pass for a new party. In 1858, by contrast with 1856, he was coming forward as a constitutionalist, and discouraged Liberals—his old foe Escosura among them—were in no mood to question his credentials. But Liberal Unionism would never acquire a soul. Manipulation and bribery and jobbery were the breath of its life; not philosophers like Ríos Rosas but wirepullers like Posada Herrera were its tutors. Parliamentary

---

[1] See Llorca, p. 165.   [2] *L'Espagne contemporaine*, p. 315.

life was the camouflage for *caciquismo*, buying and selling of votes by local bosses in return for government favours. The *bourgeois* revolution had reached a flat top or plateau beyond which it could climb no higher. All who had got what they wanted out of it, and now only desired that the hand of the clock should stand still at their meridian hour, found O'Donnell their man. He and Cánovas del Castillo, soon installed as under-secretary at the Interior, have been truly called the architects of the new polity of the new oligarchy.[1]

Everything sketched out in O'Donnell's first ministry in 1856 was expanded and developed between 1858 and 1863. Within two months of his return he partially revived the disamortization law; ecclesiastical property was included in August 1859 after long and hard bargaining with Rome.[2] Sales not only benefited the Treasury but helped for the time being to prime the pump of economic expansion. Foreign investors recovered confidence, and there was a fresh influx of capital, chiefly French, and a regular spate of books by foreigners trumpeting the country's progress.[3] In the decade ending 1856 a total of 1,517 kilometres of railway had been built; for the next decade the figure was 5,368.[4] Mon, Ros de Olano, Gándara, Córdova, Lersundi could all be found on railway directorates. There was renewed activity in mining. A cadastral register was organized at last, and a new law of hypothec, another thing the Bienio had not had time for, enacted. Creation of fresh jobs, and some consequent improvement in wages, made the working class less mutinous. But economic progress was uneven, and the corruption and hollowness of public life helped to set limits to it. There was wild speculation; a heavy adverse trade balance was piling up. Disamortization was diverting fresh sections of the investing middle class into a land-ownership still essentially parasitic; and the agricultural reformer

---

[1] Ramos Oliveira, p. 85; cf. the whole survey of Liberal Unionism on pp. 80–87.

[2] On the importance of foreign capital see, for example, M. C. T. Straquinescu, *España en 1861* (San Sebastian, 1861), pp. 9–10.

[3] E. Bonnaud, *L'Espagne et son avenir* (Paris, 1860); J. L. Vidal, *L'Espagne en 1860* (Paris, 1860); J. Defontaine, *L'Espagne au XIXe siècle* (Paris, 1860); J. Lestgarens, *La situation économique et industrielle de l'Espagne en 1860* (Brussels, 1861); Villiaumé (1861). Cf. Religious Tract Society, *The Spanish Peninsula* (London, 1861), pp. 284–5; A. Malengreau, *Voyage en Espagne* (Brussels, 1866), 2nd part.

[4] Boag, p. 5; cf. details of railway progress in F. Caballero, *Reseña geográfico-estadística de España* (2nd ed., Madrid, 1868), pp. 35 ff., and Cambó y Batlle, vol. i, pp. 124 ff.

Caballero appealed in vain to the enlightened self-interest of land-owners to allow the cultivator somewhat better terms in order to 'avert the threatening tempest' of socialism.[1]

In 1861 the peasantry of the south revolted again, this time in Narváez's own district of Loja. He could not have shown more proficiency than O'Donnell in suppressing them. But before Spain could settle down into the stagnant calm of the later nineteenth century one more upheaval on a national scale was needed to frighten throne, Church, army, and property into a more closely articulated combination. O'Donnell fell at last in 1863, and no one after him succeeded in keeping Isabel under anything like rational control. Meanwhile industrial prosperity ran down: railways began to lose money, the Crédito Mobiliario closed its doors. Again the social peril loomed large. After quelling an army rising in Madrid in June 1866 O'Donnell was himself contemplating another *Vicalvarada* before he died in November 1867. Narváez pronounced his funeral oration, and half a year later followed him to the grave.

The army was ready to get rid of Isabel. It stood, for the last time, for some hazy kind of constitutionalism; and as always it wanted to forestall serious rebellion by guiding it into a well-regulated channel. Prim took the lead; it was Serrano who won the battle of Alcolea, a bigger Vicálvaro, on 28 September 1868. Next day Isabel fled to France with husband, lover, and confessor. She was still under forty, though with all youthful looks long since swallowed up in fat. Rebellion burst the bounds of the channel traced by the army, but found none much better to flow in. There was a painful search round Europe for a successor; the reign of Amadeo of Savoy, who gave up and went home in 1873; the stormy republic of 1873–4. It was the Bienio over again, on a larger canvas. Once more a new Constitution was debated, and excise taxes and conscription were denounced, and relations with Rome broken off; once more Carlism took the field, Barcelona's labour movement came into the open, peasants seized land.

A striking difference was that Madrid was not leading the country as it did in 1854–6, and that instead Federalism was threatening to break Spain up into a collection of cantons. The defeat of July 1856 was a shock from which Madrid and the country had scarcely recovered; not so much the defeat at the barricades as the betrayal of the people by their leaders. Espartero's vast popularity had been an expression of the country's faith in itself, and in a united destiny. Now he was reposing in peaceful old age at Logroño, and no new leader could fill his place because there was no new hope or illusion potent enough to inspire all Spain. None was to arise, in fact, until another three-quarters of a century had passed.

From this point of view the grand failure of the Bienio was that of its younger men to digest its lessons and be ready next time with a practical line of action, a programme of social and economic reform. Democrats had argued hotly among themselves in the sixties about association and *laissez-faire*, but as a party they were as hesitant and divided when the time came as the Progresistas before them. Their social legislation was meagre; agrarian reform still eluded them, socialism was still a mystery. Democracy in office proved an end instead of a beginning. Late in 1874 a general made a *coup d'état*, and next year monarchy returned. What was being restored, with Alfonso XII, was the reign of the oligarchy, with the landed interest at its core and neo-Catholicism as its creed. Cánovas was its man of affairs; he had for foil Sagasta, personification as he has been called of a radical middle class scared by mass revolt into a humble place behind the dominant groups.[1]

It is easier to detect the errors and shortcomings of those who had really hoped and lived for progress than to point out what they should or could have done, given the material and moral balance-sheet that Spanish history had bequeathed to them. Most problems of nations as of individuals have been insoluble as well as unsolved. After the Liberal collapse in 1856 Lord Howden had a sombre vision of Spain standing 'on the eve of that great battle of modern humanity the result of which none can foresee'. Spaniards were a race schooled by the Inquisition and the rest of what they had endured to extraordinary patience. But things were going too far, the people were being made to suffer too much. 'I believe that a frightful revolution is preparing in Spain.'[2]

[1] A. Ramos Oliveira, *Historia de España* (Mexico, 1932?), vol. ii, pp. 276–8, 296.
[2] Howden to Clarendon, no. 235 (above).

BIBLIOGRAPHY

UNPUBLISHED MATERIALS

A. Official

1. *Foreign Office archives, in the Public Record Office, London.*—Chiefly correspondence with the Madrid legation, 1853–6 (Class F.O. 72), and the legation records (F.O. 185).

2. *Foreign Ministry archives, Paris.*—Correspondence with the Madrid embassy, 1853–6, in the series *Espagne*, and Consular reports (Political series).

3. *Foreign Ministry archives, Brussels.*—Chiefly correspondence with the Madrid legation, 1853–6, in the series *Correspondance politique reliée: Légations: Espagne.* All references to Belgian documents, when not otherwise described, are to this series. Also *Correspondance politique reliée: Consulats*, vol. v. These Belgian records provide a valuable neutral check on the British and French. They are admirably preserved and arranged, and I owe particular thanks to their keeper, M. Desneux, and his assistant, Mme Nisol, for help in using them.

4. *Foreign Ministry archives, Madrid.*—Correspondence with the legation (sometimes embassy) at Paris and legation at London. Papers here are useful especially in connexion with activities of Carlist émigrés. They are in loose bundles, mainly belonging to two series, *Francia* and *Londres*, in the class: *Correspondencia: Embajadas y legaciones*. There are separate series of miscellaneous papers, *Francia: Política* and *Gran Bretaña: Política*. All dispatches cited belong to the category 'D.P.' ('Dirección de Política').

B. Private

1. *The Cowley Papers*, in the P.R.O., Class F.O. 519.—The first Earl Cowley was then ambassador at Paris. There are many references to Spain, especially in letters from Lord Clarendon, Foreign Secretary, and L. C. Otway, secretary of legation at Madrid.

2. *The Clarendon Papers*, in the Bodleian Library, Oxford.—These letters of the 4th Earl include many to or from Lord Howden, minister at Madrid, Otway, and other correspondents in or interested in Spain. I have to acknowledge with gratitude the kindness of the present Earl of Clarendon in allowing me to make use of them.

3. *The Blackwood Papers*, in the National Library, Edinburgh.—Letters from Frederick Hardman while in Madrid as a foreign correspondent in 1854–5.

PUBLISHED MATERIALS

A. Bibliographical

Jaime del Burgo, *Bibliografía de las guerras carlistas y de las luchas políticas del siglo XIX* (Pamplona, 3 vols. 1954–5; vol. iv, *Suplemento*, 1960). This is the indispensable reference-work for nineteenth-century Spain.

B. Sánchez Alonso, *Fuentes de la historia española* (3rd ed., Madrid, 1952).

Índice Histórico Español (published quarterly by the Centro de Estudios Históricos Internacionales at Barcelona, from 1953).

Vol. xcii, *Spain*, of the British Museum *Reading-Room Catalogue*.

B. Official Collections

Colección Legislativa de España (cited as C.L.). This contains all laws, decrees, &c., arranged according to the Ministry their business relates to. From 1856 dates of publication are given separately; my references, when not otherwise described, are to dates of signing.

Diario de las Sesiones (cited as D.S.): the verbatim record, printed daily, of the proceedings of the Constituent Cortes, 1854–6. It runs to 15 volumes, with continuous page-numbering.

Dirección General de Aduanas:
    Cuadro general del comercio exterior de España . . . en 1850 (Madrid, 1852).
    Estadística general del comercio exterior de España . . . en 1862 (Madrid, 1864).
Comisión (or *Junta General*) *de Estadística:*
    Censo de la población de España (Madrid, 1857 and—for Dec. 1860 census —1863).
    Anuario estadístico de España (Madrid, 1859)—an invaluable mine of information.

Documentos relativos a las negociaciones seguidas con la Santa Sede desde el 1 de diciembre de 1854 hasta el día (Madrid, 1855).

Parliamentary Papers: trade reports of the period from Spain.

C. Newspapers

Madrid newspapers chiefly quoted are the *Clamor Público, Nación, Novedades, Iberia* (Liberal); *Diario Español, España, Heraldo* (conservative); *Estrella, Regeneración* (clerical-reactionary); *Soberanía Nacional, Discusión* (Democrat). See in Chap. 1 a brief account of the Spanish Press. Many papers were ephemeral, and not all files have survived.

Scarcely any foreign newspapers had special correspondents at Madrid. The London *Times* is an important source, especially from Jan. 1854 to July 1855, when Frederick Hardman was working for it there. (See *The History of The Times*, vol. iii, London, 1935, pp. 184, 277.) He knew Spain well, and was writing also for *Blackwood's Magazine*. I am indebted to Captain D. R. Wilson, of *Blackwood's*, for information about him. The *Times* man at Paris, O'Meagher, had been at Madrid earlier, and brought much Spanish news into his column.

Numbers following newspaper references (3/8, 4/6, &c.) denote page and column of the issue cited.

D. Other Periodicals

Annuaires des Deux Mondes (Paris, 1853–7). Well-informed surveys of events in each country in turn.

Asamblea del Ejército (La) (Madrid, vol. i, 1856). An unofficial monthly army review.

Economista (El) (Madrid, 1856–7). Fortnightly.

Escenas Contemporáneas (Madrid, vols. i and ii, 1857). Political and literary.

Ilustración (La), Madrid illustrated weekly, edited by A. Fernández de los Ríos.

Padre Cobos (El) (Madrid, 1854–6). Right-wing satirical paper, every five days.

Semanario Económico, Mercantil e Industrial (Madrid, 1856).

E. Books and Pamphlets

I have tried to consult all books and pamphlets, contemporary or later, bearing on the politics of this period. Many of them are referred to in the notes; they are too numerous for the titles to be repeated here.

INDEX

(Note. Names of places are given here and in the text in their English form where there is one (e.g. Corunna instead of Coruña). Titled individuals are referred to by their family names when they were habitually known by these, as was most often the case: titles of nobility hung loosely on Spaniards, and might be ignored by the public, except ancient titles borne by a man like the then Duke of Alba who had nothing else of note about him. Titles and ranks acquired subsequently to the date of this study are not noted. In family names 'de' was often optional, and in such cases is put in brackets; it was seldom used in practice. Spanish custom adds to an individual's paternal surname that of his mother (with or without 'y', or *and*, as a link); the latter is only given here in cases where both names were habitually used together, or when both are required to establish identity. Espartero was so known because he preferred this democratical family name to the one (Fernández) which he would normally have gone by.)

1902), 12, 33, 37, 66, 78, 80, 85, 132–3, 145–6, 168–9, 251.
Franco, N. de, 105.
Franquet, Cirilo, 160, 163.
Freemasonry, 7, 24, 31, 47, 84–85, 100.
French Revolution (1789), 3, 6, 8, 107, 126, 142, 214.
Frith, Rev. A., 130 n. 2.
Fuente Andrés, Manuel, 150, 226.
Fulgencio, P., 133.

Galicia, 3, 22, 28, 35–36 (famine), 105–6, 156.
Gamoneda, 68.
Gándara, Joaquín de la, Colonel, 60–61, 63, 230, 250.
García, L., 210.
García Ruiz, Eugenio (1819–83), 8, 115, 153, 182 n. 4, 189, 212, 216, 226, 230, 232.
Garrido, Fernando, 31, 32, 72, 88, 93, 106, 142–3, 165, 182 n. 4, 188–9, 212, 215 n. 1, 220, 222–3, 241, 248 n. 5, 249.
Garrigó, Brigadier, 62, 63.
Genoa, Duke of, 37.
Germany, 11.
Gerona, 236.
Gerona, Marqués de (José de Castro y Orozco) (1808–69), 38 n. 4.
Gibraltar, 19, 234.
Girardin, Émile de, 103.
Gómez de Laserna, Pedro (1806–71), 57, 183.
Gómez de la Mata, Agustín, 59 n. 2.
Gonfaus, Marcos ('Marsal'), 160, 171.
González Bravo (Brabo), Luis (1811–71), 247.
González y González, Antonio (1792–1876), 105, 183, 192.
Granada, 73, 100, 122, 209, 233.
Grimberghe, Roger Helmann de, 165.
Guitaut, Vicomte Cominges de, 243, 245.
Gurrea, Ignacio, General, 55, 76, 83, 105, 148, 178–9, 203, 237.
Gurrea, Venancio, 83, 105, 222, 226.
Gutiérrez de la Concha (see Concha).

Hardman, Frederick (1814–74), 42 n. 1, 50, 67, 78, 92, 101, 112, 254.
Hazlitt, William, 6.
Heraldo, El, 38, 43, 50–51, 56, 59.

Heros, Martín de los (1783–1859), 121, 168 n. 4.
Hierro, Mariano, 132.
Hore, Brigadier, 43, 76, 106.
Horsey, Miss, 131.
Howden, Baron (General John Hobart Caradoc) (1799–1873), 35–38, 40, 41, 43–45, 47 n. 2, 50, 66, 67, 87, 88, 91, 94, 95, 109, 111, 113–16 (political influence), 118, 121, 123, 127, 130, 132, 134, 138, 144, 171, 173, 175, 178, 183, 185, 187, 194, 201–2, 209, 212, 245 n. 2, 248, 252.
Hoyos, Isidoro de, General (1793–1876), 210.
Hoz, Pedro de la, 100.
Huelva, 132.
Huelves, Julián, 151, 161, 183.
Huerta, Francisco, 69.
Hugelmann, Gabriel, 228, 232 n. 7.

Iberia, La, 106, 121, 137, 143 n. 6, 149, 161, 171, 191 n. 1.
Iberian Union, 37, 40, 88.
Ilustración, La, 42 n. 2.
Industry, 8, 11, 19, 20, 27, 28, 96, 199 (and see Coal, Cotton, Iron).
Ineffabilis, Bull, 125, 146.
Infante, Facundo, General (1786–1873), 37, 41, 42, 99–100, 102, 116, 118 n. 3, 123, 183, 208 n. 2, 217, 221, 224, 226–30 (end of Constituent Assembly), 241.
Inquisition, 126, 129, 252.
Ireland, 35, 46.
Iriarte, Martín José de, General, 64.
Iron-works, 16, 19, 27, 122, 154, 195.
Isabel II (1830–1904), 2, 4–9 11–12 (character), 14, 16, 24, 32–37 (camarilla rule), 39–41, 45, 49–51, 54, 56–62 (Revolution, 1854), 65, 66, 71, 73, 77–82 (after the Revolution), 85, 88, 89, 93, 98, 99, 102, 109–16 (decision of Cortes), 120, 122, 127–8, 132–3, 144–7, 152, 168–70, 180, 190, 201–2, 208–9, 211, 218–27 (recovery of power), 230, 234, 240, 242, 245, 247–9, 251.
Istúriz, Francisco Javier de (1790–1871), 206, 249.
Italy, 12.

Jaén, 52, 233.

PRINTED IN GREAT BRITAIN
AT THE UNIVERSITY PRESS, OXFORD
BY VIVIAN RIDLER
PRINTER TO THE UNIVERSITY